Read to Succeed

to engage
children and young people
in reading for pleasure

Read to Succeed

Strategies to engage
children and young people
in reading for pleasure

Edited by
Joy Court

facet publishing

Published by Facet Publishing,
7 Ridgmount Street, London WC1E 7AE
www.facetpublishing.co.uk

Facet Publishing is wholly owned by CILIP: the Chartered Institute of
Library and Information Professionals.

British Library Cataloguing in Publication Data
A catalogue record for this book is available from the British Library.

ISBN 978-1-85604-747-0

First published 2011
Reprinted digitally thereafter

Text printed on FSC accredited material.

Mixed Sources
Product group from well-managed
forests and other controlled sources
www.fsc.org Cert no. SA-COC-1565
© 1996 Forest Stewardship Council

Typeset from editors' files by Facet Publishing in 10/14 pt Palatino
Linotype and Frutiger.
Printed and made in Great Britain by MPG Books Group, UK.

*Dedicated with gratitude to the
loving memory of a Dad who shared with me
his huge enthusiasm for books; and of my
big sister, who loved playing schools
and taught me to read by the time I
was three years old.*

Contents

Foreword

Ask anybody who works with children or who cares about the future of young people and they will agree on one thing: reading is the most basic of basics. The child who reads is a successful child: more likely to succeed academically; more likely to succeed socially; and more likely to be inquisitive about the world around them, maybe even to feel empowered to try to change it for the better. This is not just my opinion. It is a judgement supported by a body as influential as the Organisation for Economic Co-operation and Development (OECD).

When you read often, when it is as effortless and integral to your being as eating, drinking, sleeping and breathing, you are able to empathize, to access and order information, to interpret and explore the world around you.

I know this from personal experience. My father was a factory worker. My mother was a shop assistant. I got the reading habit at Crewe Library as an eight year-old and I have devoured novels, biographies, autobiographies, histories, plays, poetry, periodicals, newspapers, magazines, comics and quiz books ever since. I was the first person in my family to go to university. I liked the experience so much that I attended three of them! I became a teacher and later an award-winning author.

When I visit schools and libraries to talk about my books young people invariably ask who inspired me. I always give the same reply. The books and the authors who wrote them inspired me. That is only half the explanation, however. Without the guidance of many dedicated librarians I would not have gained access to the inspirational power of the written word. To paraphrase the words of the Manic Street Preachers, libraries gave me power – and that also means the librarians that staff them. A library without a librarian is … a room.

You might imagine therefore that there would be no dispute about the central place of reading in society and in the school curriculum. Sadly, this is not true. School and public libraries and school library services are under severe pressure. In difficult economic conditions, they are often at the top of the list for cuts.

The whole culture of reading for pleasure, of books, information technology, libraries and librarians requires advocacy. I have no hesitation in giving my support to *Read to Succeed*. This volume is a stepping stone on the way to a more literate and more informed society. I recommend it unreservedly.

To paraphrase something the great Liverpool FC manager Bill Shankly once said: Reading is not just a matter of life and death; it is much more important than that.

Alan Gibbons
Author
Organizer, Campaign for the Book

Contributors

Jenny Barber has a BA (Hons) degree in English from the University of Manchester and a postgraduate diploma in Library and Information Management from Manchester Metropolitan University. She has previously worked in libraries for Stockport College and the University of Manchester (main and business libraries) and now enjoys working as Reader Development Librarian for Stockport, where she has worked for the past eight years.

Andrew Blake has worked for Dorset Library Service for over ten years. He started as a Saturday Assistant, aged 16, and has worked his way up to his current position as a Reading and Learning Librarian specializing in working with young people. He has had a variety of roles within the service, including a jointly funded role as a Library Assistant/Youth Worker and Library Manager at a community library. He graduated from the University of the West of England in 2005 with a BA (Hons) in Drama and English. He has been involved in running many national initiatives in Dorset, including HeadSpace, Out of the Box and Right to Read.

Geraldine Brennan is a journalist and consultant specializing in children's literature and reading. Former Books Editor of the *Times Educational Supplement (TES)*, she now reviews for the *Observer* and has judged several literary awards, including, currently, the Frances Lincoln Diverse Voices Children's Book Award.

Kasey Butler is a marketing communications professional with over ten years' experience, based in London. As part of her role as Corporate Marketing Manager for CILIP she has managed the CLIP Carnegie and Kate Greenaway Awards and accompanying shadowing scheme since 2009. Kasey has always had a passion for arts and culture, having completed a humanities degree and being involved in various dance and drama activities in her native New Zealand. This is her first project specifically relating to children's books and the publishing world.

Wendy Cooling taught English in London schools for 20 years before becoming head of the children's section of Booktrust, a charity working to promote reading. There she set up Bookstart, which aims to encourage parents and carers to read to their babies when they are very young. Wendy now works freelance on a variety of book/reading-related projects. She was made an MBE in 2009 for services to children's literature.

Joy Court is a past chair of CILIP Youth Libraries Group and currently the National Coordinator for the Carnegie and Kate Greenaway Medals, having been a judge in 2000 and 2001 and chair of judges in 2009. She is a member of the National Council of the United Kingdom Literacy Association (UKLA), where she sits on the selection panel for the UKLA Children's Book Awards, and is a Fellow of the Royal Society of Arts. She manages the School Library and Resources Service in Coventry, where she also developed the Coventry Inspiration Book Awards in 2007. These unique awards involve the whole community in voting for their favourite books from short lists on www.myvotescoventry.org, where there are polls for every age group of children and young people, and by genre for the adults. She reviews books for the Reading Zone website, www.readingzone.com, and each month selects the Book of the Month for Foundation Stage and Key Stages 1, 2 and 3.

Prue Goodwin is a freelance lecturer in literacy and children's books who works chiefly for schools, universities, libraries and publishers. Prue has edited several books on children's books and learning to read, her most recent being the third edition of *The Literate Classroom* (Routledge, 2011) and *Understanding Children's Books: a guide for education professionals* (SAGE, 2008). She gives keynote talks at conferences all over the UK and abroad, and also returns regularly to the classroom to encourage children to become voracious readers.

Julia Hale is Young People's Services Manager for Plymouth Libraries, where she manages the children's and young people's library service for the city. She studied Children's Literature as part of her BEd at Homerton College, Cambridge, which partly explains her conversion from teaching to librarianship. She is a qualified primary teacher and librarian and began her career in Westminster Libraries, London, 13 years ago. Over the years she has planned many early years, children's and young people's library projects, targeting hard-to-reach groups or families living in deprived circumstances. Julia was the South West judge for the CILIP Carnegie and Kate Greenaway Awards from 2008 to 2010 and is a member of the national committe of CILIP Youth Libraries Group.

Bridget Hamlet has a BSc degree in English and Secondary Education from the University of Wisconsin-La Crosse and an Instructional Media licence. She moved to England to teach in 2002 and received Qualified Teacher Status (QTS) in England in 2003. She is currently a school librarian at Tile Hill Wood School and Language College in Coventry.

Celeste Harrington has a long history of involvement in books and reading. She was a manager for a large retail bookstore in South Africa for a number of years and was involved in purchasing books for the entire store, which had a strong children's section. A move to New Zealand resulted in a career change. After a time working with young children, she is now a lecturer for the Open Polytechnic in its Bachelor of Teaching degree. She specializes in the curriculum aspect of the programme and completed her MEd in children's literature in 2010.

Nikki Heath is the school librarian at Werneth School in Stockport. She graduated with a BA (Hons) in Library and Information Management in 1995, and has been working in libraries since childhood – for a frightening total of 28 years. She was awarded the title of School Library Association School Librarian of the Year in 2008. Since then, she has spoken to librarians up and down the country about her role and was on the selection panel for the Children's Laureate in 2009.

Jacob Hope is the Reading Development Manager for Lancashire County Council and is a freelance children's book consultant. As part of the Love Libraries campaign he was named as one of ten librarians of the future. He is a keen advocate for libraries, reading and children's books.

Eddy Hornby thought he'd spend a couple of years as a library assistant whilst he decided what to do with his life: he has now worked in Stockport Libraries for twenty years! Much of this time was spent in the Information Library at Stockport Central Library, where he feels privileged to have been taught the skills of reference work before the advent of the internet. He currently holds the post of Support for Learners Librarian and enjoys co-ordinating learning opportunities ranging from bounce and rhyme sessions to computer taster sessions for the terrified.

Wayne Mills specializes in children's literature and has a particular interest in boys' literacy and graphic novels. He was Chairman of the New Zealand Children's Literature Foundation from 1998 to 2004 and has been instrumental in establishing the internationally successfully Kids' Lit Quiz™ in New Zealand, England, Scotland, Wales, Northern Ireland, South Africa and Canada. He was awarded the Margaret Mahy Medal for distinguished services to children's literature in 2008, and Member of the New Zealand Order of Merit in the 2011 New Year honours. Wayne is a senior lecturer at The University of Auckland, Faculty of Education.

Natasha Roe is a published author and writer who now runs the communications and marketing consultancy Red Pencil (www. redpencilprojects.co.uk). For the last four years she has worked with The Reading Agency, where she has redeveloped the websites, social media, marketing strategies and language guidelines, and she currently looks after The Reading Agency's online editorial content and e-newsletter. She has worked with Anne Sarrag and Lynne Taylor to develop the Summer Reading Challenge's (SRC's) website for professionals and parents, and on marketing Chatterbooks and the Summer Reading Challenge to schools.

Anne Sarrag has worked for 25 years in the field of children's books and reading, starting with the Book Bus, a children's mobile bookshop and literacy charity in London. In the early 1990s she worked for Booktrust, and also acted as UK secretariat for the International Board on Books for Young People (IBBY). Anne held various marketing and consultancy roles with children's publishers in between taking the Book Bus (which she now owns) around the UK on roadshows to coincide with Children's Book Week. Whilst working as a consultant for CILIP during National Libraries Week in 1997, she met Miranda McKearney, and together they set up LaunchPad, a charity working with library services to promote the value of libraries for children through marketing advocacy and research. Anne led on starting the first Summer Reading Challenge in 1999 – which she has managed each year since. LaunchPad became The Reading Agency in 2003.

Emma Sherriff is Outreach Support Officer for Plymouth City Council, where her role focuses on engaging socially excluded young people in library services. Emma graduated from the University of Bath in 2006 with a BSc (Hons) in Sociology. Her working background is in child development research, including evaluative research projects, charting good practice and assisting with the training of children's services professionals. In 2007 Emma was named one of the Museums, Libraries and Archives (MLA) Council's Top Ten New Librarians. She was a judge for the Booktrust Teenage Book Prize in 2008. Emma currently project manages HeadSpace Efford and works closely with partners to deliver the Literacy with a Twist project to young people at risk of offending and young people with acute mental health difficulties. Emma also develops innovative events such as Frock Exchange to build new audiences for libraries.

Eileen Simpson is the freelance development officer for the CILIP Carnegie and Kate Greenaway Shadowing Scheme. Eileen has a background in libraries – having held her first library job whilst a teenager, as a Saturday helper in her local library! She worked from 2000 until 2004 as CILIP Marketing Assistant and Marketing Executive. Since 2004 she has been involved in directing the development of the Shadowing website and in 2006/7 she project managed national activity for the CILIP Carnegie and Kate Greenaway Awards 70th Anniversary. Eileen is a part-time lecturer at the Manchester School of Art, where she specializes in open source and peer-to-peer creative multimedia projects.

Lynne Taylor has worked with the Summer Reading Challenge since it first started in 1999. She is currently a project manager with The Reading Agency, working on the Summer Reading Challenge and Chatterbooks reading groups for children. Previously she was project manager for the CILIP Carnegie and Kate Greenaway shadowing scheme in schools and libraries, and marketing manager with Peters Library Service (now Peters Bookselling Services), having started her career working in sales and marketing for publishing houses Victor Gollancz and John Murray Publishers.

Helen Villers is a senior lecturer in the School of Arts, Languages and Literacies at the Faculty of Education, The University of Auckland, New Zealand. She co-ordinates Language and Literacy courses within the Graduate Diploma of Teacher Education (Primary) and in the Graduate Diploma of TESSOL (Teaching English in Schools for Speakers of Other

Languages). Her research interests include children's literature, biliteracy and bilingualism, integrated approaches to literacy and the role of professional mentoring within teacher education.

Lili Wilkinson managed Inside a Dog (www.insideadog.com.au) between 2006 and 2011. She is now a full-time Young Adult author and PhD candidate at The University of Melbourne. Her books include *Scatterheart*, *Company of Angels* and *Pink*.

Jean Wolstenholme is Children and Young People's Development Manager in Lancashire Libraries. Her whole career has been spent working in public and school library services in Lancashire, primarily leading a wide range of initiatives aimed to help every child discover that special book that switches them on to reading. Highlights in her career are involvement for 25 years with the Lancashire Book Award, the Lancashire Shout about Books literature festival, which is now an established annual event, NE1 4 Reading and Care 2 Read projects with children in care and Howzat! Dads and Lads, supported by the England and Wales Cricket Board.

Clare Wood is Professor of Psychology in Education at Coventry University and is Editor in Chief of the *Journal of Research in Reading*.

Introduction

'Read to Live' – all of the contributors to this book would very much agree with Gustav Flaubert's (1857) motto and, in all their different voices and with all their very different experiences and knowledge, they share with me the absolute and fundamental belief that it is essential for the life chances of every child, everywhere, that they can read.

In this introduction I will highlight some of the UK policy framework and international research evidence that underpins this belief. Although most of the contributors are from the UK and reflect UK experience, the issues faced and strategies developed are more universal. Every country will have its own political agenda, but readers will be able to recognize how campaigners for libraries and reading have used the current context to best advantage, and will gain insight from this. Thus the subsequent chapters will take us from the very youngest potential readers to young people on the fringes of society in some of the most deprived socio-economic neighbourhoods in the UK, covering some of the most innovative and yet long-standing and successful reading promotion strategies in the world. We have envisaged our readers as those who are trying to find out the background and context to child reader development in libraries and schools and to equip themselves to take this development forward. They may be a student librarian, a teacher or consultant concerned with reading and literacy, a practitioner in either field with new responsibilities or an established practitioner or manager looking for ideas and inspiration.

As former Children's Laureate, Michael Morpurgo, put it so beautifully in an article in *The Times* in 2009:

> Without the sunlight of literature children cannot grow as they should. We know that from books come knowledge and understanding, that they are a source of infinite joy and fun, that they stimulate imagination and creativity, that they open eyes and minds and hearts. It is through the power and music and magic of stories and poems that children can expand their own intellectual

curiosity, develop the empathy and awareness that they will need to tackle the complexities of their own emotions, of the human condition in which they find themselves. And it's through books that we can learn the mastery of words, the essential skill that will enable us to express ourselves well enough to achieve our potential in the classroom and beyond.   (Morpurgo, 2009)

The importance of libraries and librarians

The recent Schools White Paper *The Importance of Teaching* (Department for Education, 2010) indeed acknowledges that: 'Unless children have learned to read, the rest of the curriculum is a secret garden to which they will never enjoy access.' So how, then, do we unlock the door to that secret garden? Of course Terry Pratchett had the right idea: 'The way to get children reading is to leave the library door open and let them read anything and everything they want' (Pratchett, 2004).

This illustrates another underlying theme of the book: both libraries and children and young people's librarians have an important and significant role in awakening the reader in every child. In the same way that, as we shall see in Chapters 2 and 3 and in Chapter 4 from New Zealand, children need the skills of a good teacher to enable them to learn to read, they need the free access to a wealth of books that a well-stocked library can give them and a skilled librarian to help them find the right book at the right time. This cannot be said too often in a time when specialist courses to train the children's librarians of the future are disappearing (only 5 of 12 UK institutions with undergraduate and postgraduate courses in librarianship now offer this module) and when cuts and restructuring in library authorities are stripping out specialist posts, reducing budgets and closing libraries.

Current and future generations of children deserve the opportunities that the Demos report *Creative Reading* describes:

> Libraries can, and in many places do, provide platforms for development, or staging posts, to assist young people on their journey. Bookstart, library cards and book packs for the newborn, links to Sure Start, homework clubs, teenage reading groups, and help with becoming proficient in IT [information technology] are just some of the examples of the ways in which libraries can develop broad reading skills.   (Holden, 2004)

In a time of extensive cuts to public expenditure around the world, we need to remind those making these uncomfortable decisions of the underpinning rationale that makes libraries a vital public service: 'The underlying ethos of public libraries, there from the very beginning, is that reading helps us all to become better people with more fulfilled lives' (Holden, 2004). This important contribution to social cohesion was very much the conclusion reached by National Literacy Trust's *Literacy Changes Lives* research, which presented 'overwhelming evidence that literacy has a significant relationship with a person's happiness and success. It gives a clear indication of the dangers of poor literacy and also the benefits of improving literacy for the individual, the community, the workforce and the nation' (Dugdale and Clark, 2008). A literate person is more likely to be employed, to own their own home, to have children and to vote. As the Department for Culture, Media and Sport notes in its *Framework for the Future*: 'People cannot be active or informed citizens unless they can read. Reading is a prerequisite for almost all cultural and social activities' (Department for Culture, Media and Sport, 2003).

In the European Union, the European Commission (2001) recognized that reading skills play a central role in an individual's learning at school and beyond: 'The ability to read and understand instructions and text is a basic requirement of success in all school subjects. The importance of literacy skills does not, however, come to an end when children leave school. Such skills are key to all areas of education and beyond, facilitating participation in the wider context of lifelong learning and contributing to individuals' social integration and personal development.'

Reading: the evidence

Reading really does change lives and it was the 2002 OECD report *Reading for Change* which revealed that reading for pleasure is the single most important indicator of future success. 'Finding ways to engage pupils in reading may be one of the most effective ways to leverage social change.' It was clearly demonstrated that, across the 32 countries surveyed, children from poor socio-economic backgrounds who positively engage with reading score more highly than children from wealthier and more privileged backgrounds who do not engage with reading. This report was joyously received by librarians everywhere. For the first time we had hard statistical evidence that libraries can make a difference and that our role in promoting and encouraging reading for pleasure was not something soft and fluffy, but essential.

For the first time, too, it seemed that policy makers were paying attention to reading and to the link with libraries. In the UK public library sector we had the manifestation of Public Library Standards in 2001, which aimed to create a clear and widely accepted definition of a library authority's statutory duty to provide a 'comprehensive and efficient service' and for the first time set a performance-monitoring framework for public libraries. Sadly, no standard related to loans to the under-16s, but overall library provision across the UK did improve. This was followed in 2003 by the aforementioned *Framework for the Future: libraries, learning and information in the next decade* (Department for Culture, Media and Sport, 2003) and, as part of the action plan to deliver this ambitious development programme for the nation's public libraries, 'Fulfilling Their Potential', which focused on the needs of 11–19 year-olds. In Chapter 12 we can see what can be achieved on the ground as a result of this level of focus and planning.

School libraries

The period 2003–4 saw a focus on school libraries in the UK; the Department for Education and Skills (DfES) funded the *School Libraries Making a Difference* advocacy campaign, with the brochure (Department for Education and Skills, 2004a) being sent to every state school in the country. This was followed in 2004 by *Improve your Library: a self evaluation process* (Department for Education and Skills, 2004b) for both primary and secondary schools which, again, was delivered to every school in the country. This aligned a programme of self-evaluation and continuous improvement to the overall Self Evaluation Framework for schools and gave managers the tools to really embed the library into the School Improvement Plan.

Yet, despite this strategic lead, evidence on the teaching of reading from school inspections found that: 'Although some schools were successfully raising reading attainment and were teaching pupils the skills they needed to read with accuracy and understanding, few were successfully engaging the interest of those who, though competent readers, did not read for pleasure' (Ofsted, 2004). A further review of research evidence entitled *English 2000–05 A Review of Inspection Evidence* stated: 'In addition, too few schools have given sufficient time and thought to how to promote pupils' independent reading and there is evidence that many pupils are reading less widely for pleasure than previously' (Ofsted, 2005). Even more tellingly, that year a parliamentary enquiry into *Teaching Children to Read* under the auspices of the House of Commons Education and Skills Select Committee included this statement:

'Whatever method is used in the early stages of teaching children to read, we are convinced that inspiring an enduring enjoyment should be a key objective' (House of Commons Education and Skills Select Committee, 2005).

Significant Government funding over this period went into a range of initiatives with the specific intention of promoting and encouraging reading. The DfES funded the National Literacy Trust in 2004 to develop the Reading Connects campaign and website to build a network of 'reading schools' and to share and inspire good practice. As we write, the funding for this has just ended and the network is moving towards a subscription model for schools, although the website itself, with its multitude of available resources, still remains freely accessible (www.literacytrust.org.uk/reading_connects). In the same year The Reading Agency was also funded to develop the toolkit *Enjoying Reading: public library partnerships with schools* (The Reading Agency, 2004), recognizing that schools cannot grow readers alone. Chapter 6 gives us a good example of exactly this sort of partnership working.

Reading outside the school

In July of the same year attention turned to the family environment for reading and we saw additional government funding for Bookstart, which added book gifts at 18 months and at 3 years to the original one at 9 months (see Chapter 1 for the full story). In 2006 Booktime was launched, funded by Pearson and the DfES, which gave a book to every child starting primary school. That year, 260,000 children received a free copy of *Funnybones* by Janet and Allan Ahlberg. Following this inspiration, in 2007 Booked Up was born. Every secondary school was offered a free Booked Up resource pack to enable each Year 7 pupil to choose the book that is right for them. In the first three years over two million students received a free book. Both gifting schemes also had complimentary packs for use within libraries which emphasized the 'golden triangle' linking home, school and library to encourage reading for pleasure.

The year 2007 also saw the launch of the DfES-supported Family Reading Campaign. This campaign sought to ensure that reading in the home is encouraged and supported by schools, the local community, the business community, the media and wider society and, to further this aim, the announcement that, ten years on from the first one, England would have another National Year of Reading in 2008. Further book gifting was also to take place during this year, specifically aimed at Early Years settings (Book Ahead) and at improving boys' engagement with reading (Boys into Books).

This flurry of Government activity and funding may well have been a result of the latest in the five-yearly cycle of PIRLS (Progress in International Reading Literacy Study) data, which showed a very significant and embarrassing fall in the results for England's ten year-olds.

Reading scores continue to fall

The fall in the reading achievement scale for the UK from 553 in 2001 to 539 in 2006 'is one of the largest in the study' and 'children in England had less positive attitudes to reading than children in most other countries and … their attitudes were somewhat poorer than in 2001. Of particular concern is the 15 per cent of children in the sample for England who had the least positive attitudes, a significant increase from 2001. This is one of the highest proportions in all the participating countries in 2006.' Once again, the findings demonstrated that 'for England and in almost all other countries there is a positive association between frequency of reading for pleasure and reading attainment'. The Russian Federation, the highest-achieving country in this study, also had the highest response in the pupil questionnaire when they were asked how often they read outside of school for fun – 58%, compared to England's 33% and the international average of 40% (Twist, Schagen and Hodgson, 2007).

Shortly after this research was published, the author Alan Gibbons launched his Campaign for the Book, inspired by the imminent closure of school and public libraries. The first major action of the campaign was an e-petition to 10 Downing Street calling for school libraries to be made a statutory provision. This gained 5707 signatories, many of whom professed to being shocked that it was a statutory requirement to have a library in Her Majesty's prisons but not in her schools, and this despite all the evidence from both local and international sources which made the conclusive link between literacy, libraries, reading for pleasure and attainment. One of the best summaries of this international evidence is provided in the article 'Effective School Libraries: evidence of impact on student achievement' (Barrett, 2010).

Further bad news came from the latest results from the Programme for International Student Assessment (PISA) 2009, which again made reading the main focus for the international comparison of data from 65 countries and which continues to show the positive impact that reading for pleasure has on scores. The assessment indicates that students who enjoy reading the most in almost every country perform significantly better than those who do not. Unfortunately, it also shows that England has fallen further down the rankings in reading scores: from 3rd in 2000, to 17th in 2006, to 25th in 2009 (Bradshaw et al., 2010).

The Institute for Fiscal Studies, not an ally one would immediately think of in promoting reading, in its report *Drivers and Barriers to Educational Success* (Chowdry, Crawford and Goodman, 2009), produced further hard-nosed evidence about the impact of reading on attainment, in that 'young people who stop reading or playing sport between ages 14 and 16 tend to have lower Key Stage test results than young people whose behaviour does not change'. This research may or may not have impacted upon the Government's u-turn on the proposed cuts to funding for school sports partnerships announced in December 2010, but we should certainly make what use of it we can to defend expenditure on both school and public libraries.

In 2010 the National Literacy Trust conducted a further major piece of research, involving 17,089 pupils from 112 schools. This was to provide data on young people's reading habits and attitudes for the School Library Commission chaired by Baroness Estelle Morris. Once again, we have clear evidence about the impact of school libraries, public libraries and the family environment on reading. 'Young people with a reading age above the expected level for their age are twice as likely to be school library users as their peers with a reading level below that expected for their age' (Clark, 2010). This was exactly matched by results for public library use. Once again, those with a reading age above their chronological age were twice as likely to be public library users. There is, however, an interesting difference in the responses of young people who did not use the library. While many of the responses were similar to those for not using the school libraries, the dominant reason for non-use of the public library was that the family did not go to the library. The well known correlation between family support and educational attainment, and the fact that public libraries scored higher for involvement in reading outside the classroom, suggests 'that public libraries do not only have a role to play in the reading patterns of those pupils who use them, but also a unique role in providing opportunities to support learning outside of the classroom including support for family engagement' (Clark and Hawkins, 2010).

Back in 2000, the same year that the OECD was conducting its seminal research, The International Federation of Library Associations (IFLA) had published its *School Library Manifesto*, (IFLA/UNESCO 2000) which stated that: 'It has been demonstrated that, when teachers and librarians work together, students achieve higher levels of literacy, reading, learning, problem solving and information and communication technology skills.'

Ten years later, this remains, unfortunately, just an ambition in the UK. The Museums, Libraries and Archives Council/National Literacy Trust School Library Commission concluded: '[A]n effective school library acting as a powerhouse of learning and reading within a school is a unique resource. Our vision of a renewed school library system in the nation's schools is fundamentally about realising the potential of every child by exciting the latent reader and learner in all' (Douglas and Wilkinson, 2010, 20).

Making a difference

Michael Rosen, while Children's Laureate, showed how simply things could actually be turned around. In a series of programmes for the BBC in 2009 he turned a Cardiff primary school into what he termed 'a reading school'. As a result of this he brought together authors, publishers, booksellers, librarians, teachers and academics in a Just Read campaign: calling for every school to be a reading school.

> Not every child comes from a reading home. Sometimes, these children are denied the cognitive, social and cultural advantages that reading for pleasure provides because their schools do not have a reading culture either. These children are doubly let down. (Just Read, 2009)

This campaign is built upon the strong evidence from the United Kingdom Literacy Association (UKLA) Phase II research into 'Teachers as Readers', which shows that, where teachers and schools have a sound knowledge of children's books and how to use them to support children's development as readers, standards rise and the level of enjoyment increases. Even when a school cannot benefit from the presence of Michael Rosen himself, significant impact can be achieved (Cremin et al., 2008).

After more than a decade of investment, research, campaigning and policy making there are encouraging signs that the tide is turning. Even in 2009, Booktrust research (Booktrust, 2009), which asked over 1300 children about their own reading habits, found that love of reading was growing: 96% of all children surveyed said that they enjoyed reading (a 5% increase since September 2008). In 2009 Nielsen Bookscan showed that sales of children's books were up 4.9% in volume and picture-book sales were up by 13% on 2008 against an overall increase of 0.5% and, in 2010, they have suffered less than adult books as a result of the recession and were down only 2% in the UK against an overall figure of 4% (Harrison, 2010).

Similarly the Museum, Libraries and Archives Council (MLA) has recently published library service trends for 2009–10 which showed that children's borrowing of fiction books increased by 1.6%, whilst non-fiction borrowing declined fractionally, by less than 1% against an overall fall in borrowing of 2.5% (MLA, 2010). The latest Public Lending Right (PLR) figures issued in February 2011 show that children's writers dominate the charts of the most-borrowed authors from UK public libraries, taking seven of the top ten places. This is the highest number of children's authors in the top ten since PLR records began over 20 years ago and again indicates a more positive picture about children's reading. Julia Donaldson, whose book *The Gruffalo* was the most-borrowed children's title over the year, said: 'This just shows how much children need, and are entitled to, libraries and librarians. It's how they find out which books they like best and develop a love of reading' (Public Lending Right, 2011).

In the ensuing chapters of *Read to Succeed* you will find that all of the contributors, whatever their professional background and area of expertise, are indeed fundamentally concerned with maximizing the opportunities for every child to develop that love of reading.

In Chapter 1, for example, Wendy Cooling tells the story of Bookstart: an international inspiration and perhaps the first example of where positive action actually followed the research into the value of books and engaging with families. It is also, very significantly, a story of partnerships, which will be a recurring theme throughout the book. Above all, however, it is a passionate evocation of the fact that babies need books!

The next three chapters perform, I believe, a very important function in terms of the continuing professional development (CPD) of librarians. The School Library Commission recommendations call for school librarians to undertake further training: '[C]urrent professional training and formation for school librarians is not adequate. As well as the vital skills of information management and stock management they need a deep understanding of learning, pedagogy and child development' (Douglas and Wilkinson, 2010, 14). We are fortunate indeed to have three highly respected experts in their field to examine how children learn and are taught to read, and for their analysis of the role of libraries and librarians in this process.

In Chapter 2 Clare Wood gives us a fascinating insight into the psychology of reading development and valuable reinforcement and justification for current library strategies with very young children.

In Chapter 3 Prue Goodwin give us a cogent and expert guide to the pedagogy of the teaching of reading and the crucial symbiotic relationship between the teacher and the librarian. To develop young independent readers it is essential to understand what a partnership between the two can offer to the developing child.

New Zealand has a highly respected international reputation in the field of literacy teaching and libraries are themselves highly respected within New Zealand. However, the role of the school library is insufficiently recognized even there and in Chapter 4 Helen Villers makes a very impressive case for the vital links between libraries and literacy in order to meet the challenges of the 21st-century learner – ideas and practices that have much to offer schools and libraries in the UK and beyond.

In Chapter 5 Anne Sarrag and Lynne Taylor and their co-authors tell us the story of the national Summer Reading Challenge which, like Bookstart before it, has been a concept that has spread around the world. It epitomizes the crucial links between home and school and libraries, just as the School Library Commission recommends: 'All pupils should be encouraged to have a library card and be introduced to and encouraged to use their public library. The resources of the public library and the different skills sets of the staff who work there should be being harnessed to broaden and enhance the reading and information offer of the school' (Douglas and Wilkinson, 2010, 11). It has been successful not just in ever increasing participation, but in proven impact upon attainment.

The School Library Commission also tells us that: 'In many authorities the relationship between secondary schools and their feeder primaries is significant not just in terms of supporting transition but as a strategic framework for the local learning community' (Douglas and Wilkinson, 2010, 18). In Chapter 6 we see an example of this in practice. Nikki Heath and her colleagues from Stockport Libraries share their enthusiasm for a successful transition activity between secondary and feeder primary schools, with their local community library as the catalyst. The chapter also shows how local libraries can adapt and work with national offers like the Summer Reading Challenge.

We have seen that the School Library Commission feels that the current model of both teacher and librarian education is inadequate to deliver the very best from school library provision. In contrast, 'In the USA many states require a dual qualification in teaching and librarianship, and those that do not require instead a master's degree in librarianship with a specialisation in education. In Canada and Australia, teacher-librarians are dually qualified. In the UK, librarians qualify with a bachelor's degree and there is no specialist route for school librarians' (Barrett, 2010). In Chapter 7 Bridget Hamlet bares her soul to show us what can be gained from a different model of professional education: 'one young teacher's journey from the American Midwest to the English West Midlands; from idyllic teaching to disillusion in the classroom – and, ultimately, to inspiration in the library'. She generously shares practical ideas that school librarians and teachers can deploy to bring reading for pleasure back into the classroom and acknowledges what the UK does well and that she would take back to the USA.

Chapter 8 examines what has led to the success of a further historical example of innovation in reader development. The unique concept of Carnegie and Kate Greenaway (CKG) 'shadowing' originated in the early 1990s and has become a staple component of many a school's reading-promotion strategy. It has proved invaluable in raising the profile of reading, challenging literally thousands of young readers to engage with quality children's literature both in the UK and, increasingly, in other locations around the world. It has also been at the forefront of using web technology to engage young people with reading.

One result of the success of the CKG shadowing scheme has been the growth of local book awards to harness the enthusiasm generated by CKG and also to offer something which shadowing cannot give young people: the autonomy to make their own choices. In Chapter 9 Jean Wolstenholme tells us how the Lancashire Book Award originated and explores some of the challenges and opportunities of running this type of reading-development promotion. It includes practical methodologies for helping to embed such awards by maximizing their impact and looks at ways to ensure sustainability, such as engaging with partner organizations and sponsors.

A further unique example of motivating readers is considered in Chapter 10. There can be only one Kids' Lit Quiz™, and Professor Wayne Mills is definitely one of a kind. But if the reader is not fortunate enough to be in a participating country, there are invaluable lessons spelled out by Celeste Harrington, who examines why it works so well and links this to research on motivation and engagement.

Chapter 11 looks at another aspect of partnerships, this time between the library and the many facets of the book trade and between the library and local partners. Jacob Hope presents some highly practical advice and guidance to make the most of yet another symbiotic relationship that can work for the benefit of growing readers.

Young people aged 11–19 are perceived as a challenging group to engage in the library offer. Chapter 12 examines projects delivered by library services in the most deprived areas of the UK's south-west peninsula, engaging the most challenging and hard-to-reach of young people. Julia Hale and her colleagues comprehensively explain how libraries can go about removing barriers to library use through innovative schemes of outreach work.

The book concludes with an exciting look at the Australian Young Adult (YA) scene. In Chapter 13 Lili Wilkinson, herself a successful YA author, describes the vibrant virtual library offer that transforms reading from a solitary activity into something social, dynamic, interactive and creative and will leave the reader inspired by a real 21st-century vision of reading.

I would like to thank all of the contributors for their time, expertise and passionate commitment to children and young people and their reading futures. This book comes, in the spring of 2011, at a crucial time. The overwhelming weight of evidence and support amassed over the past ten years, outlined in this introduction, should be signposting a positive future for the readers still to come, and yet the timing of the crisis in public expenditure around the globe could not be crueller. We owe it to all those future readers not to let these advances gained and lessons learned be forgotten.

References

Barrett, L. (2010) Effective School Libraries: evidence of impact on student achievement, *School Librarian*, **58** (3), 136–9.

Booktrust (2009) *Book Time and Booked Up Executive Summary: children's research 2009*, www.booktrust.org.uk/show/feature/Booktime-press-release-October-2009.

Bradshaw, J., Ager, R., Burge, B. and Wheater, R. (2010) *PISA 2009: achievement of 15-year-olds in England*, NFER.

Chowdry, H., Crawford, C. and Goodman, G. (2009) *Drivers and Barriers to Educational success: evidence from the longitudinal study of young people in England*, Institute for Fiscal Studies, DCSF-RR102.

Clark, C. (2010) *Linking School Libraries and Literacy: young people's reading habits and attitudes to their school library, and an exploration of the relationship between school library use and school attainment*, National Literacy Trust.

Clark, C. and Hawkins, L. (2010) *Public Libraries and Literacy*, National Literacy Trust.

Cremin, T., Mottram, M., Collins, F. and Powell, S. (2008) *Building Communities of Readers*, UKLA.

Department for Culture, Media and Sport (2003) *Framework for the Future: libraries, learning and information in the next decade*, DCMS.

Department for Education (2010) *The Importance of Teaching – The Schools White Paper 2010*, Cm. 7980.

Department for Education and Skills (2004a) *School Libraries Making a Difference*, Department for Education and Skills.

Department for Education and Skills (2004b) *Improve Your Library: a self evaluation process*, www.teachernet.gov.uk/schoollibraries.

Douglas, J. and Wilkinson, S. (2010) *School Libraries: a plan for improvement – the report of the School Library Commission*, National Literacy Trust/Museums Libraries and Archives Council.

Dugdale, G. and Clark, C. (2008) *Literacy Changes Lives: an advocacy resource*, London: National Literacy Trust.

European Commission (2001) *European Report on the Quality of School Education: sixteen quality indicators*, Office for Official Publications of the European Communities.

Flaubert, G. (1857) Letter to Mademoiselle Leroyer de Chantepie, June.

Harrison, A. (2010) *Twilight Leads Boost in Children's Book Sales*, BBC News, http://news.bbc.co.uk/1/hi/education/8457612.stm.

Holden, J. (2004) *Creative Reading: young people, reading and public libraries*, Demos.

House of Commons Education and Skills Select Committee (2005) *Teaching Children to Read*, Eighth Report of Session 2004–05, The Stationery Office, HC121.

IFLA/UNESCO (2000) *School Library Manifesto*, www.unesco.org/webworld/libraries/manifestos/school_manifesto.html.

Just Read Campaign (2009), www.justreadcampaign.co.uk.

Morpurgo, M. (2009) Books for Schools: Michael Morpurgo says that reading for pleasure is a fundamental human right, *The Times*, 16 January.

Museums, Libraries and Archives Council (2010) *Trends from CIPFA Public Library Service*, www.mla.gov.uk/news_and_views/press_releases/2010/~/media/Files/pdf/2010/research/Trends_from_CIPFA_Public_Library_Service-Dec-2010.

OECD (2002) *Reading for Change: performance and engagement across countries – results from PISA 2000*, Organisation for Economic Co-operation and Development, www.oecd.org/dataoecd/43/54/33690904.pdf.

Ofsted (2004) *Reading for Purpose and Pleasure: an evaluation of the teaching of reading in primary schools*, HMI 2393.

Ofsted (2005) *English 2000–05 A Review of Inspection Evidence*, HMI 2351.

Pratchett, T. (2004), in *School Libraries Making a Difference*, Department for Education and Skills.

Public Lending Right (2011) *UK Children's Writers Dominate PLR's Most Borrowed Authors List*, www.plr.uk.com/mediaCentre/mediaReleases/feb2011(1).pdf.

The Reading Agency (2004) *Enjoying Reading: public library partnerships with schools*, The Reading Agency.

Twist, L., Schagen, I. and Hodgson, C. (2007) *Readers and Reading: the national report for England 2006,* Progress in International Reading Literacy Study, NFER.

1

It's never too soon to start

Wendy Cooling

[T]he first step, as you know, is always what matters most, particularly when we are dealing with those who are young and tender. That is the time when they are taking shape and when any impression we choose to make leaves a permanent mark.

(Plato, 428–348 BC)

Introduction

We all know, almost by instinct, that reading is a good thing, and we know that it is good to read to young children, but it took the Bookstart project, piloted in 1992, to support this belief with research evidence. This chapter is, in a way, a celebration of reading and a celebration of the joy that parents, carers and children experience when they share stories, pictures and rhymes as a regular and important part of their lives. This is not about teaching children to read – others are dealing with that – but about the practicalities and the benefits of reading to children from the very start of their lives.

Reading is still a good thing and, even as technological advances offer different ways of delivering text and pictures, reading continues to be central in life, and certainly in the process of education. Feeling good about books will make children keen to get to school and to learn to read, and the more they read the better readers they will become. Fast, fluent readers who have developed reading stamina will deal well with the whole curriculum and its reading demands and will grow into adults who have reading as a resource for the whole of their lives. They will be able to use books for pleasure, information, experience, solace, escape and so much more, and their lives will be enriched by their ability to access, by whatever means, the mass of fiction and non-fiction now available.

Pleasurable early reading experiences give babies and young children positive feelings about books. When a baby touches a small bath-book in the water and listens to someone who is known and loved talk about the duck and the story and is lifted from the bath, wrapped in a warm, fluffy towel, and cuddled on a knee and invited to look and listen as a beautiful picture book is read and talked about, they begin to know that books are good things. The baby doesn't know what a book is, or what a duck is, but they know that this bath-time experience is warm, secure and really rather nice. They know the voice of the reader and enjoy the rhythm and sounds of the words long before any of the words make sense.

A little later the baby may meet a book such as Helen Oxenbury's *Tickle, Tickle* (Oxenbury, 1987), the first-ever winner of the Baby Book Award (sponsored in the early years by Sainsbury's plc and now by Booktrust). This book has been hugely popular in Bookstart packs because it demonstrates many of the ingredients that add up to a really good book for a baby. The very short text is a joy to read aloud – very necessary, as anyone with children knows that favourite books must be read again, and again, and again. At a few months old babies don't understand all the words, but they respond to the voice of someone who loves them, and the sounds of words like 'Splish, splash' and 'Tickle, tickle' resonate in their heads; they're great words to say and to demonstrate, and the repetition and rhythm helps babies to develop an ear for language which, as time goes on, will take them into reading. The invitation to adult and child to join in with splashing and tickling makes this a book for interaction and fun, and so offers a memorable shared experience. The illustrations are a delight, as boldly drawn babies fill the pages: babies rule in this book giving it plenty of child appeal. And for those parents who worry excessively about learning, children who've enjoyed this board book will find that they understand such things as alliteration and onomatopoeia when they meet them at school.

So the sharing of words and pictures is, beyond everything, a bonding experience. Many parents and carers have always understood this and have made bedtime reading a normal part of their child's day; but others, perhaps those who had no such introduction to stories when they were young, need to be encouraged and empowered to become involved in their children's earliest education and to read with them. Some, of course, worry about their own reading skills and their ability to read aloud well. Very young children are not critical; they love to hear the voice of someone who loves them talking, singing and reading.

These early, pleasurable experiences with words and pictures, stories and rhymes help children to understand that although reading is complicated they will soon be able to do it. They will know that they must use their heads to read the words and make sense of the way they are ordered and what they mean, but they must also use their hearts to enter into the magic of the story. William Wordsworth's words in 'The Prelude' are worth remembering:

> Twice five years
> Or less I might have seen, when first my mind
> With conscious pleasure opened to the charm
> Of words in tuneful order, found them sweet
> For their own sakes, a passion and a power. ...

All our children may not be quite as quick as Wordsworth, may not understand about the power and passion of words before they reach the age of ten, but those who are read to every day from their very earliest days are most likely to do so.

We all have a reading history and most of us never forget the earliest chapters of it. Talk to disaffected teenagers, and some will say that they never read and all books are boring. But show them some classic picture books, and most of them will remember with pleasure lifting the flaps and finding Spot over and over again (Hill, 1980); poking their fingers through the holes in *The Very Hungry Caterpillar* (Carle, 1969); being pleasantly scared by the monsters in *Where the Wild Things Are* (Sendak, 1963); and staying awake at night wishing the Tiger would come to tea (Kerr, 1968). Reminding them of the days when reading was fun brings to mind the wonder of some of these books; soon they're talking about the skeletons in *Funnybones* (Ahlberg and Ahlberg, 1992); the safety of the hen in *Rosie's Walk* (Hutchins, 1968) and searching for the hidden characters in *Each Peach Pear Plum* (Ahlberg and Ahlberg, 1978). Sadly, some children miss out on this very early experience and don't meet these books until they reach school. They start school without that knowledge of stories and books and how they work that gives other children a strong, positive beginning. It was to offer equal opportunity and access to books to all children that the Bookstart project was introduced.

The Bookstart story

This is, inevitably, a very personal account of the beginnings of this book-gifting scheme, which has grown beyond my wildest imaginings. It could be a proper, 'Once upon a time. ...' story because the germ of the idea is the much-told story of one boy called Kevin. Working at Booktrust brought many invitations to schools, libraries, bookshops and publishers, and certainly the one to visit a school as the new reception children arrived is the most memorable. The year was 1991, nursery education was not available to all and for some children this was their first school experience. The new arrivals were nervous and excited, but their parents were almost traumatized; they didn't want to leave their little ones. The excellent class teacher gave each child a picture book to look at as she gently got the parents to leave. The children looked at their books, most of them turned the pages, pointed things out to themselves and named things out loud; some recognized their book. But Kevin did not. He bent his book, sat on it, sniffed it, tried to throw it like a frisbee and then looked round to see what others were doing and tried to copy. It was very clear that Kevin had never held a book before, didn't know what to do with it and so, in a way, failed at the very first thing he was asked to do at school. He didn't have a wealth of story experience, felt left out and different, and was having a less positive start to school than others. It seemed to me shocking that such a thing could happen – a child of four or five knowing nothing of books – and it pushed me to look further. It became very clear that Kevin was not the only one and that large numbers of parents and carers were not reading to their children – they were parents who cared for their children and wanted the best for them, but thought it was best to leave books and reading to teachers.

Reading does need to be taught, and that *is* the job of a qualified teacher, but parents can inculcate a love of books long before school. It became clear that if we wanted all homes to have books, we needed to supply them, and, since one or two books were not going to change the world, families needed to be encouraged to enrol their babies at the public library as early as possible and so have access to the wide range of wonderful board and picture books now available.

Librarians were immediately keen to be involved in a possible scheme to bring books to children, but libraries were not the places to give out the baby packs because the families who most needed the books seldom went into them. It soon became clear that the only people who saw all, or almost all babies, were health visitors. At that time babies all had a health check at around nine months and health visitors were following up on families if they failed to keep their appointment. Health visitors seemed the very best people to give out those first Bookstart packs, and tying reading in with health stressed the importance of intellectual development alongside physical development. Families accepted the importance of the health check, and receiving books at the same time helped them to focus on the importance of reading.

As always, the hardest part of setting up the pilot project was the raising of necessary funds, and a huge debt is owed to the Unwin Charitable Trust for its contribution and ongoing support. Publishers were behind Bookstart from the start and donated books for the pilot. Birmingham Library Services and South Birmingham Health Authority agreed to join with Booktrust in bringing Bookstart to 300 families with babies of eight to nine months in three areas of the city, areas reflecting the wide diversity of the population. Margaret Meek of the University of London Institute of Education offered valuable advice and wrote a letter to all parents involved. She wisely stressed the need for the project to be properly evaluated, and so Dr Barrie Wade of Birmingham University's School of Education was approached. He agreed to produce an interim report of the project and to follow the Bookstart babies into school; such research would, we hoped, really tell us whether early intervention with books does make it more likely that children start school motivated to read, and whether sharing books with babies changes parents' and carers' attitudes and their library visiting and book-buying habits. Margaret Meek's introductory letter included the paragraph:

> Why should we read to very young children? There are lots of reasons but the most important is that the sooner children enjoy reading, the more they will want to read and to become good at it. We know now for certain that the children who handle books confidently before they go to school, and have enjoyed being read to, are those who learn to read in school with most success. Also, parents and other adults who read to children report that babies love to be read to, even before they can talk.

In 1992, Booktrust and its partners produced the first Bookstart packs – simple yellow folders containing a board book, a nursery rhyme card (soon to change its name as parents wrote and said 'thank you for the place mat'), Margaret Meek's letter, a poster illustrating the joys of reading and, most importantly, an invitation to join the library. Parents and carers were also asked to complete a questionnaire to help with the research. They were asked to complete a further questionnaire six months later, designed to investigate changes in attitudes to book sharing, book buying and libraries. Joining in with the giving out of packs was a memorable experience because families found it hard to accept that they were not being asked to pay, but simply to read.

From the start, we looked at the diversity of the population and tried to have this in mind by providing materials in the home languages most used in the pilot areas. It is interesting to note that one of the poems on the first rhyme card was this poem from Ghana, beautifully illustrated, of course:

Listen to the tree bear
Crying in the night
Crying for his Mammy
In the pale moonlight
What will his Mammy do
When she hears him cry?
She'll tuck him in a cocoa-pod
And sing a lullaby.

Those first Bookstart babies were too young to really understand this rhyme but they were, almost accidentally, learning about the sounds of words, about the rhymes and rhythms of language.

Bookstart was different from other projects in that it was offered to *all* families in the chosen areas rather than being targeted at families considered to be deprived. It was clear that in all sections of the population there were adults who were not reading to their children, who thought that libraries were for when their children were older, and so we were convinced that the Bookstart gift should be for everyone. The aim was to grow the project to benefit all children in the UK.

Support for Bookstart was immediate, and the follow-up, over-subscribed conference generated huge interest and led to the setting up of 30 projects around the country, initiated by enthusiastic librarians and health visitors and supported by local authority funding. The summary of findings in the initial report, *Booktrust report number 2*, published in 1993, read:

Bookstart has been warmly welcomed by professionals and by parents. It has promoted more awareness of books, more reading and more sharing of books with very young children in the wide range of families who received the pack. Significantly more babies had enrolled as library members as a result of the pack. Bookstart had promoted book purchase and book club membership.
(Wade and Moore, 1993)

The enthusiasm spread, more areas became involved, libraries began to run sessions for adults and babies (more on this later) and to compete to get the youngest library member! We knew we had the foundation of something important, and so the struggle for money to improve and extend the project began. It was perhaps the follow-up research, looking at Bookstart babies when they started school, as well as at other local projects, that brought publicity and began to convince a wider range of people that Bookstart was good news, a project that really benefited children.

A Gift for Life, Bookstart: the first five years, by Barrie Wade and Maggie Moore of Birmingham University, was published by Booktrust in 1998 and found that many positive benefits resulted from sharing books with babies. There is not space here to review the research, which, along with later research, can be viewed on the Bookstart website, but just to say that point one of the report's summary read:

> Bookstart is a relatively low-cost scheme, but findings show it has the potential to increase book sharing, book purchase and library usage. Bookstart contributes to laying the foundations for literacy and analysis indicates its potential for raising standards in both literacy and numeracy. (Wade and Moore, 1998)

The literacy findings did not surprise; the numeracy ones did – Bookstart children had shared a wide range of picture books, including, it became clear, books about counting and shape, and so they started school ready and willing to learn how to read and how to work with numbers.

Bookstart continued to be developed by a dedicated team at Booktrust; local schemes continued to grow – there were 60 by 1999 – but the break-through came in 1999 with funding from Sainsbury's plc. Sainsbury's asked its staff and colleagues how they wanted the company to celebrate the millennium. Sainsbury's wanted to support a project for children that was about learning and that would leave a legacy for the 21st century. Bookstart, established and ripe for expansion, was chosen and for the first time universal provision was possible – by the year 2000, 92% of babies were benefiting from Bookstart. *Sainsbury's Bookstart Report* (Booktrust, 2000) reported that 91% of parents said they were reading to their babies after receipt of the Bookstart pack.

When the two-year sponsorship came to an end Bookstart was strong and established. For the first four years of the new century, Government funding from first the Department for Education and Employment and then the Department for Culture, Media and Sport enabled packs to be produced and local authorities to buy into Bookstart. The scheme was kept in the public eye and, in July 2004, the then Chancellor of the Exchequer, Gordon Brown, announced funding to entitle all families to three packs of books before school: the Baby Book Bag at around nine months, Bookstart+ at 18 to 24 months and the Treasure Chest at three to four years. At last the project had achieved its major aim, but, it must be said, only with the strong support and involvement of its many partners – especially library and health professionals and children's publishers.

The carefully chosen books are of course central in the packs, but booklists, booklets offering advice to parents and carers, and a place mat with nursery rhymes illustrated by the best of our children's illustrators that are now included give added value and added support to families. Today's book bags and boxes have been developed with creativity and have benefited from the expertise of our many partners – they bear little resemblance to the yellow folders given to those 300 families in Birmingham in 1992. Bookstart has come of age, become a part of children's early years entitlement, involved with Children's Centres, Sure Start projects and more. The *Bookstart Partnership Report* of 2003 quotes Professor Kathy Sylva's statement to the House of Commons Select Committee on Education and Employment:

> Our study has shown that the home environment can really make a difference … more important than the mother's educational qualifications is what the mother does with her child. Education matters, qualifications matter, but if the mother reads to the child, plays rhyming games, sings songs, talks about letters and sounds, and takes the child to the library, these behaviours at home are more important and can compensate for a low education level.   (Booktrust, 2003)

My only complaint with Professor Sylva is that she failed to mention fathers, for of course their involvement is equally important. My celebration is that the core beliefs of Bookstart have become accepted facts. It is somewhat ironic that, as I write this in February 2011, the country's financial situation is dire and Bookstart funding, and indeed libraries, are under threat.

The exciting developments of the last ten years have been skimmed over, but central has been the introduction of Booktime and Booked Up, giving children books as they start primary and, later, secondary school. Anyone observing the work teachers do with the chosen books will witness a real sense of excitement that any good gift can bring, as children are once again reminded of the wonders that books offer. Reading for pleasure needs to be encouraged amidst the hard work and prescription that school so often brings. Details and research findings could fill this book, but all can be found on the Booktrust website: www.booktrust.org.uk/show/feature/Bookstart-research.

The issue of diversity is one that challenges any organization seeking to intervene in children's reading development, and clearly Bookstart packs and resources need to reflect the rich and varied society in which we live.

Publishers are encouraged to include positive images of disability, to feature different kinds of families and children from a wide range of backgrounds in their books, but there is a great deal more to be done here. As readers, we remember the books that touch us, the books in which characters think a bit like us or find themselves in situations that we have experienced. Of course we enjoy the wildly fantastical and the journeys and adventures that we will never experience, but the book that makes us feel that the writer knows what's going on in our heads is always one to remember. Picture books have never been richer, but still there are some children who will never see themselves or anyone like them in any of the books they are offered. It is only necessary to observe children, say the young black child seeing the cover of Mary Hoffman and Caroline Binch's *Amazing Grace* (1991) for the first time with wonder and delight on her face, to know that this is important. This book was one of the first in the UK to show a strong and vibrant black child on a cover, and the need for this has been clearly reflected in its ongoing success.

Bookstart, a partnership project

Bookstart is, at heart, a partnership project relying on the support, advice and co-operation of a range of professional groups and organizations. Booktrust produces Bookstart packs and co-ordinates the project nationally. Packs are then supplied to centres around the country and local delivery is managed by library, health and education agencies in each local authority. Every effort is made to reach all families, so organization must be flexible and locally sensitive if Bookstart is to help in the tackling of social exclusion. Ways must be found to identify children with special needs, and organizations such as Home-Start, Scope, the National Deaf Children's Society (NDCS), the Royal National Institue of Blind People (RNIB) and Mencap have been valuable and generous in the sharing of their expertise. Booktouch, a special resource pack for children up to four years old who are blind or partially sighted, and Bookshine, a pack for deaf children, have benefited enormously from the co-operation, experience and advice of experts. Bookstart's list of partners continues to grow and widen as the Bookstart team seeks to reach traveller and refugee families and respond to the language needs of families and the literacy needs of parents and carers – delivering Bookstart to *all* our children is an ongoing challenge.

A small group of very special librarians in Birmingham were Bookstart's first partners, and librarians have continued to be central partners as the project has grown. They are involved in inserting local library information into packs, inviting and encouraging library membership, delivering packs to families and offering activity sessions that support the reading message. In 1992 parents regularly told us that they were afraid to take their babies to the library in case the baby damaged books or made too much noise. I can't imagine hearing such comments today, for libraries have responded to these concerns and today's children's libraries welcome babies and toddlers and support the adults with them as they choose books. More and more parents enrol their babies at the library, and libraries offer them an excellent service. My own local library has displays to support Bookstart, offers a wide range of board books and picture books, reassures adults who may be concerned about books getting chewed or torn and, in fact, offers a friendly space in which children and adults are happy to spend time together.

Activities offered for parents and children vary from area to area but almost always include Bounce and Rhyme Sessions, Storytimes, Bookstart Rhymetimes, etc. that entertain children and, more importantly, model reading for adults who are nervous and uncertain about how to read to their children. Watching a good librarian share books with children really is a great way for parents to begin to see how to go about sharing books and talking about them with their children. These sessions are aimed at the babies and children and so are non-threatening to even the least-confident adults. The work of librarians continues to strengthen the Bookstart message: the six books each child receives before school are a wonderful gift, but it is the regular diet of books from the library that helps children to develop into real readers and book lovers. Now, in 2011, library budgets and libraries themselves are under threat; we lose these services at our peril, for their disappearance would change the educational chances of many of our children.

Librarians are not just passive partners; they bring expertise and ideas to Bookstart. Just one activity can be mentioned here: Bookstart Book Crawl, an idea from Croydon Libraries, a library-joining incentive that has generated millions of library visits. The scheme is very simple: young children collect special stickers when they borrow books and are awarded a certificate after six library visits. This proved very popular, so the idea has been picked up by the Bookstart team and disseminated throughout the country – it is now run in libraries in over 90% of local authorities. It was reported in the Booktrust publication *Reading for Pleasure: reading for life* (Booktrust, 2010) that 195,206 Bookstart Book Crawl Certificates were awarded in 2009, representing 420,824 library visits. Children completing 10 Crawls receive a Gold Certificate, which equates to 60 library visits. The certificates are beautiful, illustrated by such popular children's book illustrators as Tony

Ross, Jane Ray, Jan Ormerod and Nick Sharratt, and many families seek to collect the whole set. This inexpensive, attractive idea is just one example of the additional value that libraries have brought to Bookstart.

Health professionals too have been involved in Bookstart from the beginning and Bookstart baby packs and Bookstart+ are still usually gifted via the family's health visitor. This partnership is invaluable and the gifting during an essential health-care check-up gives the books a greater importance in the eyes of some parents. Health professionals value being part of Bookstart and see it as contributing to parental bonding, early listening and communication skills, development of attention span, pre-literacy skills and social skills. And it is still a fact that parents with babies are more likely to be reached in this way than in any other.

Bookstart could not exist without the support of children's book publishers. Over four million books are purchased every year at a nominal cost, but with a value of over £21 million. Publishers submit books for selection, books that are positive and inclusive, reflecting our society and celebrating gender, race and ethnicity. The chosen books, from classic authors to the very newest talent in writing and illustrating, spark the child's imagination and curiosity, use language well, show words and pictures working together, and can be enjoyed repeatedly by children and adults. Kate Wilson, then Director Children's at Pan Macmillan, gave a publisher's view of Bookstart for the *Bookstart Partnership Report June* in 1993:

> Bookstart is, without question, the most exciting cross-agency project I've ever
> been involved in. As a publisher, we are so impressed by the commitment
> demonstrated by the national team and by the librarians and health visitors who
> give their skills and time so unstintingly. It is a wonderful thing for the book
> industry to have parents and carers of the youngest potential readers exposed to
> the experience of books and book sharing, and is worthy of the strongest
> possible support from us all. (Booktrust, 1993)

This support is offered in so many ways, not just in the continuing publication of exceptional books, but in supporting other aspects of the project – particularly the production of a give-away book for Bookstart Day, providing books for piloting new projects to reach special groups of children and making it possible to offer dual-language books to children whose home language is not English. Publishers provide Bookstart with the tools for the job, board and picture books rich in language and illustration that will leave children wanting to read more.

Conclusion: the wider picture

All around the world people and agencies who care about reading have heard of, and picked up on, the Bookstart idea. The first country to bring Bookstart to its children was Japan: Izumi Satou of Bookstart Japan believes that: 'All people seek the happiness of their children and that is what Bookstart gives to every child.' Izumi's book telling the story of ten years of Bookstart Japan was published in 2010, sadly only available in Japanese. Asian countries such as Korea and Taiwan introduced Bookstart to remind parents of the pleasure of book sharing as concern was growing about the fast-paced, competitive nature of their schools. Parents were taken up by the need for children to achieve, paying for extra classes and supervising learning, but making no time for enjoyment. Today Bookstart projects are happening from Australia to Thailand to Columbia to the Falkland Islands and many places in between. There are affiliated schemes in many European countries – the German Government committed to seven years of funding in 2010. Projects work in ways appropriate to each country – books can be given out through Buddhist temples or by volunteers, according to what works best. International meetings offering opportunities to share ideas and disseminate good practice have been held at IBBY (the International Board on Books for Young People) conferences and at the Bologna Book Fair, and the message is spreading. The idea, as has already been said, is a very simple one, but delivering it to all children is a challenge in any country and requires the support of a wide-ranging group of people. As Bookstart spreads around the world, Britain is once again fighting for the necessary funding to keep the book gifting going at the present level and to respond to changing needs. A project with wide reach, demonstrating the strength of partnership working, and supported by solid research, cannot be allowed to disappear.

The last word goes to a character in Terry Jones's 1997 book *The Knight and the Squire*. The book is set in the 14th century, a time when few children could read. Tom and his non-reading friend find themselves hiding in a library in France:

> Not a library such as the village priest had back home; the priest's library consisted of one perhaps two books at most. This library was different.
>
> If Tom could have counted them all, he would have been able to count eleven thousand volumes sitting on shelf after shelf – and all round the room, and from the floor to the ceiling. There was even a gallery running around above their heads, with ladders up to it and more books stretching on above that. And each book was secured by a chain.

Tom tries to explain to his friend what reading is like:

It's like … not being blind … It's like … standing on the edge of a cliff and knowing you can fly.

And why he's so glad he can read:

walking in here … I suddenly saw that the whole world – more – is in books. It's like being able to see beyond the horizon!

Bookstart's wish is for all children to see the impossible, to see beyond the horizon, for this, as Izumi Satou from Japan says, could be one of the keys to happiness.

References

Ahlberg, J. and Ahlberg, A. (1978) *Each Peach Pear Plum*, Puffin.

Ahlberg, J. and Ahlberg, A. (1992) *Funnybones*, Puffin.

Booktrust (1993) *Bookstart Partnership Report June*, Booktrust.

Booktrust (2000) *Sainsbury's Bookstart Report*, Booktrust.

Booktrust (2003) *Bookstart Partnership Report June*, Booktrust.

Booktrust (2010) *Reading for Pleasure: reading for life*, Booktrust.

Carle, E. (1969) *The Very Hungry Caterpillar*, Puffin.

Hill, E. (1980) *Where's Spot?*, Puffin.

Hoffman, M. and Binch, C. (1991) *Amazing Grace*, Frances Lincoln.

Hutchins, P. (1968) *Rosie's Walk*, Random House.

Jones, T. (1997) *The Knight and the Squire*, Puffin.

Kerr, J. (1968) *The Tiger Who Came to Tea*, HarperCollins.

Oxenbury, H. (1987) *Tickle, Tickle*, Walker.

Sendak, M. (1963) *Where the Wild Things Are*, HarperCollins.

Wade, B. and Moore, M. (1993) *Bookstart:: Booktrust report number 2*, Booktrust.

Wade, B. and Moore, M. (1998) *A Gift for Life, Bookstart: the first five years*, Booktrust.

2

How children begin to read

Clare Wood

Introduction

One of the reasons why I work in the area of children's reading development is because my brother experienced substantial difficulties learning to read and write and was finally identified as experiencing developmental dyslexia at the age of 35. I watched him labour over reading activities and struggle with expressing himself in writing, and I watched the impact that these experiences had on his confidence and behaviour during childhood and early adulthood. His difficulties contrasted starkly with my own love of reading and writing, and this made me reflect on why he experienced so much difficulty in something that I saw as effortless and enjoyable.

As a researcher, I know that reading is something that is learned, and therefore is something that must be taught. Children at risk of reading and writing difficulties can be identified early in childhood and supported with the right tuition and resources both at home and at school. My own work has been concerned with these issues of early identification and effective intervention, but there is still a great deal to be learned about effective literacy tuition.

This chapter is intended to offer a simple introduction to the topic of early reading development, which will give an idea of the initial stages that readers go through on their journey towards skilled, fluent reading. This is followed by some more practical material on what skills and activities appear to be important for reading development at different stages of the journey. The aim of this material is to offer the reader some food for thought on how both typically and atypically developing readers can be supported during these early stages of reading through activities that you can try out both as an individual and professionally in the context of library-based sessions with children. Much of this is based on my own research interests and personal views, and what is offered here is a taster of what the research literature has to offer, rather than being an exhaustive overview of everything we currently know on the topic. I hope that you find it as interesting as I do.

Stages and phases of early reading development

In the academic literature there has been some debate over whether it is appropriate to describe children as passing through stages or phases of reading development. Stages imply a fixed sequence of changes, whereas phases imply a looser pattern of development. However, both stage theories (e.g. Frith, 1985) and phase theories (e.g. Ehri, 1997, 1999) describe a broadly similar pattern of development.

At first, children 'read' without reference to the alphabetic principle. That is, they may be able to tell you what a word 'says', but they will be doing so based on visual recognition of the word as a whole, or on the basis of significant features of a word rather than because they know what sounds the individual letters make. For example, Bloodgood (1999) found that young children were able to read their own name or those of their friends, but this was achieved without any relevant letter–sound knowledge. Similarly, Gough, Juel and Griffith (1992) found that pre-school children learned to read words that were associated with a thumbprint faster than conventionally presented words, but the thumbprint was what cued the reading of the associated word, and over half of the children could not read the word when the thumbprint was missing. This is similar to the phenomenon of when young children appear to be able to read product names on packaging or signs: whilst children can read words like 'Pepsi' when they are presented in the context of a product logo, they appear to do this on the basis of visual cues alone; if they see 'Xepsi' written within the traditional product logo, they will still read it as 'Pepsi' (Masonheimer, Drum and Ehri, 1984). This example shows the limitations of children's use of salient visual cues as the basis for word reading in our alphabetic script. It is useful for providing children with an initial sight vocabulary, which enables them to understand the idea that letter-like forms 'say something', but there are limits to how many words children can learn and use in this way before confusions between similar-looking words will start to occur. For example, an unfamiliar word like 'ship' or 'shell' may be persistently misread as a visually similar known word, like 'shop', by children who are in this phase of development.

Children eventually begin to develop an awareness of the alphabetic principle: that each letter or set of letters represents a given sound in speech, and that they can 'decode' text by learning these letter–sound combinations. For languages like English, there is not a perfect association of one-to-one correspondence between letters and their sounds, but it is a good starting point from which to learn commonly occurring patterns, and then rules about exceptional spellings, which are often based on words derived from other languages. Reading during this phase of development can feel laboured because children are consciously applying their knowledge of letter-sounds and rules about how words are written as they are reading.

Over time and with practice, children start to recognize longer letter strings as commonly co-occurring (e.g. '-ing', '-ough') and this speeds up their processing of text. Eventually children achieve a level of automatized, fluent reading ability where word recognition is instantaneous and effortless, and this frees up mental resources for processing the content of what is being read. This is an important point to note: this chapter is focusing primarily on the earliest stages on the journey towards skilled reading and is best thought of as being about how children 'decode' text. With the heavy emphasis on phonics in most primary school classrooms in the UK, you might be forgiven for thinking that when children can decode the words on the page they can 'read', but of course the ultimate aim is to read for meaning (reading comprehension). Decoding is the first (but very necessary) step on this journey towards skilled reading, but it is not the only step. Other chapters in this book will be discussing comprehension in more detail, but it is important to note here that decoding text is a means to an end, not the end itself.

Reading together

Studies of family literacy practices show that what you do with your children in the early years does make a difference to their early reading development. If there is one consistent research finding in the literature on pre-school family literacy practices, it is that regular reading of a storybook with your child will impact positively on later reading development (e.g. Weinberger, 1996; Wood, 2002a). A study by Wood (2002a) of 61 UK pre-schoolers showed that the majority of parents engaged in daily joint storybook reading, weekly games and occasional singing activities, and that parents who fell into this group had children with better vocabularies and reading performance a year later in school than did those children whose parents who reported engaging in little or no literacy-based interaction with them, or who sang with them but did little else. More frequent joint storybook reading was also linked to better awareness of letter sounds and short-term memory. Such research underscores the importance of local libraries in resourcing such activity, as well as book-gifting projects such as those run by the Booktrust charity in the UK (see Chapter 1).

It is worth noting, however, that simply reading aloud to a child is not sufficient to promote literacy benefits: in the words of the song, 'it's not what you do; it's the way that you do it'. For example, one study of pre-school teachers found that the more that the teachers read to their children, the less well the children subsequently did on their reading. This was likely to be because the time spent reading to the children displaced other activities that might benefit literacy development, and because also this form of reading to children puts the children in a somewhat passive role. It is important to involve children in the reading process by encouraging their engagement with the story as it is read and the text as it is presented. One way of ensuring this is to use *dialogic prompts* with the children as you read with them. That is, you should ask open-ended questions about the story, expand on the children's responses to these questions, praise the children and build their interest in the story.

One model for dialogic prompting is based on the CROWD acronym and is recommended by Grover Whitehurst, who has been a prolific researcher in this area (Figure 2.1).

Completion prompts: These are where you leave a (predictable) word off the end of a sentence, which allows the children the opportunity to join in by completing the sentence for you.
Recall prompts: These are where you ask the children to recall what has happened in part or all of a story. This can be done at the end of a book-reading session, or at the beginning if you are re-reading a favourite book with them.
Open-ended prompts: These are used in conjunction with pictures and take the form of 'Can you tell me what is happening here?'
Wh- prompts: These are prompts using 'wh-' words like 'why', 'where' and 'what', and are used to help to build the children's vocabulary and understanding of words and events in the story.
Distancing prompts: These are used to encourage children to make links between elements of the story and their own ideas and experiences. These can take the form of encouraging the child to think about recent events or visits, or their own likes and dislikes, and linking these to the events and characters in the story.

Figure 2.1 *The CROWD model of dialogic prompting*

There has been extensive research into use of dialogic reading prompts with pre-school children, and this has found that they promote vocabulary development, narrative skills and understanding of word order (e.g. Arnold et al., 1994; Hargrave and Sénéchal, 2000; Hay and Fielding-Barnsley, 2007; Whitehurst and Lonigan, 1998; Zevenbergen, Whitehurst and Zevenbergen, 2003).

So, when children are in the early years, and even before they can read for themselves, we can boost their chances of later reading success by regularly reading storybooks with them (rather than reading 'to' them), taking care to engage the children in a discussion around the story as we progress through it.

Finding time for rhythm and rhyme

The ability to hear and recognize when two words rhyme is something that seems so obvious that we can often take it for granted. Children's books in the early years have long recognized that children enjoy hearing and playing with rhyme from a young age, and books of nursery rhymes and poetic stories like *We're Going on a Bear Hunt* (Rosen and Oxenbury, 1989) are commonly found in pre-school children's bedrooms and libraries. However, not all children are as aware of rhyme as we might think. Children with reading difficulties are characterized by difficulties in hearing patterns of sounds in speech, such as whether or not two words rhyme, or if they start with the same sound (alliteration) (e.g. Bradley and Bryant, 1978; Wood and Terrell, 1998).

The ability to recognize that speech comprises smaller units of sound that make patterns in this way is known as 'phonological awareness'. There has been a substantial amount of research to examine the relationship between phonological awareness and reading development and there is consistent evidence that phonological skills can predict later reading development, and it is proposed that phonological skills underpin reading achievement in a causally important way (Adams, 1990). Another type of phonological awareness is awareness of speech rhythm, and, like the other forms of phonological skill, it also appears to be implicated in reading development, although the nature of its contribution is one that is still being understood. We do know that individuals with reading difficulties appear to have difficulties perceiving aspects of speech rhythm (Wood and Terrell, 1998; Wood, Wade-Woolley and Holliman, 2009). One reason why it is important for reading is because of the links between intonation, word stress and comprehension of language – how we use our voices changes the intended meaning of our utterances, and being able to represent these features appropriately is linked to reading with expression and comprehension skills. But there is also some evidence that speech rhythm sensitivity is linked to decoding skills, too.

It is relatively straightforward to engage young children in activities that will help them to develop phonological awareness. In very young children, practising favourite poems or rhymes is a good idea, and if you can do so in combination with completion prompts this will encourage them to reflect on why certain words 'fit' the gap. If you can pick poems with a strong metrical pattern or 'beat' to them, this will offer the chance to develop the children's awareness of speech rhythm, too. Library sessions such as Rhyme Times, Baby Bounce and Rhyme are good examples of appropriate activities of this kind. Such activities can be made even more fun (and noisier) with the use of drums and tambourines, which the children can use to beat out the emphasis on stressed words in the poem. Ask the children if they can think of any other words that also rhyme with a particular word, to see how well they understand the concept and to support them to think of strategies for building words that rhyme. In slightly older children this can be done using magnetic letters, words or cards or even Scrabble tiles to make words and see what happens when you substitute one letter with a different one. If they struggle with 'hearing' the differences between sounds or rhymes, try drawing their attention to how they use their lips, tongue and voice differently when they make different sounds, as a way of highlighting the contrasts to them in a way that they will understand. Putting their hand on their throat as they make different letter sounds, or even just in front of their lips, will make them 'feel' the differences in sounds, even if they cannot distinguish them clearly in sound (e.g. try saying /g/ and /k/ in this way!).

Encourage children to make up their own rhymes – the sillier the better! With older children, asking them to recite their favourite poems is a good way of getting them to think about speech rhythm, and it may be worth modelling the correct reading of the poem for them in terms of expression and timing if this is something that they struggle with. In terms of hearing them read prose, again encourage them to think about introducing more expression into their reading – this will require them to think about the events in the story and how the characters feel and so on, but appropriate use of dialogic prompts will support the children to reflect on these aspects and how to express them in their reading aloud.

Fun with phonics

Phonological awareness is important because children have to move on to mapping speech sounds onto printed letter combinations. The teaching of letter–sound combinations is referred to as *phonics*, and there has been much debate recently over the different forms that phonics tuition can take and which ones are more effective. The bottom line, however, is that phonics tuition is an important feature of effective literacy tuition in the context of alphabetic languages like English. Parents who are interested in how to support or supplement the phonics tuition that their children receive at school should always talk to the school first, but there are a number of excellent resources available that can be ordered from bookshops, of which *Sound Linkage* (Hatcher, 2000) is perhaps one of the best that is easily available and based on a solid research foundation.

One of the messages from the research literature is that phonics should be taught in the context of 'real books' rather than reading schemes. That is, many reading schemes are constructed to emphasize phonological regularities or high-frequency words in English. However, research suggests that the letter–sound correspondences that are taught in the context of phonics tuition enable children to read more words in regular children's books than they do words in reading schemes (Solity and Vousden, 2009). Children's literature therefore offers a better basis for teaching and practising phonic rules than many reading schemes do. So, if children are using a reading scheme at school, it may be a good idea to supplement this with regular visits to the local library where children can select their own books from popular children's literature.

So much emphasis is placed on phonics that children can become bogged down with such activities, which can also seem to be increasingly divorced from reading for pleasure. It is important to maintain children's motivation to read by allowing them to choose their reading material and supporting them to read content that they want to engage with, without making judgements about whether the level of the text is going to be too hard for them to cope with. If they have your support during reading in the home or library, this is not necessarily a concern, and it is worth remembering that joint book reading is ideally placed to support children with this type of activity.

Some children see 'books' as closely associated with schoolwork, and it can therefore be hard to engage them in phonic activities outside of school, especially if they have had some negative experiences or already sense that they find this type of activity difficult. However, there is a free computer-based resource aimed at early readers that can be accessed via the internet and that adopts a game-based interface. Developed in Canada by researchers at Concordia and McGill Universities, ABRACADABRA is a suite of game-based activities that support a wide range of reading activities, including phonic work, storybook reading, reading with expression and appropriate speed, comprehension and spelling. There are printable resources to go with it and, most importantly, there are resources aimed at teachers and parents which explain what each activity is designed to teach and how to use it. Intervention programmes that have been developed based on these materials have been found to support the development of early reading skills and are particularly engaging for readers who have difficulty maintaining their attention with traditional book-based activities (Comaskey, Savage and Abrami, 2009; Deault, Savage and Abrami, 2009). ABRACADABRA can be accessed at http://grover.concordia.ca/abra/current/index.php.

From the known to the new

Once children have acquired a sight vocabulary of words that they can recognize and they have some knowledge of letter–sound correspondences, they can be encouraged to reflect on how they might be able to work out how to read unfamiliar words that look similar to words that they do know. Known in the academic literature as 'orthographic analogy' or the 'clue word' technique (Goswami, 1993), this can be easily achieved just using some words written down on pieces of card. Begin by showing the child a word that is familiar to them and ask them to read it aloud. Then put a new word that is less familiar but that is visually similar immediately below it, and point out to them the similarities between the two words and ask them to sound out the unfamiliar part. Then ask them to guess at what the new word might be. So, for example, you could take a word like 'look' and put beneath it a word like 'shook' and ask the child if they know what sound 'sh' makes and see if they can work out what the new word might say. Rhyming words are often the easiest ones to start with, but the technique also works on words with different middle and ending letters (e.g. bin–ban or beak–bean). There is evidence that as long as children have some reading experience and some phonological and alphabetic knowledge, this is a strategy that is available to even beginning readers, although it is not necessarily one that they will spontaneously use without some initial direction to do so (Wood, 1999, 2002b).

Reading in the digital age

There is no doubt that children are exposed to the influence of digital technology from the earliest stages of their development and that this impacts on what and how children read (Marsh et al., 2005). For some this is a cause for concern, and much has been written in the media about declining literacy standards amongst children and young people, with the blame being attributed to the increased use of personal digital devices such as mobile phones and computers. Our own data shows that children are receiving their first mobile phone as young as five years old. However, much of this concern is expressed in the absence of any direct evidence that this is the case. My own personal interest has been in relation to children's text-messaging behaviour on mobile phones and its impact on reading and spelling.

There has been an assumption that children's use of texting slang (or 'textisms') such as 'CU L8r' and 'anuva' is undermining children's understanding of standard spelling and is compromising their literacy development as a result. Spelling attainment is relevant to discussions of early reading, as it has been suggested that children's understanding of the alphabetic principle is driven, initially at least, by their early attempts at spelling (Frith, 1985). So, we (my colleagues and I) have investigated whether there is any connection between children's understanding and use of text-message abbreviations and their literacy attainment on standard tests. The results of these studies have surprised many, as not only have they demonstrated positive associations between textism use and both reading (Plester, Wood and Joshi, 2009) and spelling (Plester, Wood and Bell, 2008), but there is also evidence that use of textisms contributes positively to children's spelling development over the course of an academic year (Wood et al., in press, a). The reason for these positive associations is because most of the textisms that children like to use are phonologically based and, as such, they are enabling children to practise their understanding of letter–sound correspondences. Such language play is also likely to offer motivational benefits and the technology is affording children practice at reading and spelling on a daily basis.

This leads to the question of whether we should buy mobile phones for our children and encourage them to use them in these ways. The research suggests that, where children already own mobile phones and use them to text message, they do no harm and appear to benefit the children's literacy, and so there is no cause for concern. We did conduct a study which looked at the impact of giving mobile phones to nine and ten year-old children who did not already own them, and this showed no detrimental impact, but no strong benefits either (Wood et al., in press, b). The modest nature of the effects observed was, however, likely to be down to the limited nature of the intervention – to ensure that the study addressed ethical concerns at the time, the phones were basic and access was restricted to weekends and half-term break for only a ten-week period. When we compare this to the types of phone they usually own and the ways in which they are normally used by young people, this intervention did not offer children the chance to fully embrace the technology. So the suggestion is that if you have a child who is keen to own a mobile phone and they are mature enough to cope with owning it and interacting with other children using it, then there is no reason to be concerned. The technology is certainly supporting literate activity, and in some cases where the children are avoiding other types of print, there may be real benefits to be obtained here. But I would not recommend that parents go out of their way to obtain a phone for their child if it was something that they were not considering otherwise, for practical reasons such as the expense, and the risk that the child him or herself may not be ready or happy to engage with the technology. What the studies do underscore is the importance of language play, phonological skills and regular literate activity outside of school. This may be via mobile phone, social networking sites (where children are afforded the same opportunities for language play) or through the creation and consumption of their own words and those of others. The technology and availability of quality texts afforded by local libraries therefore have the potential to impact on children's literacy development by both formal and informal routes.

Conclusions

There are at least three key areas in which we can support children's reading – their motivation, their decoding skills and their comprehension of text – and each area is dependent on the others. Take any single aspect away, and the whole fragile structure comes down, much like a deck of cards. Decoding is pointless if a child lacks either the motivation to read or the ability to comprehend the words on the page. Comprehension is redundant if the child does not want to read in order to learn and is impossible if decoding has not yet been acquired. Motivation will be short lived if the skills or resources to feed this enthusiasm are not available. It is important that we recognize the role that we can potentially play in providing a supportive learning environment, at home, in school, in early years settings and in public libraries, for children starting this journey to literacy in relation to each of these three aspects of reading skill.

References

Adams, M. J. (1990) *Beginning to Read: thinking and learning about print*, MIT Press.

Arnold, D. H., Lonigan, C. J., Whitehurst, G. J. and Epistein, J. N. (1994) Accelerating Language Development through Picture-book Reading: replication and extension to a videotape training format, *Journal of Educational Psychology*, **86**, 235–43.

Bloodgood, J. (1999) What's in a Name? Children's name writing and name acquisition, *Reading Research Quarterly*, **34**, 342–67.

Bradley, L. and Bryant, P. E. (1978) Difficulties in Auditory Organisation as a Possible Cause of Reading Backwardness, *Nature*, **271**, 746–7.

Comaskey, E. M., Savage, R. S. and Abrami, P. (2009) A Randomised Efficacy Study of Web-based Synthetic and Analytic Programmes among Disadvantaged Urban Kindergarten Children, *Journal of Research in Reading*, **32**, 92–108.

Deault, L., Savage, R. and Abrami, P. (2009) Inattention and Response to the ABRACADABRA Web-based Literacy Intervention, *Journal of Research on Educational Effectiveness*, **2**, 250–86.

Ehri, L. C. (1997) Sight Word Learning in Normal Readers and Dyslexics. In Blachman, B. (ed.), *Foundations of Reading Acquisition and Dyslexia: implications for early intervention*, Laurence Erlbaum Associates.

Ehri, L. C. (1999) Phases of Development in Learning to Read Words. In Oakhill, J. and Beard, R. (eds), *Reading Development and the Teaching of Reading*, Blackwell.

Frith, U. (1985) Beneath the Surface of Developmental Dyslexia. In Patterson, K., Coltheart, M. and Marshall, J. (eds), *Surface Dyslexia*, Lawrence Erlbaum Associates.

Goswami, U. (1993) Towards an Interactive Analogy Model of Reading Development: decoding vowel graphemes in beginning reading, *Journal of Experimental Child Psychology*, **56**, 443–75.

Gough, P. B., Juel, C. and Griffith, P. L. (1992) Reading, Spelling, and the Orthographic Cipher. In Gough, P. B., Ehri, L. C. and Treiman, R. (eds), *Reading Acquisition*, Erlbaum.

Hargrave, A. C. and Sénéchal, M. (2000) A Book Reading Intervention with Pre-school Children Who Have Limited Vocabularies: the benefits of regular reading and dialogic reading, *Early Childhood Research Quarterly*, **15**, 75–90.

Hatcher, P. (2000) *Sound Linkage: an integrated programme for overcoming reading difficulties*, 2nd edn, Whurr.

Hay, I. and Fielding-Barnsley, R. (2007) Facilitating Children's Emergent Literacy Using Shared Reading: a comparison of two models, *Australian Journal of Language and Literacy*, **30**, 191–202.

Marsh, J., Brooks, G., Hughes, J., Ritchie, L., Roberts, S. and Wright, K. (2005) *Digital Beginnings: young children's use of popular culture, media and new technologies*, University of Sheffield.

Masonheimer, P. E., Drum, P. A., and Ehri, L. C. (1984) Does Environmental Print Identification Lead Children into Word Reading? *Journal of Reading Behavior*, **16**, 257–71.

Plester, B., Wood, C. and Bell, V. (2008) Txt msg n school literacy: does texting and knowledge of text abbreviations adversely affect children's literacy attainment? *Literacy*, **42**, 137–44.

Plester, B., Wood, C. and Joshi, P. (2009) Exploring the Relationship between Children's Knowledge of Text Message Abbreviations and School Literacy Outcomes, *British Journal of Developmental Psychology*, **27**, 145–61.

Rosen, M. and Oxenbury, H. (1989) *We're Going on a Bear Hunt*, Walker.

Solity, J. and Vousden, J. (2009) Real Books vs. Reading Schemes: a new perspective from instructional psychology, *Educational Psychology*, **19**, 373–97.

Weinberger, J. (1996) A Longitudinal Study of Children's Early Literacy Experiences at Home and later Literacy Development at Home and School, *Journal of Research in Reading*, **19**, 14–24.

Whitehurst, G. J. and Lonigan, C. J. (1998) Child Development and Emergent Literacy, *Child Development*, **69**, 848–72.

Wood, C. (1999) The Contribution of Analogical Problem Solving and Phonemic Awareness to Children's Ability to Make Orthographic Analogies when Reading, *Educational Psychology*, **19**, 277–86.

Wood, C. (2002a) Parent–child Pre-school Activities Can Affect the Development of Literacy Skills, *Journal of Research in Reading*, **25**, 241–58.

Wood, C. (2002b) Orthographic Analogies and Phonological Priming Effects, *Journal of Research in Reading*, **25**, 144–59.

Wood, C. and Terrell, C. (1998) Poor Readers' Ability to Detect Speech Rhythm and Perceive Rapid Speech, *British Journal of Developmental Psychology*, **16**, 397–413.

Wood, C., Wade-Woolley, L. and Holliman, A. J. (2009) Phonological Awareness: beyond phonemes. In Wood, C. and Connelly, V. (eds), *Contemporary Perspectives on Reading and Spelling*, Routledge.

Wood, C., Meacham, S., Bowyer, S., Jackson, E., Tarczynski-Bowles, M. L. and Plester, B. (in press, a) A Longitudinal Study of the Relationship between Children's Text Messaging and Literacy Development, *British Journal of Psychology*.

Wood, C., Jackson, E., Hart., L., Plester, B. and Wilde, L. (in press, b) The Effect of Text Messaging on 9–10 Year Old Children's Reading, Spelling and Phonological Awareness, *Journal of Computer Assisted Communication*.

Zevenbergen, A. A., Whitehurst, G. J. and Zevenbergen, J. A. (2003) Effects of a Shared-reading Intervention on the Inclusion of Evaluative Devices in Narratives of Children from Low-income Families, *Journal of Applied Developmental Psychology*, **24**, 1–15.

3

Creating young readers: teachers and librarians at work

Prue Goodwin

Introduction

Every Tuesday, in my local library, there is a gathering of about 60 very young 'readers' who, as yet, cannot decode a single printed word but who certainly have all the characteristics of book-lovers. They are members of the Baby Bounce and Rhyme group. Every Friday, there is Story Time for the under-fives. The children listen, laugh, gasp, shout out and are totally absorbed in the narrative and pictures shared with them by the librarian.

Having spent my whole career teaching reading, it is delightful for me to observe events where children are having such a pleasurable introduction to literacy. Whatever may or may not happen in their homes, these children will start school knowing about books, aware of the enthralling power of stories and having had experiences with language in engaging, playful ways. I cannot imagine any teacher or parent thinking that these library-based activities are just time fillers or entertainment for children. When it comes to preparation for more organized literacy education, few activities could be better than playing with the sounds of English and listening to stories.

The library where the activities take place has always been a good one but, like other public libraries, it is run by an ever-decreasing number of staff, who are enthusiastic and hard working, but unqualified as librarians. Despite this, a library manager has taken on the responsibility of contacting schools, encouraging membership and ensuring that there is a lively children's collection available. For older primary children there are holiday activities, a well-supported Summer Reading Challenge (see Chapter 5) and a Children's Book Award. These book-focused activities keep children interested in reading over the long summer break and let them see that it is not only teachers who promote the pleasures of reading. Librarians and teachers both want the same thing – to help youngsters to become confident, life-long readers. At a time when we are regularly told that standards in reading are not good enough, it would seem an obvious step to capitalize on the skill and support offered to schools by libraries.

Debates about the teaching of reading have been a major feature of social and political discourse throughout my career in primary education in the UK. In 2010, following two decades of direct Government intervention in literacy teaching in English schools (involving a national curriculum and a more specifically targeted national literacy strategy), standards are still not 'as expected' and criticism is still being directed at primary teachers. Perhaps more to the point, as Government has taken responsibility for the curriculum, and even for pedagogy, little has been achieved by way of improving politicians' knowledge of literacy learning. However, it is clear even to the least well-informed that there is much more likelihood of successfully improving reading standards if children have access to well-stocked libraries and, even more importantly, to enthusiastic and experienced librarians.

Over the last few decades, the relationship between teachers and librarians has gradually changed. Despite the continued mutual interest in children's development as readers, the withdrawal of schools' library services in many local authorities and an assessment-driven literacy curriculum in primary schools have led to a situation where teachers no longer request the invaluable support of a librarian when planning to teach reading. This chapter seeks to restore the close connections between schools and libraries. It aims to explain to fellow professionals the processes and pedagogies involved in teaching reading from a teacher's point of view. Although not exclusively related to young children, the teaching of reading is predominantly the task of early years practitioners and primary teachers. The chapter will suggest that, if Government targets in reading are to be met, links between libraries and primary schools should be re-established.

In order to explore the relevant issues, the chapter brings together personal experience, judgement and opinion, combined with recent research into literacy learning. It considers:

- what teachers and librarians need know about the nature of reading
- how reading is taught in English primary schools in the early 21st century
- the development of young independent readers
- how schools and libraries can work together.

Becoming a reader

If learning to read were as simple as is sometimes implied, there would be no non-reading school-leavers. Teachers work very hard to ensure that all their pupils learn to read successfully, but most have at some time taught children for whom learning to read has proved a difficult task. In a class where one or two children are struggling to learn there will be others making excellent progress, and yet more plodding along in a consistent but unremarkable way. Struggling to learn is usually neither the child's nor the teacher's fault but a consequence of the unpredictable nature of learning. We tend to use reading as a measure of intelligence, despite it being common knowledge that some of the most admired thinkers in the past (e.g. Einstein, Churchill and, possibly, Leonardo da Vinci) were slow learners when it came to reading. Many children who struggle to read are very able in other aspects of learning; however, without literacy skills they are unlikely to succeed in most educational contexts. People who imagine that learning to read is straightforward are usually those who confuse reading with word recognition. It certainly is essential to be able to decode the symbolic representation of language by working out the words, but that is not the same as reading. Reading involves understanding meaning from the printed word.

If children are to become competent, confident readers they need to know:

- how to read (lifting the intended meanings from the page through a combination of word recognition and language comprehension)
- about reading (its purposes – both functional and aesthetic)
- about being a reader (the development of individual and highly personal relationships with reading).

As acknowledged in the Bullock Report, *A Language for Life* (Department for Education and Science, 1975), which had a considerable impact on the teaching of literacy in the UK:

> reading is more than a reconstruction of the author's meanings. It is the perception of those meanings within the total context of the relevant experiences of the reader – a much more active and demanding process. Here the reader is required to engage in critical and creative thinking in order to relate what he reads to what he already knows; to evaluate the new knowledge in terms of the old and the old in terms of the new.
>
> (Department for Education and Science, 1975, 79)

This description clearly places being able to read far beyond the ability to apply basic decoding skills in order to construct literal levels of meaning. Of course, that may be where small children start, but thinking that they have finished learning to read because they can sound out a string of words – however accurately – is to deny the 'active and demanding process' in which all readers are engaged. It is useful to remind ourselves in a little more detail of what all readers, young and old, have to do in order to understand what they read.

What readers do

Readers encountering a new text have to determine what the words are, what they mean and how the words combine to make coherent, yet sometimes cryptic, meanings. Initially, for inexperienced readers, meanings may be literal, but it is not long before the subtleties of language reveal meanings beyond the literal, between the lines or hidden in figurative expression. As we read, we bring emotion to the text and respond to its meanings accordingly. In other words, to fully comprehend what is read requires the reader to understand at three levels simultaneously:

1 at the literal level – seeing and translating symbolic representation of language into speech sounds and literal meanings
2 at the level beyond the literal – applying prior knowledge, judgement and experience to uncover deeper meanings
3 at a personal level – having individual and emotional response to the impact of the text which, arguably, informs understanding more profoundly than any other aspect of reading.

Of these three levels of understanding, the first involves learned linguistic decoding skills, the second, literary experience combined with intellect and the third, emotional response. The eye, the mind and the heart are all employed. Full engagement of the heart distinguishes a reader from someone who is merely able to read.

Literal level of meaning making

Readers access the literal meaning of text by decoding print through a combination of graphic and visual information (letter shapes, punctuation marks, etc.), phonic information (speech sounds), syntactic information (grammar and language structure) and semantic information (literal meanings in context). It is important that children are systematically taught the grapho-phonic word-recognition skills (often referred to as phonics), as this knowledge is unlikely to be acquired through any other means than direct, systematic teaching. However, high-quality 'direct' teaching can be motivating and enjoyable – especially when rhymes, word play and excellent children's books are involved alongside the more pedantic learning of phonemes and graphemes.

Children acquire syntactic and semantic knowledge from the minute they hear language. They become familiar with speech patterns and word order and they learn new vocabulary every day. They use what they have learned in their developing ability to talk.

At the early stage of learning to read, syntactic knowledge is about how the rhythm of the speech patterns language as we read. When we give words 'expression', we are applying the rhythms and cadences required by the sentences to give them the intended meaning. For example, the phrase 'a cup of tea' will mean different things depending on the pattern of sounds it makes when being read.

For example:

What would you like? **A cup of tea**, please.
A cup of tea? No, thank you.
This is a **cup of tea!** I asked for coffee.

To learn how word order alerts a reader to how printed words should 'sound' when read, children need to hear a lot of texts read aloud. This entirely functional purpose is only one tiny aspect of the value of reading aloud to children. Reading aloud is highly pleasurable – but is also an essential element of teaching reading. It continues to be so throughout education.

The four linguistic skills – phonic, graphic, syntactic and semantic – only enable readers to access literal meanings. It is possible for children to learn how to decode a page of text word by word, sometimes even giving it expression, without having any understanding of what they have read. However fluent they may sound, they are not reading unless they comprehend meanings.

Meanings beyond the literal

Ways of understanding meanings between and beyond the literal include visualization, inference, prediction, use of intertextual reference and the application of personal experience. The starting-point for understanding beyond the literal is prompted by the expectations readers have of texts.

Young children learn how books work and the purposes of different texts (bibliographic knowledge) from sharing all sorts of literary items with adults. In addition to concrete knowledge of books, they learn abstract concepts, such as how narratives work. Being read to regularly is, arguably, the most important literacy experience they can have, but browsing through books, joining in rhymes and retelling familiar stories all contribute to what they need to know in order to understand beyond the literal. By recognizing familiar themes, characters and situations, they begin to be able to predict how a narrative will unfold, often responding by relating the fiction to their own lives. For example, children sharing the picture book *Farmer Duck* (Waddell and Oxenbury, 1991) may make comments such as: 'I've been to a farm' (personal experience); 'It might be the Ugly Duckling' (intertextual reference); or 'He's sad' (empathy). Instead of being passive receivers of the words, they become active participants in the construction of meanings. If time spent sharing books has been positive, children anticipate the pleasure of a new story or of revisiting an old favourite.

As readers become more independent and are able to decode with relative ease, reading beyond the literal is reasonably straightforward for adults to demonstrate and discuss. Teaching young readers how to interpret plot structure, characterization and setting shows them how authors use literary devices to move stories forwards. More abstract ideas contained in subtext, metaphor and narrative voice can also be identified as readers become confident. The more children discuss and explore books, the deeper their knowledge and experience of 'being readers' becomes. Engaging creatively with books (through role play, artwork, problem solving, music making, drama, etc.) always entails involvement with the complexities of language. It is important that adults take an active part in children's reading development by engaging children in genuine conversations about books, demonstrating that it is both normal and refreshing that readers make different interpretations and have different responses to what they read. Recognizing the 'rights of the reader' (Pennac, 1994, 145) to have individual response is a very important message to give young readers.

Responding to reading

Once an individual reader has control of the decoding skills and recognizes that shades of meaning lie between the lines, the ability to enhance understanding is entirely related to personal response. It is possible to teach children a level of competency with decoding skills and to help them to understand beyond the literal; what cannot be explained with any accuracy are the emotional responses readers may have to texts. Feelings can be described but not taught, yet experienced readers know that it is their feelings about what they read that directly influence how and what they understand. As previously stated, full engagement of the heart – i.e. individual personal response – distinguishes a reader from someone who is merely able to read.

A good teacher ensures, right from the start, that children learn to value their feelings as they read. It is possible to do this by making sure that youngsters have plenty of opportunity to respond emotionally to texts, being encouraged to express their feelings regarding the whole experience of what has been read. Seeking personal response goes way beyond the simple question, 'Did you like it?' True comprehension is reached when young readers are able to share opinions, feelings, questions and insights with each other. To help children to do this, teachers create opportunities that provide time to think, to talk, to return to the text and to respond to it in a variety of creative ways.

> Examining the text to support and justify response means that we are a world away from simplistic notions of likes or dislikes. Of course, each reader will create their own meanings so that no two readers will read the same text in the same ways (and that is a challenging thought for any teacher) but 'to go back to the text to support … response' means the parts played by both the text and the reader are recognised and given status in the classroom. There is no difference between response and comprehension.
> (Martin, 2011, 89)

Children need to be aware that being 'lost in a book' – that is, intellectually and emotionally engaged by what is being read – is what happens to most readers. The phrase 'lost in a book' accurately describes the powerful change of consciousness that occurs when we read. It is as though the individual reader is under some form of enchantment; the real world is going on around them but they are part of a different universe. Readers become absorbed in the meanings they are making; they may be engrossed by the story, fascinated by the facts or gripped by the content of whatever it is they are reading. It is only when they stop reading that readers become aware of having been emotionally engaged (entertained, informed, scared, amused, exhilarated, etc.). After the event, when the reader has relinquished the enchantment of being 'lost in a book', intellectual and emotional responses to the text can be considered objectively. The fact that there is no physical manifestation of this experience does not mean there is no 'product' as a result. It may not always be made apparent to others, but 'while the act of reading may produce no physical outcome, it does produce an outcome of value – a changed person, with more knowledge or more emotional depth or both' (Holden, 2004, 25). When experienced readers talk to each other about books, there is almost always a tacit agreement that they have developed positively in some way as individuals as a result of their reading.

Teaching reading

When I read I enter into the worlds and minds of others – I know what it feels like to be in a certain place, in a certain situation, facing a certain dilemma. When I read my feelings are engaged; I sympathise and empathise with the characters I am reading about and often my emotions are as raw as theirs. When I read I learn things; I gain new information; my bank of knowledge is enlarged. When I read I hear others' opinions and I evaluate them against my own viewpoint and against what I know of the writer. When I read I know what to do; I follow the instructions to make the IKEA bookcase, to cook that new recipe, to find an address. When I read I enjoy the delights of language, of laughing as the joke plays with the meanings of words, of struggling with hidden meanings as I complete the crossword, of revelling in the craft of the skilled wordsmith. Friends and family recommend books to me, colleagues show me where to find out certain information, the Internet takes me on unending journeys of discovery. Reading is a part of me and my life – without reading my life would be poorer. How do I begin to teach that?   (Perkins, 2011, 15)

The words of Dr Margaret Perkins reflect the thoughts of many people involved in teaching literacy. Where do I start, to teach something so complex, so important and so personal? Reading, in particular how it is learned and taught, has been the focus of academic research by psychologists, educationalists and linguists for decades. Every piece of research has value, but, despite all the different ways in which reading has been explored at an academic level, it is unlikely that there will ever be a single teaching method that ensures that all children become competent readers. As the Bullock Report pointed out:

> There is no method, medium, approach, device or philosophy that holds the key to the process of learning to read. We believe that the knowledge does exist to improve the teaching of reading, but that it does not lie in the triumphant discovery, or rediscovery, of a particular formula. Simple endorsements of one or another nostrum are of no service to the teaching of reading. A glance at the past reveals the truth of this. The main arguments about how reading should be taught have been repeated over and over again as the decades pass, but the problems remain. (Department for Education and Science, 1975, 77)

Organizing the teaching of reading

When organizing reading in the primary classroom there are two major elements of reading experience that teachers have to provide for their pupils. The first concerns pedagogy. Teachers must actively intervene in the development of their pupils' skills, knowledge and experience of understanding the written word in all its forms. The second element is about supporting each child, intellectually as well as practically, as he or she becomes an independent reader. Schools must provide the conditions and materials which ensure that all pupils are enabled to read and to develop their potential as individuals who can choose to enhance their lives through literacy. The two elements, teaching reading and encouraging independence, work parallel to, and in co-operation with, each other. Skilful primary practitioners interweave formal and didactic teaching with less academic, more creative interactions with texts, creating a mix of literary experiences that support a diverse group of young readers. For each child, progress will be monitored and records kept. Unfortunately, because the process of becoming a reader is difficult to pin down, it is also very hard to assess. It is possible to test linguistic skills or literal levels of comprehension, but neither set of results will indicate levels of readership. That can only be judged by observing pupils' attitudes to reading and their engagement with literacy.

Teaching

There are certain practices, approaches and principles related to teaching reading that are applicable throughout the years of primary school. They are adaptable to any age, stage of development or previous experience that children may have had. For example, it is essential that teachers read aloud to children every day, but the books (or other texts) being read aloud to 4 year-olds will vary tremendously from those read to 11 year-olds. Key classroom practices should include:

- reading aloud to children: for the pleasure of listening; for learning about literacy and literature; and to make links to children's independent reading
- shared reading, when teachers:
  — demonstrate how to construct meaning from text
  — engage children in discussion that extends comprehension
  — lead and direct learners towards new literacy competencies
  — share reading materials that raise expectations and achievement
- guided reading, when groups of learners apply what has been taught during shared reading and there is an emphasis on discussion about texts, articulating thoughts and feelings that can lead to deeper understanding
- individual reading, when each child reads alongside an adult and talks about what is being read
- independent reading, when children can:
  — read to themselves from books they have selected
  — share a book with a friend
  — bring reading materials from home
  — browse in the library
- 'booktalk' (Chambers, 1985), which involves children in open discussion and debate about literature, invites them to contribute their own opinions and to develop personal literary preferences, and also provides a time to make book recommendations to each other or for teachers to introduce new titles and authors to the class
- literacy sessions to help pupils to develop:
  — literary appreciation of narrative, poetry, picture books and plays
  — knowledge of a range of written texts, including ICT and media texts
  — information retrieval and study skills
  — creative response (through play, drama, art, problem solving, etc.) to what has been read.

All these approaches, adapted by professionals to support their particular groups of learners, have been demonstrated over time to be effective

(Holdaway, 1980; Chambers, 1993a; Booth, 2006). They are also advocated by current curriculum documents for teaching English across the UK. However, to be successful, they are dependent on all primary teachers having literary attributes, such as:

- explicit knowledge of the nature of reading and of being a reader
- experience of 'interrogating' text in order to comprehend at every level
- willingness to share their personal responses to texts with children
- ability to guide children in discussion about the interpretation of a text.

In order to employ these approaches with the same class throughout a school year, all primary teachers need a wide, confident knowledge of children's books.

Developing independent readers

Above all, independent reading should be about pleasure. There is plenty of evidence that reading for pleasure leads to improved reading attainment (Clark and Rumbold, 2006; Cremin et al., 2008), which means that schools should aim to get children reading for pleasure in order to raise standards. Adult readers identify pleasure in reading chiefly as being associated with being 'lost in the book'. No one can 'get lost' in something they are struggling to read. It follows, therefore, that the books children are offered to read to themselves should always be well within their decoding ability.

The point at which children become independent readers cannot be calculated by their age or by the year group they are in. Nor is independence anything to do with which book a child is currently reading. Although related to the ability to read, independence has far more to do with gaining personal satisfaction, enjoyment and enlightenment from reading than with how the task is performed. Whether children become genuine readers can depend on how they perceive themselves and what they believe 'achievement' in reading is. Some pupils are given the false impression that making progress as a reader is about increasing the number of words in a book rather than becoming engaged in its contents. Confusion in the minds of children (and parents) is made worse by the discourse surrounding independent reading and the traditional ways in which 'reading books' are regarded. In some schools, a great deal of time is spent deciding what 'reading book' each child should be on until they have reached the status of being a 'free reader'. But I would ask, free of what? And what sort of readers are the children who are not free? Prisoners? Being a 'free reader' has become the way to indicate that a child has finished learning to read. A great deal of anxiety is caused by this competitive model of progress, in which adults become so obsessed with colour bands, numbers and other methods of organizing materials that learning to be a reader gets forgotten. Instead, there are pointless arguments about the benefits of using reading schemes or 'real' books, and pressure to put children 'up' a level, based on a false concept of how children make progress as readers. Before we consider the needs of independent readers, some myths about books need to be dispelled.

What are reading books for?

The purpose of a 'reading book' is for a child to discover that they can read with ease. Reading with ease enables children to practise new-found skills that have been taught during literacy sessions and consequently to become confident in their growing ability as readers. Struggling to decode a text has the reverse effect, with every 'next book' making children feel that reading is difficult. The flow of meaning is lost in the effort to decode unfamiliar words and meaning making is abandoned. Progress is perceived as climbing a contrived ladder of attainment instead of increased fluency, engagement and enjoyment. It is unfortunate that many children have been put off reading whilst in primary school because they have been led to believe that getting to the end of the reading scheme is the point of learning to read. A 'book-based' model of progress leads them to perceive reading as a competition instead of continuous growth in what should be life-enhancing, literary experience.

'Real' books and reading schemes

There are two sectors of UK publishing associated with child readers: trade and education. Both are important; both have their place in classrooms. Trade publishers are the childhood equivalent of adult publishing; their market is the book-buying public, which includes specialists who buy for libraries and schools. Educational publishers produce textbooks, reading schemes and teaching resources; their market is schools and a few educationally aspirational parents. Debates about the teaching of reading have led to all sorts of misguided opinions and arguments about the differences between trade (sometimes termed 'real') books and educational materials. The products from trade and educational publishers serve completely different purposes in classrooms.

Educational reading packages

Reading materials produced by educational publishers in the UK today are a long way from the scrappy booklets some adults remember reading at school. Many of these resources are well written and beautifully illustrated, providing enjoyable reading experiences for young readers at the early stage of their development. My limited knowledge of early reading in other English-speaking nations (gained when visiting to speak at conferences in Australia and the US, and meeting teachers from the Caribbean, Canada and New Zealand in the UK) suggests that there has been a similar pattern of improvement in the production of teaching materials. This is to be welcomed, as there is a role for well-produced educational materials. However, no package of books can teach a child to read. Experienced readers (teachers, of course, but also family members, librarians, volunteer helpers and friends) teach willing learners of all ages to read, usually finding engaging learning resources to help establish the early skills. For children in schools, the resources are often contemporary educational reading packages. Learning to read does not fit easily into any uniform pattern of development (it is not schematic) so it is not possible to provide a sequence of books that will match every child's learning needs. Most children take about two years to establish a confident use of decoding skills, but many quickly pass the point of needing graded materials, while others may need supportive texts well into their junior years. It is the job of teachers to make professional judgements about which materials to use with each child. Many children have suffered as a result of being 'put on the scheme' inappropriately and, as a consequence, have experienced the negative effects of failure before they have had a chance to succeed (Goodwin, 1994).

Children often miss vital steps in development either by being kept on educational publications of limited literary value or by leaping straight from highly controlled reading materials to a 'free' selection of junior novels. Both these problems are caused by mistaken assumptions that reading ability develops because children are constantly moving on to longer, less illustrated books with more complex vocabularies. Unfortunately, such experiences lead to reluctance to read in children who are either not yet confident enough to tackle much print or who are able to decode but not to read beyond the literal. A limited book-by-book approach also causes children, even those reading well, to miss many important literary experiences of childhood (e.g. particular genres, such as traditional tales, classic texts, picture books) in the pursuit of winning an imaginary competition to complete a 'reading book' ladder of achievement. Children (and their parents) need reassurance that learning to read is not a race; a number or colour band on a book provides little or no information about a reader and there is no evidence that people become better readers by reading books based on increasing linguistic difficulty.

Newly independent readers

Children begin to develop the attitudes to reading that will bring about true independence long before they can make meanings from print. Reading for pleasure is at the heart of becoming a reader. Enjoyable experiences, such as listening to stories and looking through superb picture books, allow the youngest of children to anticipate what being a reader will be like. For most children the transition to being independent readers will occur over several months, between their sixth and ninth birthdays. By the age of six most youngsters are proficient enough at decoding to tackle more varied texts than those provided in reading packages. The point at which youngsters find that they can read an entire book without adult intervention marks a crucial moment in their development. At that point, far from needing the 'next book' from a graded list, children should be encouraged to choose from a specially selected collection of books that are all within their decoding capability. Newly independent 'readers' need plenty of time to consolidate their new-found skills with books they want to read and that they can read with ease. From this point on, there is no such thing as a book that is too easy.

The books they are offered must be attractive, at the same time as providing fledgling readers with opportunities to:

- practise their ability to decode to a point at which the skills become automatic
- establish a confident expectation of reading success
- build up reading stamina
- develop their ability to understand at and beyond the literal
- learn how to select what they want to read.

It is important that children are encouraged to behave as would readers of any age and are offered books that support their growing interpretive competencies. That is, books, for example, which combine a range of beneficial features such as:

- being well written by good children's authors

- having engaging content, whether it be enjoyable stories or fascinating information
- being easily within the decoding ability of inexperienced readers, whilst avoiding unnecessarily restricted vocabularies
- having unthreatening amounts of print on a page
- introducing literary devices such as humour, inference and plot-twists
- having lively, appealing illustrations by talented artists.

To reinforce children's newly acquired independence, reading materials should allow them to wallow in books. As they gain confidence in themselves as readers, children will acquire further attributes of being literate, such as being selective, developing preferences and having opinions about their reading.

Making children into readers

Once pupils are past the 'newly' independent stage it is very important that they are motivated to read for themselves, if they are to become thoughtful and reflective readers. Children who have not discovered the pleasures of reading easily lose their motivation to read and, as with any set of skills, without practice their ability to comprehend deteriorates. If the time spent learning to read has not established an expectation of pleasure, it can be difficult to get children reading independently, and insisting that they do is counter-productive (Goodwin, 1994). As Daniel Pennac puts it in the opening of *Reads like a Novel*:

> The verb 'to read' is averse to being put in the imperative, an intolerance it shares with certain other verbs, such as 'to love' and 'to dream'. One can always try, of course – so try: 'Love me!' 'Dream!' 'Read!' 'So read for heaven's sake, I'm ordering you to read!' Which produces? Nothing. (Pennac, 1994, 3)

Those of us who read for pleasure do so because we want to. We cannot make children into successful, independent readers by forcing them to read. They need to be supported, stimulated and motivated to pick up a book and let themselves get absorbed in its contents. In any primary classroom there could be 30 individuals with differing tastes in reading materials, differing levels of competency and different perceptions about reading. Ideally, teachers should know enough about children's books to be able to suggest titles to individual independent readers, but it is unrealistic to expect every teacher to know hundreds of books. Even if we regularly update ourselves, we will never know enough. This is the time when contact with libraries and librarians becomes essential. With expert support, teachers can create the conditions in a classroom where reading for pleasure is the norm. Librarians, teachers and children should spend time together just chatting about books, making recommendations to each other and generally sharing the joy of reading. It may seem a little informal, but the effect on reading would be remarkable, far greater than forced silent reading or writing book reviews. A good supply of high-quality books is essential, but, no matter how extensive the resource collection, the most important element of the 'conditions' to create readers is the presence of adults who are themselves readers – adults who read to pupils, talk about books and involve them in all sorts of literary activities.

Libraries and librarians

Libraries have always been important to schools, but mostly as collections of materials for pupils who can already read. Laying the foundations of literacy is the work of primary schools, but the role that can be played by librarians is seldom fully recognized. Activities and events that are already happening in libraries across the UK are having positive outcomes which benefit children and schools. The impact research report on the Summer Reading Challenge (SRC), for example, has evidence that its contribution 'not only raised levels of motivation and commitment to reading' (Kennedy and Bearne, 2010, 10) but also maintained levels of reading competence over the long summer months. Imagine the impact that the SRC would have if all schools were required to get involved. Where local authorities fund links between libraries and schools there are book awards, author visits and book festivals organized by librarians, with hundreds of children taking part. Rather than increasing workloads, events such as these make the job of a teacher much easier.

Then there are the very young – infants, toddlers and pre-school children. The babies bouncing and the pre-school story listeners gain far more than 30 minutes' worth of entertainment, or even of language and narrative experience.

> Young children who go to the library will also play at 'going to the library'. The rich, meaningful quality of symbolic play is, generally, that it is for real. Literacy begins not only in being read to, where the adult is in charge, but also as symbolic play. (Meek, 1991, 79)

Children who have visited them know what libraries are for; when more formal schooling begins, symbolic play transforms into behaving like readers. Children are familiar with the space, the purpose and contents of a library; they know how to browse the book boxes, to lounge on the cushions with books and they understand the concept of being a book borrower. Older primary pupils delight in a place, away from school, where anyone can borrow books and enjoy the companionship of fellow readers. They can be truly independent readers in a library, able to choose whatever they want to read, with interested adults close by who are happy to give informed advice.

Teachers need libraries and librarians

For teachers of reading there could not be a more useful group of people to know than librarians. Teachers choose their careers for many reasons; they may love working with children or have a desire to teach a favourite subject (mathematics, PE, history, etc.). Only a few will set out with a passion to teach literacy, but teaching reading is the prime function of the primary school, so every teacher has to acquire a confident knowledge of the elements of learning to read, in conjunction with as many effective teaching methods as possible. Added to this, each teacher needs quality children's books to read aloud, to use during shared or guided reading and to discuss with pupils during booktalk sessions. As Aidan Chambers pointed out, all teachers of reading need a 'store' of at least 500 books that they can rely on to support youngsters in becoming enthusiastic readers (Chambers, 1993b). This seems a daunting number, unless you can turn to an expert for continual advice and support, not just about books but about all aspects of literature and information handling. Unlike many primary teachers, librarians choose their job because they love reading.

> Librarians have always been a special breed of literates. They now mastermind a range of resources unknown to their predecessors: charts, film loops, micro-bibliographies, summary pages. They guard copyright from the users of photocopiers. They study the different ways in which information may be presented, including computers.
> (Meek, 1991, 176)

Teachers urgently need librarians beside them when they set out to create confident young readers.

Conclusion: the 'symbiotic relationship'

The skills and knowledge offered by librarians have never been as necessary as they are now, when successive governments have imposed a didactic reading curriculum and many teachers have lost confidence in their intuitive use of literature with their pupils. The primary curriculum is set to become even more related to assessment; we are informed that, in addition to the established tasks, six year-olds will be tested on their phonic knowledge. In education we need the support and positive input of librarians to reinvigorate the teaching of reading. Any enlightened government would ensure that teachers and librarians were encouraged, and funded, to establish and develop close relationships. Ironically, at the moment libraries are struggling to survive, despite the obvious connection there is between having a nation of readers and valuing literacy professionals. In a logical world where learning is valued, teachers and librarians would be working side by side and, no doubt, achieving their own and the politicians' aim of the highest possible standards of reading for every child.

References

Booth, D. (2006) *Reading Doesn't Matter Anymore*, Stenhouse Publishers.

Chambers, A. (1985) *Booktalk: occasional writing on literature and children*, The Bodley Head.

Chambers, A. (1993a) *Tell Me: children, reading and talk*, Thimble Press.

Chambers, A. (1993b) The Difference of Literature: writing now for the future of young readers, *Children's Literature in Education*, **24** (1), 1-18.

Clark, C. and Rumbold, K. (2006) *Reading for Pleasure*, National Literacy Trust.

Cremin, T., Mottram, M., Collins, F. and Powell, S. (2008) *Building Communities of Readers*, UKLA.

Department for Education and Science (1975) *A Language for Life* (The Bullock Report), HMSO.

Goodwin, P. (1994) *Reluctant to Read?* Reading and Language Centre.

Holdaway, D. (1980) *Independence in Reading*, Ashton Scholastic.

Holden, J. (2004) *Creative Reading: young people, reading and public libraries*, Demos.

Kennedy, R. and Bearne, E. (2010) *Summer Reading Challenge 2009 Impact Research Report*, UKLA, www.readingagency.org/children/summer-reading-challenge/.

Martin, T. (2011) Readers Making Meaning: responding to narrative. In Goodwin, P. (ed.), *The Literate Classroom*, 3rd edn, Routledge.

Meek, M. (1991) *On Being Literate*, The Bodley Head.

Pennac, D. (trans. Daniel Gunn) (1994) *Reads Like a Novel*, Quartet Books.

Perkins, M. (2011) Making Space for Reading: teaching reading in the early years. In Goodwin, P. (ed.) (2011) *The Literate Classroom*, 3rd edn, Routledge, 15–23.

Waddell, M. and Oxenbury, H. (1991) *Farmer Duck*, Walker Books.

4

The six dimensions of the 'honeycomb' model, and its implications for literacy, libraries and literature in New Zealand

Helen Villers

Introduction: the New Zealand context for literacy

It is argued in this chapter that New Zealand's reputation as a 'highly literate and print-orientated society' (Wilkinson, 1998, 144) has been due in part to the isolation and independence borne originally of our geographical position or 'islandness' and, through the 20th century in particular, to a strong 'home grown' literacy teaching and learning pedagogy in our schools, high rates of library membership, newspaper and magazine readership, a strong commitment to the wide canon of literature and, more recently, to our own burgeoning adult and children's literature.

The argument, however, has been sorely tested in recent times. Like many other countries in the Organisation for Economic Co-operation and Development, New Zealand has been challenged to maintain literacy standards in English in the face of worldwide instantaneous communication, globalization and access to popular culture, mobility and mass migration, socio-lingual and cultural diversity and, more recently, effects on the literacy achievement of those most likely to struggle in times of economic constraint. To add complexity to an already challenging field, the very notion of what it means to be literate has shifted from simply being able to read and write to the wider concept of *literacies*: the range of functional, academic, 'new literacies', multi-literacies and critical ways of 'reading the world' (Freire and Macedo, 1987; Gee, 2008; Healy, 2008; Kalantzis, Cope and Cloonan, 2010; Lankshear and Knobel, 2003; Leu, 2000; Wink, 2010).

Healy encapsulates this shift in emphasis when she suggests:

> Many students in their everyday lives connect to an array of texts that bear little resemblance to the book, and to a vast digital network that transcends more

traditional forms of text. Of particular concern to the focus of this discussion are issues surrounding access to information, and to the libraries that typically support inquiry learning.   (Healy, 2008, 1)

Libraries and librarians have now the opportunity, and the obligation, to powerfully reassert their place as key information providers in classrooms, schools, communities and homes as the intersecting lines of knowledge, skills and communication and the literacy curriculum, inquiry processes and information resources become the pivotal drivers of 21st-century life.

The *School Library Manifesto* of the International Federation of the Library Associations (IFLA) states:

> The school library provides information and ideas that are fundamental to functioning successfully in today's information and knowledge-based society: The school library equips students with lifelong learning skills and develops the imagination, enabling them to live as responsible citizens.
>
> (IFLA/UNESCO, 2000)

The New Zealand Curriculum (Ministry of Education [MoE], 2007) reiterates the importance of this in a key competency entitled 'Using language, symbols and texts':

> Students who are competent users of language, symbols and texts can interpret and use words, number, images, movement, metaphor and technologies in a range of contexts ... [and] they confidently use ICT (including, where appropriate assistive technologies) to access and provide information and to communicate with others.   (MoE, 2007, 12)

In an extensive review of information and learning in New Zealand, however, the Education Review Office (ERO) found that:

> Information literacy was a particularly weak area. In most primary and secondary schools, teachers had incorporated aspects of information literacy (for example, information skills and library skills) into their teaching, but there were few examples of a school wide, integrated approach using an information process model.
>
> (Education Review Office, 2005, 2)

While it can be argued that teachers cannot do it all and that libraries and librarians and the expertise, resources and support they offer students in an information age are more important than ever, New Zealand confronts, like many other countries in the Western world, the budgetary battle for school libraries, library professional development, qualifications, commitment to dedicated space, technology upgrades, ICT expertise and, lastly but critically, quality multimedia collections.

There is nothing more certain in the lives of 21st-century learners than the speed of change and, *ipso facto*, the uncertainty this delivers. The verbs 'to learn' and 'to know', and 'knowledge' as an outcome, must be continuously redefined in 21st-century terms to include active, critical enquiry and resource-based approaches to teaching and learning. Teachers, and the library professionals who support them, need an increasingly sophisticated repertoire of pedagogical-content knowledge and information-technology skills as well as subject knowledge if they are to assist students to work independently and collaboratively in authentic, problem-solving situations, to consider multiple points of view and to come to their own evidence-based conclusions. What a far reach this is from the rote-learned, regurgitated, finite and culturally bound versions of learning and knowledge considered appropriate barely a generation ago!

The challenge is for educators and librarians alike to embrace a wide view of literacy: the pedagogies and professional relationships, the materials and resources, and the necessary skills and understandings required for knowledge creation, as well as a comprehensive knowledge of children's and young adult literature – and this at the same time as focusing on a narrow view of the learner. Idiosyncratic developmental pathways must be carved out for each individual as they make their way down the 'information highway'. How best to achieve all this?

Responding to contemporary challenges in literacy teaching and learning

In this chapter the New Zealand response to the challenge is discussed, and linked to the six contemporary dimensions of effective literacy practice. Expectations of students, instructional strategies, knowledge of literacy learning, knowledge of individual learner need, engaging learners with texts, and partnerships within and beyond the classroom will all be discussed with regard to literacy achievement in New Zealand and the implications this has for teachers, librarians and the literacy (and literary) practices and traditions in this country. While these dimensions are drawn directly from the curriculum-linked handbooks for teaching literacy for Years 1 to 4, Years 5 to 8 and secondary levels Years 9–13 (MoE, 2003, 2006, 2004), it must be pointed out that this author is making the connections between libraries and literacy – the texts do not! Libraries have, nonetheless, a privileged place in the social, recreational, intellectual and professional lives of New Zealanders and, as it will be argued, have a great deal to do with the quality of literacy education and student achievement for most, but by no means all, in New Zealand schools.

The Arcadia of the South Pacific

New Zealand is a small island nation of some four million people where oral storytelling, reading and writing have always been greatly valued. Traditionally, we have depended on story, in one form or another, as a way to describe, to explain and to explore the very essence of what it means to live in a land at the far end of the earth that Rudyard Kipling (1893) once described as the 'last, the loneliest and the most lovely'. Others in the early years saw the country as an 'arcadia' for social experimentation and an opportunity to create a perfect and highly literate citizenry: a fresh beginning in a land where each one of us can claim heritage from somewhere across the ocean – we have all come by way of canoe, sailing ship, ocean liner or jumbo jet. Telling stories about the world and reading and writing 'home' for new settlers was always, and still continues to be, a fundamental way of life and a key factor in purposeful literacy practice in this country, irrespective of one's origin, language, cultural heritage and even the method of communication used. Twenty-first century New Zealand is a considerably different place from that encountered by our first settlers – first Maori and then the Pakeha (those of European descent), Asiatic, Indian and Pasifika peoples who followed. This is now a multicultural and highly diverse nation as counted on most OECD indicators; no longer isolated in the South Pacific, but connected at a mere digital touch with the rest of the world.

Schools and libraries

The partnership between schools and libraries has played a critically important role in shaping a literate tradition and, it is contended, a sense of identity for a people who generally view themselves as a nation of readers. Informal measures of readership suggest a highly literate society in print-based terms; bookshops, library membership, newspaper and magazine subscriptions, local publishing, book clubs and literary festivals all indicate a healthy literate lifestyle. This is reflected in the teaching principles and practices of our schools and the value placed on library access and use.

A pedagogy founded on 'real and purposeful' reading and writing, and practices which include modelling, sharing, guiding and fostering independence through inquiry processes have been valued as pivotal to effective teaching and learning. The literacy programme has been viewed for many years as an integrated part of the wide curriculum and most young teachers are quick to recite, and put into action, the truism 'learning to read, reading to learn'. While the curriculum has consistently endeavoured to capture an outward-looking, worldwide perspective, New Zealanders also recognize and admire in themselves resourcefulness and a 'can do' attitude. Innovation and invention has been the mainstay of a country so far from the rest of the world. When something needed doing or fixing, the problem had to be solved within the local context.

This ethos endures, and nowhere is it better illustrated than in literacy learning and the supporting resources – material and human – that it depends on. In the past, libraries were often far flung and hard to reach, particularly for rural schools and homes. In response to this the Country Library Service was established as a type of 'mail order' service to readers, and in time this was extended by 'book buses', which took the books directly to the people. The School Library Service was developed along similar lines, and the best of both national and international material was made available to readers from one end of the country to the other. Today the school library network, as part of the National Library of New Zealand, continues to serve New Zealand children well. Curriculum Services (Te Puna Matauranga o Aotearoa) offer free advice to teachers and to teacher librarians about library management, professional development and collections. Teachers can select texts by topic, access level, genre and media as appropriate. Currently as many as 1.5 million texts are borrowed each year from the collection of over a million items and, as many teachers will attest, there is nothing more exciting for their students than the big brown box of books and other resources arriving just in time for a research project, a novel or author study, a theme-based approach or a focus on recreational reading and writing.

If schools are in the fortunate position of having a qualified teacher librarian, the administration and supply of books and their promotion and use, often accompanied by information and study skill development, will extend the dimensions for both teaching and learning even more effectively.

This is consistent with the Ministry of Education and National Library of New Zealand School Library Guidelines (2002), which outline six key principles for library development and curriculum implementation, focusing on the provision of information literacy, service, reading, access, information resources and place. Ideally, each aspect should dovetail seamlessly into the range of dimensions for effective literacy practice and translate into student progress and achievement.

Effective practices through the literacy dimensions

As briefly described above, among the significant resources underpinning literacy and learning in New Zealand schools are a series of teacher handbooks: *Effective Literacy Practices in Years 1 to 4* (MoE, 2003) and *Effective Literacy Practices in Years 5 to 8* (MoE, 2006) for the primary school and *Effective Literacy Strategies in Years 9 to 13* (MoE, 2004) for teachers in all subject areas in the secondary school. These texts, inclusive of oral, written and visual modes of language, are designed to underpin site-based professional development, 'best' practice in the classroom and self-review (through critical action research and self-review) nationwide. Texts with a more specific focus on oral language (MoE, 2009c, 2009d) are also available. The suite of texts all link to the national curriculum (MoE, 2007) and are reflected in the *Literacy Learning Progressions* (MoE, 2009a) and, even more recently, are measured in terms of individual student achievement by the controversial *New Zealand Curriculum Reading and Writing Standards for Years 1–8* (MoE, 2009b).

Literacy, as described by these texts, depends on three key factors: the ability of a reader/writer to learn the code (decoding and encoding), to make meaning (fluency and comprehension) and to think critically (MoE, 2003, 25). Each aspect depends on engagement with texts. Literacy teaching and learning in New Zealand is envisioned through a graphic model produced in the literacy handbooks for teachers (MoE, 2003, 2006, 2004) and fondly known as the 'honeycomb' (MoE, 2003, 12). The model demonstrates how the six dimensions of effective literacy practice (expectations; instructional strategies; engaging learners with texts; knowledge of the learner; knowledge of literacy learning; and partnerships) fit together, using the metaphor of the honeycomb's interconnection and strength, to produce a cohesive and research-informed approach to literacy planning, pedagogy and assessment. It is this model, and each of the literacy dimensions it describes, that will be explored in more depth in this chapter.

Knowledge of literacy learning

This dimension defines literacy as 'the ability to understand, respond to, and use those forms of written language required by society and valued by individuals and society' (MoE, 2003, 19). While this appears to be a rather limited way to describe a complex set of factors involved in contemporary literacy acquisition, it does include reference to text in its broadest sense, and therefore to the complementary strands of oral and visual literacy as well, signalling that the 'new literacies' and the widening range of multi-literacies and communicative forms will have a significant bearing on the literate practices of the school, community and beyond. The oral, written and visual strands, whether productive (speaking, writing and presenting) or receptive (listening, reading, viewing), will involve the elements of the framework described above; the model accepts that decoding and encoding are necessary but not sufficient, that making meaning involves construction of one's own text or the deconstruction of that of others, and that all text demands to be questioned, analysed and critically reflected on for purpose, audience and, more provocatively, for its ability to include or exclude, to privilege or to marginalize (Luke and Freebody, 1999).

In the middle decades of the 20th century questions of this nature probably remained largely unanswered. The texts children read at school and the literature their families enjoyed at home did not always reflect who we were as a people or what we aspired to be, or to have, as an independent nation. Luminaries such as Sylvia Ashton-Warner (1963) and Elwyn Richardson (1964), among others, however, shook the conservative, highly structured model of the New Zealand curriculum to the core with multidisciplinary, integrated and arts-based programmes of learning which, once mainstreamed, became known as 'organic learning' and 'language experience'. Local research into literacy practice and assessment (Holdaway, 1979; Clay, 1991; Elley 1992a, 1992b) informed, reflected and responded to a more socially just and inclusive approach to Maori students in particular and to the rapidly increasing diversity of New Zealand classrooms, borne of migration from the Pacific and Asia (Rata and Sullivan, 2009). Eventually, from this 'home grown' pedagogical base, and coupled with research borrowings from abroad (Smith, 1985; Goodman, 1965; Cambourne, 1988) came models of reading and writing based on socio-cultural and socio-linguistic frameworks for literacy acquisition. Learning to be literate, it was believed, was a socially interactive construction or co-construction (Vygotsky, 1978) based on the socialization of learners into the literacy practices valued by their communities and contingent on prior knowledge, experience and individualized patterns of progress.

This approach, when coupled with the use of children's literature or 'literature like' school readers, began to describe the so-called era of 'whole language'. New Zealand's approach to literacy began to be identified internationally as the 'teaching of literacy as wholes of language rather than fragments' (Cambourne, 1988, 203). While educationalists in this country protested the use of the 'whole language' and argued instead for an interactive, compensatory approach (Rumelhart, 1985) based on meaning, structure and grapho-phonic information (Clay, 1991), the moniker stuck, and was applied with enthusiasm and, arguably, rather uncritically, both here and overseas.

At best, this engaged learners in rich, real-life experiences with texts which, if read in a similar manner to bedtime story reading, would assist the development of 'book language' (front cover, author, illustrator, etc.), concepts about print (one-to-one letter or word matching, reading left to right, etc.) (Clay, 2002) and a range of key strategies, including the use of context as a first pass and sounding out or decoding as a fall-back position when an unknown word was encountered (Smith and Elley, 1997; Braunger and Lewis, 2006). Phonemic awareness and attention to phonological skills, however, became, for some, a neglected aspect of this approach and left some children, particularly those for whom English was a new language, grappling to make sense of the reading process (Tunmer and Chapman, 1999).

The pedagogical response was developing simultaneously, but theory and pedagogy overlap, and endure long after the empirical studies have been argued out. The 1980s ushered in new terminology – this became known in New Zealand as the 'Balanced Reading Programme' (MoE, 1985, 1996). It called for reading 'to', reading 'with' and reading 'by' in equal measure. Of significance to this discussion is the dramatic effect the pedagogy had on books in schools, and subsequently on library use, particularly after Elley (1992a), pondering the success of New Zealand students in the International Association for the Evaluation of Educational Achievement (IEA) study of 15 countries, designed, tested and generalized the findings of a 'Book Flood' in Fiji (teacher 'read alouds' from a wide variety of children's literature). This suggested that:

> Providing an abundance of high interest books in the classroom enables teachers to adapt their reading instruction to the pre existing motivations of students.
> Such adaptation may explain the relatively high association between the size of

a classroom library and student reading achievement which has been documented across multiple nations. (Guthrie and Wigfield, 2000, 413)

If ideas about the book flood had an advantage, it was in a renewed commitment to children's literature and library use. The methodology appears to work for students in the 'mainstream' or largely mono-cultural English-speaking classrooms; but, with increasing socio-linguistic diversity, largely borne of increased international migration, has come disparity of achievement between students in high-decile schools (schools in higher socio-economic areas) and those in low-decile schools. Disturbingly, the evidence (Wilkinson, 1998) suggests significant issues of retention and literacy achievement for Maori and Pasifika students in general, and for boys in these schools in particular. While a raft of research projects (Bishop and Glynn, 1999; Phillips, McNaughton and MacDonald, 2000; Lai et al., 2009) continue to identify causal factors and a range of interventions likely to lift achievement, including the identification and pedagogical structuring of literacy practices more consistent with student heritage and language backgrounds, the situation appears to be curiously resistant to positive change. As a result, successive governments have placed enormous emphasis on literacy (and numeracy) initiatives to lift achievement, in particular for Maori and Pasifika students and/or those in low-decile schools.

In 1999 the Ministry of Education (MoE, 1999) selected a 'task force' of literacy experts to conduct a full review of literacy teaching, learning and assessment and as a result a wide range of 'best evidence syntheses' interventions, initiatives and resources have been implemented in a bid to lift student achievement overall and that of underperforming groups in particular. This has involved a raft of change in terms of policy, teachers' professional development, research-informed literacy practices and assessment strategies to raise student achievement. Of note, however, is the fact that attention to the role of the teacher librarian in lifting student achievement and the importance of library qualifications as an endorsement to a teaching degree (currently unavailable as postgraduate qualifications from the major teacher education providers) has not yet featured in the list of interventions deemed to be likely to improve outcomes for our most vulnerable students. The audit of student learning in the information landscape undertaken by the Education Review Office (ERO) in 2005, however, advocates strongly for collaborative approaches between teachers and librarians by:

developing a shared educational philosophy and commitment by all staff to fostering student development of information literacy; establishing a school-wide cross-curriculum approach for student information literacy development that features the explicit and systematic use of an information process model; designing whole-school professional development in teaching and assessing information literacy skills; linking the school library's role in supporting information literacy and students' attitudes to reading with the school's overall vision and direction; aligning the various parts of the school's information infrastructure – principally the school library (including school library ICT) and other ICT within the school – with a clear rationale for their respective complementary roles in contributing to student learning; allocating the appropriate mix of teaching and library management expertise to the school library to ensure it is not only well-managed, organised and promoted, but also plays a central role in supporting student learning; improving assessment of both information literacy and student attitudes to reading to inform future planning for positive student outcomes; improving assessment of the school library's impact on student achievement to inform future planning for positive student outcomes; developing programmes and strategies based on identified needs, for improving Māori students' learning in the information landscape; and identifying and addressing any specific barriers that low decile (both primary and secondary) and small and rural (primary) schools may face in developing students' positive attitudes towards reading. (Education Review Office, 2005, 5)

The ERO has subsequently recommended that the appropriate agencies take a leadership role in the implementation of this advice and make links to national initiatives such as the Digital Strategy, the Literacy and Numeracy Strategy and the ICT Strategy (see www.minedu.govt.nz). What, then, is the likely impact of this for the individual learner?

Knowledge of the learner

The second literacy dimension of the honeycomb provides a focus on the individual: a child-centred approach to effective literacy practices. If teachers are to be successful, then it stands to reason that they must understand and be ready to respond to the differentiated route to literacy that each of the students in their care will take. The application of their theoretical and professional knowledge is meaningless without acknow-ledgement of the more predictable characteristics of learners and literacy in general and the very specific strengths, needs, gaps, attitudes and interests of each. A carefully planned and orchestrated approach to the developmental pathway is necessary and this is contingent on the information gleaned by assessment, be it by informal observation, anecdotal information, diagnostic testing or formal examination.

In New Zealand it is expected that teachers working with students in the primary and intermediate schools (Years 1–8) will collate information about learners from a variety of sources and using a range of assessment methodologies. They are then required to make an 'over all teacher judgement' (MoE, 2009b) in order to determine next learning steps, access levels, text selection, goals etc. Teachers need knowledge of the literacy practices and understandings, and the prior knowledge and experiences children bring with them to school. Are they familiar with narrative text through bedtime story reading or are they more comfortable with recitation, storytelling or directive approaches and observation? Are they aware of how different forms of text work? Do they know that that there are certain 'concepts about print' and that words and ideas can be recorded in a variety of ways and those texts are structured with predictable and stable conventions and purposes? Teachers must support understandings about meaning or semantic sources of information and about the structural or syntactical sources of information that provide the grammar of text. They need to know that grapho-phonic information (the sound and visual aspects of letters and words) is an essential source of information, as is the visual language, and the ways in which signs, symbols, illustration or gesture can create meaning too. All these sources of information must be integrated and drawn on accurately, strategically, fluently and automatically if the child is to comprehend or to create text that is comprehensible to others.

School and public libraries can play a significant role in effective literacy learning for individual students. Libraries are places where students and texts can be matched for level, topic and interest. The 21st-century school library, if well set up and effective in the support of information literacy, will be able to respond to the complex developmental pathway and inquiry processes or ICT skill required by the learner or, indeed, that of the teacher. Libraries are pivotal to teacher knowledge and, from the staffroom shelf or resource room to the school or university library, teachers' knowledge needs to be supported by access to contemporary and seminal research and professional literature.

Ideally, qualified librarians should be at hand to direct, support, advocate and guide professional development in library and information skills. Theory and practice can develop directly from staff collaboration and librarianship and focused professional development. Libraries are places to select text and try out the skills and understandings borne of a teacher's professional knowledge of literacy development. Schools where practice is research-informed and where professional reading is an expectation are those most likely to have knowledgeable teachers and successful learners (Alton-Lee, 2003). Above all, the motivation to become a reader and the reading 'mileage' required to become so (Stanovich, 1986) may well begin in the library. Moore and Trebilcock (2003) suggest that the quality of the school library programme is a powerful predictor of reading achievement. They quote Gniewek's (1999) summary of American research, which indicated that in well-resourced school libraries, where a qualified librarian is in place, students are more likely to 'score higher on standardised tests, read at higher levels, and achieve more in all subject areas, regardless of the socio-economic and education levels of their parents' (Moore and Trebilcock, 2003, 20).

Libraries are also sources of assessment information and resources. They make available assessment exemplars and professional reading material to inform and challenge teachers' decision making about individual learners and the groupings they belong to. From libraries come the texts necessary to create informal reading inventories for the assessment of reading and models of text type for the assessment of writing: the narrative fiction, plays, poetry, graphic novels, other forms of visual text and non-fiction material used to inform teaching and learning and to create both formative and summative assessment. Libraries provide the integrated and cross-curriculum resource base for teacher-made tests as well as the place where the archives of examinations and assessment exemplars are stored and where the rigour and reliability of tests can be cross-checked. In the secondary school this is imperative. In the modern primary and intermediate school it is increasingly desirable. This level of expertise is often beyond the reach of the classroom teacher, and for this reason a qualified librarian is essential, particularly if this person is also well briefed on the forms of pedagogical strategies used in the classroom.

Knowledge of instructional strategies

The 'Matthew Effect' (Stanovich, 1986) describes a phenomenon in reading that suggests 'the more you read (and write) the better you get'. This is the basis upon which New Zealand schools have embraced approaches as guided reading and writing, shared reading and writing, sustained silent reading, as well as 'reading to' and modelling in writing, all of which place emphasis on real reading for real purpose within a scaffolded context for instruction at both the functional and aesthetic levels. Each of these approaches is transferable from one curriculum area to another. It is common in New Zealand classrooms to see a guided reading group grappling with an excerpt from a scientific text in the science programme, or a teacher modelling persuasive text in a health lesson. The boundaries of the timetable in most New Zealand schools are fluid, and the approaches flow from one end of the day to another.

The National Education Guidelines (MoE, 2010b), however, do insist that precedence be given to literacy and numeracy, and many schools run 'long mornings' in order to accommodate the key strategies as they fit within integrated-inquiry learning topics. It is important, therefore, that a classroom be rich in reading material and have easy access to the library. At the most pragmatic level, children's engagement with books, read aloud by the teacher or selected and read independently by the child, provides access to words, ideas and experiences that help to construct and reconstruct and to challenge the understandings of the world the child lives in. Freire and Macedo (1987), in this regard, have discussed the way children read the world in the first instance and then begin to read the word, but that the words continue to provide ways of reading the world in an empowering cycle of increasing advantage.

Children's literature is one of the very important ways in which the learner can, almost effortlessly, encounter the world and engage in an often seamless integration of speaking, listening, reading and writing activities through dance, drama, music and the visual arts, and critical thinking. Literature can provide the context for wider curriculum content and the springboard to non-fiction text. Children's literature is the grist to an effective literacy programme and, for so many children, the rich reward of the functional and sometimes decontextualized approaches to learning to read and write. It allows learners to step inside the lives and the minds of others. It brings together the languages and cultures, beliefs and values, and the creative, imaginative spirit of not only the writer and the reader but also the wider audience; a dynamic collaboration that has an indisputably powerful impact on the life of the classroom and, arguably, on the life of an individual forever. The library and the librarian are pivotal in this, and as important in the digital age as they were in an imagined era of dark and dusty shelves of books and scary witches at the front desk, similar to Eoin Colfer's rather unflattering description in *The Legend of Spud Murphy*:

The library seemed to go on forever. Row after row of wooden
bookshelves, bolted to the floor at the bottom and the ceiling at the top.
Each row had a ladder with wheels on the upper end. Those ladders
would have made great rides, but there was zero chance of children ever
being allowed to have fun in here.   (Colfer, 2004, 21–2)

The extent to which the school library can be seen as an inspiring (and fun)
place to be is, without doubt, the key to the engaged reader.

Engaging learners with texts

It was not until the late 1950s that children's literature in general and
educational publishing in particular began to reflect more accurately the
world that young New Zealanders were growing up in. The 'Janet and John'
readers and the McKee series, among others, borrowed from the UK and the
USA, were dismissed in favour of our own 'Ready to Read' series for
younger children and the 'School Journals' (see www.thechair.
minedu.govt.nz) for more able readers. For the very first time the unique
profile of New Zealand society, urban and rural, Maori and Pakeha, became
visible in the 'little books' and the magazine-type format of the journals.
These free-issue texts became central to the reading curriculum of the
nation's primary schools. Their legacy lives on in contemporary and often
electronic versions of the same, reflecting and challenging both the local and
the global world the students live in.

Contemporary New Zealand children's literature and classroom reading
material is in fine fettle, depicting a young, confident and
bicultural/multicultural nation and, in spite of a worldwide return to the
'basics' of textbooks and phonics-based programmes, young New
Zealanders have typically been taught in an integrated, experiential, holistic
and literature-based manner, as described earlier. While this has suited the
developmental needs of children in 'mainstream' English-medium
environments it may well have compromised the aspirations of those who
come to our schools with languages other than English and distinctly
different literacy traditions. Worryingly, languages policy in this country is
in flux, and Pasifika versions of the 'Ready to Read' books and other such
texts in Samoan, Tongan or Cook Island Maori, for example, have been
(temporarily) withdrawn for MoE review and audit purposes. It is critical
that text, from the classroom bookshelves to the downtown libraries, reflects
and responds to who our learners are, the languages they speak, the

interests they have and the potential they possess. As McNaughton (2002) has said, our students arrive in our classrooms (and libraries) not at risk, but full of promise. For both teachers and librarians the focus is on supporting students to become engaged and motivated readers who are confident to access, select, use and evaluate text for educational, informational and leisure-time purposes and be able to fulfil this promise. So often, however, this rests on our willingness as professionals to put in place realistic and appropriately high expectations of our students, their 'knowledge and expertise, their progress and their achievement' (MoE, 2003, 15).

Expectations

Expectations are based on personal and professional beliefs and understandings about literacy and the very manner in which literacy and literature are perceived. Applegate and Applegate (2004) have discussed the 'Peter effect', based on a parable from the Bible which asks, 'How can I give that which I do not myself possess?' In this sense, the attitudes of teachers and librarians towards literacy and their motivation to be seen as readers and writers themselves can be shown to have a significant effect on a student's own self-efficacy. This can be even more profoundly affected by the ideas held by teachers about children's capacities for learning. Teachers' expectations shape all aspects of their professional practice and have a direct impact on learners' self-esteem, their patterns of progress and their achievement:

> All the research shows that the more children love reading, the more
> they will read, and the more they read, the better their literacy, their
> academic achievement, their learning outcomes and their attitudes. This
> is irrefutable, but sometimes overlooked. The school library is a
> foundation for the school's literacy programmes and a catalyst for the
> development of lifelong readers. It is where they get the spark that turns
> them from learning to read to enjoying reading.
>
> (National Library of New Zealand, 2010)

Setting expectations and establishing goals for an individual learner requires evidence. Teachers in New Zealand have a variety of assessment options available for both formative and summative assessment (as discussed earlier). Specifically, teachers in the lower end of the primary school might use running records (Clay, 2002) and simple writing analysis methodology (MoE, 2011a) to determine a child's level of access and next learning steps. Standardized testing enables 'broad brush' decisions to be made, while more detailed analysis and diagnosis of older students can be gained from 'e-asTTle' measures (MoE, 2011b). This is an electronically delivered and 'marked' assessment measure of reading, writing and mathematics and is available in both English and Maori. The advantage of this form of assessment is that individual attainment can be compared with a classroom or school cluster cohort, by decile or for the testing of national standards. While there are obvious dangers in this, it does assist a teacher to design realistic and appropriate learning pathways and expectations for a student, or groups of students, which provides for support as well as challenge and, ultimately, permits a 'best fit' by course of study, particularly in the upper levels of the primary and intermediate schools, and beyond, into the secondary school.

Librarians too, in collaboration with classroom teachers, are able to use this information to tailor specific information-skill teaching and learning and text selection and use with whole classes, groups or individuals. Expectations are evidence-based and learning outcomes are focused. Students need feedback about their learning, as do their families and caregivers, and to be informed about next learning steps and personal goals. It is important that these are delivered with clarity, aligned to assessment outcomes, reviewed and reflected on. Above all, they should mirror who the student really is, the interests and expertise they have, the potential they bring to learning and the expectations that all involved in the learning partnership hold. This is where librarians, along with other specialists in the school, can add to the classroom teacher's assessment. This calls for partnerships, the last of the six literacy dimensions described by the MoE (2003, 2006, 2004).

Partnerships

The importance of multiple 'voices' in the literacy development of a single student has long been acknowledged. The oft-quoted Korean adage that it takes a whole village to raise a child is equally important when the essential role of the school in the socialization and education of students in, and for, the 21st century is considered. Partnership, as the sixth dimension of the honeycomb, is described as collaborative relationships that:

contribute to and support student learning. Each learner lives in a network of significant people including their teachers, family, peers and specialist teachers. Effective teachers recognise the need for, and actively promote, partnerships within these networks. (MoE, 2003, 15)

In earlier times teachers might have been expected to close the door of the classroom and work to a curriculum based on bounded notions of knowledge, skills and understandings. We now live in an era where quite the reverse is true. Classroom doors have been flung off their hinges to embrace globalized teaching and learning. Knowledge is no longer lodged in the authority of individual teachers or, indeed, individual texts. Knowledge is generative and, as Leu (2000, 745) would insist, 'deictic', or in a constant state of transformation:

It is the rapid and continuously changing nature of literacy, literacy as technological deixis, that requires our attention as we consider research in this area and the implications for literacy learning.

Because technology is involved and because inquiry processes and information skills and technology prescribe the pedagogy of the future, our relationships within the library, and beyond into the digital world, are contingent on libraries and qualified librarians.

Hay and Foley (2009) agree, and suggest that classrooms and libraries have a critical role to play in the partnership relationship with schools. The job of the librarian, they insist, is to build capacities – of the students, teachers and themselves – to establish a well-organized centre for literacy and information that aligns to curriculum and content, to extend the human resources and facilities available, to build up a collection which reflects the needs and the aspirations of a particular school, to collaborate with all educational professionals, including specialists, to promote, deliver and implement professional development and qualification upgrades and endorsements, to manage the library effectively, to communicate with clarity and to work for funding and continuous improvement for what should be the most important resource centre in the school.

Partnerships in this sense can involve parents and families as well, and, where appropriate, the library might be seen as the welcoming gateway to the school and the various activities that take place within it.

Luke and Freebody (1999, 5) have said:

Literacy education is ultimately about the kinds of citizens/subjects that

could and should be constructed. Teaching and learning isn't just a matter of skill acquisition and knowledge transmission or natural growth. It's about building identities and cultures, communities and institutions. And 'failure' at literacy isn't about individual skill deficits – it's about access and apprenticeship into institutions and resources, discourses and texts.

If we are, as the rhetoric suggests, riding a knowledge wave that is leading us towards a 'knowledge economy', then surely literacy and library partnerships are where it begins.

Conclusion

The future of teaching and learning is undoubtedly collaborative, inquiry-based, digital, online and library or 'information centre'-based. In the future, traditional forms of reading and writing must compete with Web 2.0 approaches for student motivation and engagement. The MoE recognizes the importance of this and the challenges of ensuring that each student in this country has equitable and successful access to 21st-century pedagogies, and urges teachers to reconsider their current beliefs:

> To design courses that motivate students' engagement, teachers often have to put aside their preconceived ideas about e-learning, re-think their traditional teaching approaches, and plan authentic and active learning environments in which they are facilitators rather than lecturers. In blended learning, traditional teaching and learning approaches can be integrated with the approaches made possible through technology. (MoE, 2010a)

It is important to remember, however, that the ability to read fluently, with confidence, comprehension and motivation, is fundamental to being able to participate effectively in the world today. It is the essential foundation for all other literacies, digital literacies included. Students will not become information-literate without high levels of reading literacy. High-quality teacher education and investment in library and ICT qualifications are critical aspects of this. Libraries and librarians, teachers and classrooms will have to work together in well-informed, pedagogically aligned and integrative ways to ensure that this is made possible.

And there is another dimension to keep in mind as well; in our haste to embrace technology, let's not lose sight of the greatest of all gifts to our students: children's and young adult literature. Unlike the latest deictic 'techno tool', literature will endure. The winners will be our children who know how to read, how to write and how to learn – and, importantly, how to enjoy a good book. As *Newsweek* magazine (1991) commented so long ago: 'If reading is the cornerstone of learning then the best foundations are built in New Zealand.' The honeycomb model provides just such a foundation, and it is our job now to fill its dimensions with the skills, knowledge, understandings and enthusiasms appropriate for a new era we all know so little about.

References

Alton-Lee, A. (2003) *Quality Teaching for Diverse Students in Schooling: best evidence synthesis*, Ministry of Education,www.educationcounts.govt.nz/goto/BES.

Applegate, A. J. and Applegate, M. D. (2004) The Peter Effect: reading habits and attitudes of pre-service teachers, *The Reading Teacher*, **57** (5), 554–64.

Ashton-Warner, S. (1963) *Teacher*, Simon and Shuster.

Bishop, R. and Glynn, T. (1999) *Culture Counts: changing power relationships in education*, Dunmore Press.

Braunger, J. and Lewis, P. (2006) *Building a Knowledge Base in Reading*, 2nd edn, National Council of Teachers of English and International Reading Association.

Cambourne, B. (1988) *The Whole Story: NATURAL learning and the acquisition of learning in the classroom*, Ashton Scholastic.

Clay, M.M. (1991) *Becoming Literate*, Heinemann.

Clay, M. M. (2002) *An Observation Survey of Early Literacy Achievement*, Heinemann.

Colfer, E. (2004*) The Legend of Spud Murphy*, Miramax Books.

Education Review Office (2005) *Student Learning in the Information Landscape*, Education Evaluation Reports.

Elley, W. (1992a) *How in the World Do Students Read?* The Hague International Association for the Evaluation of Educational Achievement.

Elley, W. (1992b). Acquiring Literacy in a Second Language: the effect of book-based programs ,*Language Learning*, **41** (3), 375–411.

Freire, P. and Macedo, D. (1987) *Literacy: reading the word and the world*, Bergin and Garvey.

Gee, J. P. (2008) *Social Linguistics and Literacies: ideology in discourses*, Routledge.

Gniewek, D. (1999). School Library Programs and Student Achievement: a review of the research, www.libraries.phila.k12.pa.us/misc/research-sum.html [inactive].

Goodman, K., (1965) A Linguistic Study of Cues and Miscues in Reading, *Elementary English*, **42** (6), 639–43.

Guthrie, J. T. and Wigfield, A. (2000) Engagement and Motivation in Reading. In

Kamil, M. L., Mosenthal, P. B., Pearson, P .D., and Barr, R. (eds), *Handbook of Reading Research*, Vol. 3, Erlbaum.

Hay, L. and Foley, C. (2009) School Libraries Building Capacity for Student Learning in 21C, *Scan*, **28** (2), 17–26.

Healy, A. (2008) Expanding Student Capacities: learning by design pedagogy. In Healy, A. (ed.), *Multiliteracies and Diversity in Education: new pedagogies for expanding landscapes*, Oxford University Press.

Holdaway, D. (1979) *The Foundations of Literacy*, Ashton Scholastic and Heinemann.

IFLA/UNESCO (2000) *School Library Manifesto*, www.unesco.org/webworld/libraries/manifestos/school_manifesto.html.

Kalantzis, M., Cope, B. and Cloonan, A. (2010) A Multiliteracies Perspective on the New Literacies. In Baker, E. A. (ed.), *The New Literacies: multiple perspectives on research and practice*, The Guilford Press.

Kipling, R. (1893) *The Song of the Cities*, retrieved from www.poetryloverspage.com/poets/kipling/song_of_cities.html.

Lai, M., McNaughton, S., Amituanai-Toloa, M., Turner, R. and Hsiao, S. (2009) Sustained Acceleration of Achievement in Reading Comprehension: the New Zealand experience, *Reading Research Quarterly*, **44** (1), 30–56.

Lankshear, C. and Knobel, M. (2003) The 'New Literacy Studies' and the Study of New Literacies. In Lankshear, C. and Knobel, M. (eds.), *New Literacies: changing knowledge and classroom learning*, Open University Press.

Leu, D. (2000) Literacy and Technology: deictic consequences for literacy education in an information age. In Kamil, M. L., Mosenthal, P. B., Pearson, D. P. and Barr, R. (eds), *Handbook of Reading Research*, Vol. 3, Longman.

Luke, A. and Freebody, P. (1999) *The Four Resources Model*, Reading Online, www.readingonline.org .

McNaughton, S. (2002) *Meeting of Minds*, Learning Media.

MoE (1985) *Reading in Junior Classes*. Learning Media.

MoE (1996) *The Learner as a Reader*, Learning Media

MoE (1999) *Report of the Literacy Taskforce*, Ministry of Education.

MoE and National Library of New Zealand (2002) *The School Library and Learning in the Information Landscape: guidelines for New Zealand schools*, Learning Media.

MoE (2003) *Effective Literacy Practice in Years 1 to 4*, Learning Media.

MoE (2004) *Effective Literacy Strategies in Years 9 to 13*, Learning Media.

MoE (2006) *Effective Literacy Practice in Years 5 to 8*, Learning Media.

MoE (2007) *The New Zealand Curriculum*, Learning Media.

MoE (2009a) *Literacy Learning Progressions*, Learning Media.

MoE (2009b) *The New Zealand Curriculum Reading and Writing Standards for Years 1–8*, Learning Media.

MoE (2009c) *Learning through Talk: oral language in years 1–3,* Learning Media.

MoE (2009d) *Learning through Talk: oral language in years 4–8,* Learning Media.

MoE (2010a) *Effective Practices for E-learning: how do we engage learners?* http://akoaotearoa.ac.nz/effective-practice-elearning.

MoE (2010b) *The National Education Guidelines (NEGs),* www.minedu.govt.nz/NZEducation/EducationPolicies/Schools.

MoE (2011a) *Assessment Exemplars in English: Te Kete Ipurangi – The Online Learning Centre,* www.tki.org.nz/r/assessment/exemplars/eng/index_e.php.

MoE (2011b) *e-asTTle; Te Kete Ipurangi – The Online Learning Centre,* http://e-asttle.tki.org.nz/.

Moore, P. and Trebilcock, M. (2003) *The School Library Team: what does it do to influence teaching and learning?,* Monograph No. 2, Auckland College of Education.

National Library of New Zealand; Te Puna Matauranga o Aotearoa (2010) *Services to Schools,* http://schools.natlib.govt.nz/curriculum-services-who-are-we.

Newsweek (1991) *In New Zealand, Good Reading and Writing Come Naturally,* 2 December, 41f, www.newsweek.com/1991/12/01/in-new-zealand-good-reading-and-writing-come-naturally.html.

Phillips, G., McNaughton, S. and MacDonald, S. (2000) *Picking up the Pace: effective literacy interventions for accelerated progress over the transition into decile 1 schools,* Ministry of Education.

Rata, E. and Sullivan, R. (2009) *Introduction to the History of New Zealand Education,* Pearson.

Richardson, E. S. (1964) *In the Early World,* New Zealand Council of Educational Research.

Rumelhart, D. E. (1985) Toward an Interactive Model of Reading. In Singer, H. and Ruddell, R. B. (eds) *Theoretical Models and Processes of Reading,* 3rd edn, International Reading Association, 722–50.

Smith, F. (1985) *Reading,* Cambridge University Press.

Smith, J. and Elley, W. (1997) *How Children Learn to Read,* Longman.

Stanovich, K. E. (1986) Matthew Effects in Reading: some consequences of individual differences in the acquisition of literacy, *Reading Research Quarterly,* **21**, 340–406.

Tunmer, W. E. and Chapman, J. W. (1999) Teaching Strategies for Word Identification. In Thompson, G. B. and Nicholson, T. (eds), *Learning to Read: beyond phonics and whole language,* International Reading Association and Teachers College Press.

Vygotsky, L. (1978) *Mind in Society: the development of higher psychological processes,* ed. and trans. M. Cole, Harvard University Press.

Wilkinson, I. A. G. (1998) Dealing with Diversity: achievement gaps in reading literacy among New Zealand students, *Reading Research Quarterly*, **33** (2), 144–67.

Wink, J. (2010) *Notes from the Real World*, 4th edn, Pearson.

5

The Summer Reading Challenge in libraries: a continuing success

Anne Sarrag, Lynne Taylor, Natasha Roe and Geraldine Brennan

What inspires 750,000 children in the UK to read over 3 million books during the summer holidays for pleasure?

The Summer Reading Challenge is one of the largest creative reading opportunities available to children in the UK. It introduces children to one of the best free resources for their minds that they have on their doorsteps – the local library – and focuses on developing skills that are vital for their life chances and life skills – reading and a love of reading.

> Alan Yentob, Creative Director of the BBC, speaking at the Summer Reading Challenge Conference 2009: Celebrating 10 Years and Looking Ahead

The Summer Reading Challenge is great fun for everyone. It's free, it's simple: read six books over the summer holidays, chosen from the library. There are stickers and incentives to collect along the way to keep children motivated, and at the end they have a real sense of achievement, marked by libraries and schools issuing Summer Reading Challenge certificates and medals, hosting celebration events in libraries, schools, theatres and other community venues.

The scheme benefits children in several ways. Not only are they rewarded for completing the Challenge, they are encouraged to swap ideas and recommendations. The idea is that they form closer relationships with their libraries, hopefully becoming 'readers for life'. 'The children have the freedom to choose their own books,' says The Reading Agency's Lynne Taylor. 'It gives them a real sense of personal achievement that they associate with the library.'

We also know that this simple idea makes a real difference to children's reading habits. Research has shown that children who take part are more enthusiastic about reading and that taking part can help prevent the 'summer holiday reading dip', when they lose their reading momentum and motivation (Kennedy and Bearne, 2010).

This chapter will look at how the Summer Reading Challenge works. We will trace its beginning, expansion and development over the last 13 years – working with schools and other partners, growing into a catalyst for volunteering in libraries and now running in countries overseas. We will examine the effects this has had on the provision of resources and opportunities for library staff, and the difference it makes to children and young people.

How the Summer Reading Challenge started

Working closely with children's library professional groups ASCEL (Association of Senior Children's and Education Librarians) and YLG (Youth Libraries Group), freelance consultants Miranda McKearney and Anne Sarrag set up LaunchPad, a charity to promote the value of libraries for children through advocacy, marketing and research. It created the first Summer Reading Challenge, *The Reading Safari*, in 1999 to address the fragmented way that each UK library authority was trying to keep children reading over the summer by designing its own reading activities, the quality of which varied from the fantastic to the mediocre or even nothing at all. It also wanted to monitor and evaluate the Challenge so that information could be gathered nationally about the effects of keeping children reading over the summer.

Libraries immediately benefited from having professionally designed, high-quality print items, which were cheaper for them than producing their own materials, as well as having robust professional research and evaluation that they could use in their own reports, and everyone benefited from the higher profile that a national scheme could achieve with the general public.

What a lease of life the Summer Reading Challenge has given to summer activities in public libraries since 1999, and what a great lever it has been in getting us into schools and working with partners in both the public and private sectors.

Mike Treacy, Kingston Libraries, Royal Borough of Kingston upon Thames, in
The Reading Agency, 2009

How the Summer Reading Challenge works

By creating a fun, creative summer holiday activity, the Summer Reading Challenge aims to:

- get more children reading more
- build children's confidence and enthusiasm about reading
- build children's and families' use of public libraries
- help children and families to benefit from cultural experiences
- help young adults to experience rewarding volunteering activity through library work
- ensure that disadvantaged children are included in the challenge.

The independent charity with a mission 'to get more people reading more', The Reading Agency, now runs and manages the Summer Reading Challenge and each year creates a set of printed materials for any library authority to buy to enable it to run the Challenge, and a dedicated website. There is a different theme each year (see Figure 5.1), which the promotional materials, incentives and interactive website reflect. Past years, themes have included sports themes for Olympics in 2000 and 2008, The Reading Relay and Team Read respectively. In 2007 The Big Wild Read had an environmental theme

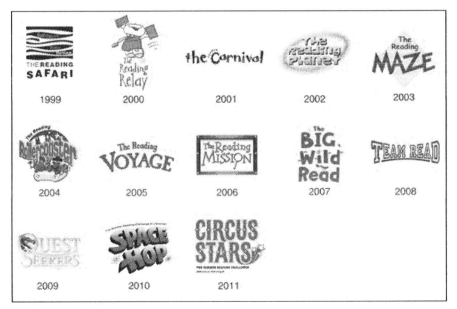

Figure 5.1 *Summer Reading Challenge themes*

that was linked to a BBC children's campaign. Space Hop in 2010 was inspired by the huge wave of interest in the 40th anniversary of the first lunar landing the previous summer, and in 2012 the Summer Reading Challenge will explore the themes of the Olympics, again through a Challenge linked to stories and cultural exchange.

Children are consulted in the planning for each Challenge through a library advisory group of regional representatives who then work with selected children. Children help select the illustrator each year by responding to sample illustrations from a short list of guest illustrators. They also provide feedback on the proposed theme and ideas for the website. With support from library staff, these children also help to finalize the annual book collection: a list of thematic and top new summer reads displayed in a bespoke display unit. These are not, however, required reading, since an essential element of the Summer Reading Challenge is that children can read any book they choose from the library – but many library authorities do rely on these as an inspiring selection to top up their bookstock for the busy summer ahead.

Involving children has helped The Reading Agency to know what children like about the Challenge, what matters to them, and what is relevant to them and their peers.

The website has proved a particularly useful tool for engaging children with the Summer Reading Challenge themes and in supporting their literacy development. Typically, a Summer Reading Challenge website has games based on the theme, places where children can discuss books and places where they can talk to the authors who are lending their support to the Challenge that year.

The Reading Agency provides the Summer Reading Challenge materials in different formats for visually impaired children, and in Welsh/English bilingual versions. The information leaflets for parents are available in 20 different languages.

Authors and publishers

Michael Rosen is patron of the Summer Reading Challenge and one of the authors who regularly contributes to the website. Over the years, over 80 authors and illustrators have been filmed or have sent in blogs and messages, engaging with thousands of children taking part in the Challenge.

Authors and illustrators are also involved in hundreds of workshops throughout the summer holidays that are linked to the Challenge, often supported by publishers. Publishers also pay a small fee when their books are included in the annual Summer Reading Challenge book collection, which goes towards the overall costs of running the Challenge.

Partners and sponsors

Over the years, the Summer Reading Challenge's simple structure has appealed to partners and sponsors. For example, in 2007 The Big Wild Read had an environmental theme linked to a BBC campaign. Children were given wild flower seeds to plant as one of the incentives and collected tree tokens, which enabled The Woodland Trust to plant 20,000 trees in UK woodlands.

In 2011 Tesco Bank will be the Associate Sponsor of the Summer Reading Challenge Scotland 2011. Tesco Bank (whose main offices are in Scotland) approached The Reading Agency asking if it could include the Challenge in its Tesco Bank Community portfolio. Its support is funding free additional materials for Scottish library authorities, which should mean that more children in Scotland are able to take part, as well as a series of family-focused events.

Reaching into communities

As part of running the Challenge, libraries organize a wide range of events in many different community settings, incorporating music, dance, poetry, art and performance. In summer 2010 there were 15,000 different events linked to the Space Hop theme, which 250,000 children (and their families) attended. These events link Summer Reading Challenge families with their local communities and engage them with cultural and learning experiences.

Libraries can use these events to showcase their role in the community, and local media often feature positive stories of children and their families joining in at events and getting a real buzz from creative activities.

Making a difference to children

Key findings from impact research carried out in 2009 into the Summer Reading Challenge shows that the Challenge makes a significant impact on the children who take part.

The research, carried out by the United Kingdom Literacy Association (UKLA), a registered charity committed to promoting good practice nationally and internationally in literacy and language teaching and research, found that children undertaking the Summer Reading Challenge saw it as an 'overwhelmingly positive experience'. They tend to be 'committed readers' before they take the Challenge, but 80% of children believe they are better readers as a result of taking part. The research found that they enjoyed it a lot and wanted to take part in it again the following year. They also liked visiting the library a lot, and now visit the library more often than children who do not take part in the Challenge.

The Summer Reading Challenge 'boosts children's inclination to read at home' and widens the range and repertoire of the things they read. Children who took the Summer Reading Challenge read far more books over the summer than those who are keen readers but who did not do the Challenge.

Through their reading, and the library activities around the Summer Reading Challenge theme, children are learning to recognize authors and finding new favourites. They are learning new things and responding creatively to the books they read. They enjoy talking about the books with adults in the library and they think about books after they've finished reading them.

Significantly, the research found that the Summer Reading Challenge can contribute towards preventing the 'summer holiday dip' in children's reading motivation and attainment. Teachers said that more children who had taken part in the Challenge either maintained or improved their reading than those who had not, and far fewer dipped in their reading levels after the summer holidays (Kennedy and Bearne, 2010).

Case study 5.1 The Malak family, from Luton

The Malak family – mother Samia and three children, Shiza (8), Humza (13) and Fizzah (10) – from Luton use the Wigmore Library and are big fans of the Summer Reading Challenge. They have been doing the Challenge since 2003 and explain why it means so much to them, and the difference it has made to their family.

How they take part in the Summer Reading Challenge

At their local library, the librarians put up lists showing how each child is progressing through the Summer Reading Challenge. This is a great incentive and also an important public acknowledgement and celebration of what Samia's children have achieved. The Malak family now race down to the library to see who's coming first. Their library also does Summer Reading Challenge activities related to reading, such as hosting artwork displays and pulling together reports on what the children and young people like reading.

'I think the very important thing about Summer Reading Challenge is that we are doing something together as a family and it doesn't cost us anything. We like going to the library anyway but we look forward every year to the Summer Reading Challenge,' says Samia.

What they gain from the Summer Reading Challenge

'The difference the Summer Reading Challenge has made to our family over the years is shown clearly in our home, where all the walls have been taken up with the posters the children have done or the certificates they have won and I've had to pinch ribbons from chocolate boxes for all their medals! The Summer Reading Challenge offers something fresh and different each year and we always look forward to doing it,' says Samia.

'I used not to read books much but the Summer Reading Challenge got me into reading them. You get encouragement to read books because you get more and more rewards,' says Humza.

Case study 5.2 The Glaister family, from Reddish in Stockport

The Glaister family, from Reddish in Stockport, are also enthusiastic supporters of the Summer Reading Challenge. Jack Glaister, 10, has done three Summer Reading Challenges using giant print books from the RNIB Library and his local library. Jack has been visually impaired from birth.

How they take part in the Summer Reading Challenge

'He first got involved with the Summer Reading Challenge via his local library when his older sister Katy was doing it and he asked if he could do it too. At first we used audio books and chose short books.

'Getting books to read through the RNIB library and his local library is important for Jack. Unlike other kids, he can't just go and buy a book in the high street. At our local library, we know a couple of the staff well, they have a good relationship with him and they are very aware of his vision.'

What they gain from the Summer Reading Challenge

'It is important for Jack to be able to do what other kids his age are doing and he also quite liked the idea of writing about his favourite stories and then getting a reward at the end, like the stickers. It gave him something to aim for and made him feel that he could do it.

'Reading has improved his imagination. Since he has been doing the Summer Reading Challenge his teachers have said that he is now writing stories he's made up, with really quirky ideas, and they think he's getting this from reading.

'They've also told me that his reading is now on a par with others' in his class. Because of his impairment he was behind, but now they are saying he has caught up – that's a significant result and I'm proud of him for that.'

The Summer Reading Challenge in public libraries

The Summer Reading Challenge has a very useful strategic role in helping to deliver public library services. It provides a cost-effective way for authorities to support local reading and literacy strategies and also links them in with key partners in the community. As Janene Cox, Strategic Commissioner for Culture, Leisure and Tourism, Staffordshire County Council explained at the Summer Reading Challenge Conference in 2009: 'It's helped us embed our service in key strategic outcomes and delivery plans at County, Directorate and District level, and it's enabled our stakeholders and partners to understand and value our role.

'In difficult times it becomes even more important for libraries to demonstrate that they provide a good library service for children, and they can show through the Summer Reading Challenge the difference they are making to communities.'

Case study 5.3 Lambeth Library

Sandra Davidson, Senior Children's and Young People's Librarian at Lambeth, talks about the difference the Summer Reading Challenge has made to the library service, and how running the challenge has given library staff the experience and confidence to run even more events and activities for children and families.

How it runs the Challenge

'We have been running a form of the Summer Reading Challenge for 12 years. We started running our own summer scheme; then, when the national offer became available it was very attractive to us. We didn't have to think about a theme and the materials and prizes were more exciting than anything we could afford to produce ourselves.

'It was good to be part of something with a national identity. I belong to a network of heads of children's library services and we have been able to share experiences of the Challenge because we are all working with the same programme.

'The core programme is for 4 to 11 year-olds but we encourage younger children to join in because we want to attract families. Lambeth has pockets of severe deprivation, so free activities are important.'

What they gain from the Summer Reading Challenge

'We have been able to run successful community events that target particular groups of children that we want to bring into the library. We are able to do this because the Challenge has given us confidence in putting on events, promoting books for reluctant readers and encouraging reader development in an informal way that is different to working on literacy levels. For example, we have worked with a local group of children's writers and illustrators to run a four-week creative writing workshop for children, which was oversubscribed. We have thought about how to create a good learning experience for whole families and organized a training course for librarians on sharing books with parents.

Case study 5.4 Essex Libraries

Sarah Mears, Children's Services Development Manager, Essex Libraries, talks about its approach to the Summer Reading Challenge and how it focuses on staff training, with a special emphasis on the child's experience of the Challenge.

How it runs the Challenge

'We have been running the Summer Reading Challenge since it started and ran our own challenge before that; then our own programme evolved into a national activity, which we were pleased with. We also have our own extension of the Challenge for older children. So the ideas behind the Summer Reading

Challenge are well established with our staff.

'The next move for us was to get staff to think through how we could make the best use of the Challenge to support book sharing activities in which children express ideas about books. You take a quick and practical activity such as children sorting books into boxes related to how much they enjoyed the book, and customize it for the Challenge. For example, when we had a fantasy theme children put books they didn't like in the Dragon's Mouth and gave those they liked to the Wizard.'

What it gains from the Summer Reading Challenge

'We use some of the approaches in our training for school group visits to our libraries, so it's very useful. We have held a successful role-play workshop on talking to children – what to do when a child won't speak, or the parent speaks for the child, or the child speaks too much. Another successful session was on addressing a school assembly, because we want to get every primary school in the county to have an assembly on the Summer Reading Challenge. When an assembly goes well and you keep it simple and make it sound exciting, it really does increase the number of children from that school who take part and you can see the results right away.'

The Summer Reading Challenge in schools

From its own annual monitoring and evaluation, The Reading Agency knew that teachers liked the Summer Reading Challenge and thought that it benefited them. However, The Reading Agency needed more specific research to assess the impact on educational standards.

In 2009 Rebecca Kennedy and Eve Bearne from UKLA carried out a research project involving teachers from 11 different schools, to assess the impact of the Summer Reading Challenge on children's reading motivation and attainment. This research identified, as has been mentioned earlier, the important role that the Challenge provides in maintaining children's reading motivation and standards over the long summer holiday, but also found that it instils a positive attitude to reading and learning in schools. Teachers commented that children were more confident in talking about their reading and have improved self-confidence. Participants brought in resources and books for topic work that they'd researched in the library as part of the Challenge.

The researchers also found that the role of the head teacher is critical in supporting children's readiness to engage with the Summer Reading Challenge. In those schools where the head teacher was centrally involved more children were engaged with the Challenge and benefited from it.

The impact research showed that the Summer Reading Challenge works best where there are strong links between schools and libraries. A high number of libraries (89%) visit schools to encourage children to take part in the Challenge. Half of the libraries targeted specific schools and intensively promoted the Challenge. These included schools where take-up of the Challenge had been low, and schools where there were lower literacy attainment results, particularly schools in deprived areas.

Where they do target schools, libraries report that more children take part in the Challenge and more complete it. The libraries also have a closer working relationship with the head teacher/teachers in those schools they work with to promote the Summer Reading Challenge.

Case study 5.5 Walsgrave Church of England Primary School

Walsgrave Church of England Primary School actively promotes the Summer Reading Challenge. Head teacher Kim Docking and Bryony Harrison, the Year 5 teacher and the literacy co-ordinator at Walsgrave, talk about how it has become an integral part of the school's literacy improvement plan. Bryony has responsibility for literacy levels across the school and is keen to promote reading for pleasure, seeing it as an essential way to raise attainment.

How it promotes the Summer Reading Challenge

In Walsgrave Church of England Primary School there is a real commitment to providing good, pertinent bookstock to complement the topics being studied by the children, and the school uses Coventry Schools' Library Service, which it values highly. But it also wants children to read widely outside of school, and the Summer Reading Challenge provides a really good opportunity for them to do this. Librarians come into the school assemblies to talk about the Challenge and encourage the children to take part.

Bryony explains how the school promotes the Challenge to its children. 'During the summer term we'll do things in class to promote the Summer Reading Challenge, like having children who've done it before talk about their experience, and having people from the library talk about the Challenge. We visit the local library, so the children can meet the librarians and know where it is! Nearer to the summer holidays I'll do an assembly showing them the website, and in ICT classes they can play on it. We send a letter home to tell the parents about the Reading Challenge and what it involves. We also link very closely to the Showcase Cinema, which runs a programme called Bookworm Wednesdays, where children can see a film for free if they bring a book review. We link that in to the Summer Reading Challenge by saying that they can write a review for some of the books they read and get in to the cinema.'

Kim explains: 'We don't have a library on our doorstep, so it's about educating the children to persuade their parents to take them to the library.'

What it gains from the Summer Reading Challenge

'You can very much see the children who have taken part in the Summer Reading Challenge and the ones who haven't,' says Bryony. 'They're coming back into school and they're naturally engaging – their brains haven't been to sleep over the whole summer holidays!

'There's one boy who liked books, but they were all very short, picture-type books linked to films, or computer games and sticker books and things like that. Through the Summer Reading Challenge, when we went to the library, the librarian said "if you like books about films why don't you try these?" and he started reading Harry Potter for the first time. So for him, it's given him the experience of longer reads and he's loving it, he's really drawn into it.'

Kim talks about the benefits to the whole school: 'The reason why we promote the Summer Reading Challenge is we can never have the size and scale of the local library and have all the updated books and the range, the books that really fire up the children's imagination, so we encourage all the children to use the public library. For us, it's about narrowing the gap and making sure all children have equality of opportunity.'

The Summer Reading Challenge in local authorities

The Summer Reading Challenge has proved to be a discrete incentive that libraries can use with groups of harder-to-reach children because it's appealing and easy for them to understand.

So far, library authorities have used the Summer Reading Challenge to engage children in local authority care (looked after children), traveller families, asylum seekers, young carers, children of homeless families, children of parents in prison and children with physical or learning disabilities. The scheme's simplicity means that it works well with any group of children who may have barriers to accessing books and reading. Plus, it is also good for home-educated children, who can take part in the scheme, share reading experiences and connect with other children in the community.

Case study 5.6 Norfolk Libraries

Norfolk Libraries has used the Summer Reading Challenge as a way to involve looked after children in the library. Lisa D'Onofrio, co-ordinator of Opening Doors, talked about a three-year project that aimed to encourage looked after children to read and access libraries, working with Norfolk Library and Information Services.

How it uses the Summer Reading Challenge

'Everyone here knows the benefits and joys of reading, but for looked after children I think these are tripled. When working with vulnerable children we need to be aware that some kids might have never owned a book, and some might not even be sure of what to do with one.

'Norfolk Library and Information Services has developed strong partnerships with the Children's Services summer schools for looked after children. Each year the community librarian works very closely with the summer school team to plan activities around the Summer Reading Challenge specifically, as well as reading in general.

'The librarian puts together a Summer Reading Challenge collection of a variety of picture, poetry, factual and story books for the children to borrow and use during the summer school. This range of books is carefully selected to suit all needs, even if children aren't literate or find reading frustrating or demanding. Library staff also confer with workers about the best way to support each child, so they feel included at every step.

'On their first visit, the librarian reads the children a selection of different stories using a variety of different voices and props to get them interested and encourage them to take part. The looked after children are then invited to join the Summer Reading Challenge (they don't have to have a library card) and they are given the various Challenge materials.

'We then visit the schools twice more, bringing in specific books the children have requested or items about topics they are interested in and we read more stories and talk to the children about what they have read so far, asking about plot, characters, style, etc. They then get Summer Reading Challenge stickers.

'There are medal and certificate presentations either in the Summer School venue or at the library. Either way, we invite an audience of relevant bodies and civic dignitaries, which leads to a real sense of achievement for the children.'

What it gains from the Summer Reading Challenge

'At these return visits we have seen the children display more confidence in their reading and they enjoy sharing their reading discoveries more with us and the team. Many of the children we have introduced to the library via the Summer Reading Challenge are now regular repeat library visitors. Often the same children will do the Challenge year after year. Recently, a librarian went to visit a high school, and re-met Jane, who had participated in the Summer Reading Challenge with him for several years. She was now an enthusiastic and well-regarded assistant in her school library and said that her involvement with the Summer Reading Challenge was what had started her reading for pleasure. Our input gave her the help she needed to have confidence to volunteer in the library. She now really enjoys introducing other young people to books.'

The Summer Reading Challenge and youth volunteering

In summer 2010 the Reading Agency set up a volunteering programme with v, the national youth volunteering charity for 16- to 25 year-olds, that was funded by v and the John Laing Charitable Trust. The Reading Agency ran training for libraries on making the best use of volunteers and produced a guide which libraries could use to train their volunteers while v ran an online recruitment campaign on its v-inspired website.

Twenty authorities took part in a trial and recruited 634 volunteers aged 14 to 25. The volunteers were appointed by Summer Reading Challenge team leaders and worked with staff at larger libraries for several months before the Summer Reading Challenge started. They helped to plan activities and events and to select the books and worked out their volunteering roles. Volunteers with good ICT and design skills were used as media promoters and gave presentations at local school assemblies, wrote blogs and generated a Twitter campaign. Volunteers in Hounslow were specifically trained in interviewing, editing and design skills.

All the young volunteers gained valuable work experience and a reference to help them find employment. They gained confidence and social skills while doing something good for their community. Many of the library authorities developed schemes that meant young people's volunteering also counted towards national award schemes relating to leadership and citizenship, such as the Duke of Edinburgh's Award. The Reading Agency produced a guide for volunteers to show how they could gain an accredited v50 Award for 50 hours' volunteering.

The first scheme was a great success. All 20 library authorities wanted to continue working with volunteers and 75% of the volunteers wanted to continue volunteering in a library. Further funding from John Laing Charitable Trust means that the Summer Reading Challenge volunteering programme will run in 50 local authorities in 2011, and John Laing Charitable Trust has agreed to fund a further three years' development, with the aim of having Summer Reading Challenge volunteers in all library authorities.

Case study 5.7 Tameside Metropolitan Borough Council

Ruth Lomas, Young People's Service co-ordinator for Tameside Metropolitan Borough Council, has been successful in setting up an accredited award for young people specifically for contributions to the Summer Reading Challenge. Tameside has been using volunteers aged between 12 and 18 to help with the Challenge since 2008.

How it involves volunteers in the Summer Reading Challenge

'We have a ready-made structure for working with our volunteers, as all our libraries run an hour-long activity session for every week of the Summer Reading Challenge, which they might repeat if they have a lot of children. For the Space Hop programme in 2010, which attracted nearly 4,000 children, we devised weekly themed sessions called things like Blast Off and Space Chase, and finished with an Aliens' Party. The aim is to draw more children into the Challenge, find out what they are reading and teach them library skills. We devise the activities using the theme of the Challenge but introduce our own ideas. Every week includes a treasure hunt in the library to find information, which the volunteers lead.

'We wanted to give our Summer Reading Challenge volunteers credit for what they do with a recognized award. We have set up a programme whereby if they volunteer for more than one year, they can build up their accredited awards. In the first year, they can take a Leadership Skills in Voluntary Work Level 1 certificate accredited by the AQA (one of the major English exam boards), followed by a certificate in Assisting with a Children's Summer Reading Challenge Scheme, and we are working on a third unit: Volunteering on a Summer Placement with Children. We hope experienced volunteers will help us deliver training to new volunteers. Some of the older volunteers have also acquired awards through the volunteering charity v.'

What it gains from the Summer Reading Challenge

'Some of our wonderful, fantastic volunteers stay connected with the library service through our Youth Forum of 10 young library leaders aged 14 to 19, who contribute to planning services and activities for World Book Day and our annual book festival. We use the Forum and other volunteers to help us promote the Challenge in schools. In 2010 we visited 70 primary schools and gave presentations about the Summer Reading Challenge at 58 assemblies.' ▓

The Summer Reading Challenge and international partners

In 2003 the Summer Reading Challenge went international by producing a bespoke version of the Challenge each year for the British Council, which uses the Challenge to support its Learning English programmes around the world at British Council centres and partner schools. The materials look almost identical to those in the UK but there are subtle changes to the wording, including removing 'summer' from the title to reflect that it is run at different times of year in different countries.

Approximately 11,000 to 13,000 children take part in the Challenge each year in 25 countries and some of them send in messages to the website, connecting up with children from the UK. 'I finished my Space Hop competition in British Council, Sri Lanka. It was the most interesting I've ever had' (Nidula, Sri Lanka).

The British Council staff run the Challenge to suit the different needs of the local region. The Chennai (India) office said that one of the things it valued about the Challenge was the opportunity it gave its children to engage with children from other parts of the world. In Oman, the co-ordinator said: 'I really hope that the Reading Challenge continues next year, as we have had great success here in encouraging children to read – not an easy matter in a country which doesn't have a reading culture!' (Laws, 2011)

In the Palestinian Territories many of the children who took part have little access to good-quality English materials, and some are in areas badly affected by the violence in Gaza. The British Council works with the Ministry of Education and non-governmental organizations to deliver the Challenge in schools, particularly in marginalized areas such as refugee camps, where there is a huge demand for English language. Local English-language teachers run the sessions after receiving training sessions run by British Council staff.

In 2010, Prince Harry launched the British Council Summer Reading Challenge at Mophane Primary School in Botswana with 1000 students. Prince Harry spent an hour with the school, talking to the children about which books they had chosen to read for Summer Reading Challenge. It was a great opportunity to emphasize the importance of extensive reading for pleasure and enjoyment, and the role the British Council can play in helping students develop reading skills.

The Challenge is also used in libraries through the Republic of Ireland and in Army Services in Germany. Library leaders in other parts of the world have also expressed an interest in the Challenge, and so the Summer Reading Challenge may be reaching even further. The Challenge team is currently looking at creating an affiliate scheme that may involve digital versions of the Summer Reading Challenge materials, which can be printed in-country, and models where overseas partners can use their own illustrators to reflect their culture and creativity.

What makes the Summer Reading Challenge successful?

At the heart of the Summer Reading Challenge's success is its simplicity: a simple concept with fantastic results in terms of the numbers of children involved and the numbers of books read. It's an ideal way to get children moving into extended and independent reading. The sense of competition makes children want to join in – they want to read the six books to get their reward.

It combines reading with creative and cultural activities and an online offer to develop children's literacy skills at the same time as building a habit of using a public library. Children can choose from the complete range of books in the library and are helped by the library staff to find books that appeal to them.J89

Being run on a local level is another key part of the Summer Reading Challenge's success. Although it is a national programme, the Challenge is delivered by local library staff. There's a strong sense of ownership and staff enjoy using the theme to generate lots of fun and excitement around reading, which in turns helps the children and their families to feel that it is relevant to them. They can see lots of local activities that they can join. This generates positive publicity for libraries and helps to illustrate their essential role in the community and showcase the work that they do in reader development.

As Hazel, aged 9, from Stoke-on-Trent said after doing the Summer Reading Challenge 2010: 'I love the library and I think it is awesome that you can be part of them for free. I have really enjoyed Space Hop and I want to do it again next year. But just because Space Hop is over that doesn't mean that I'll stop reading and borrowing books from the library' (The Reading Agency, 2011).

Plans for the future – what lies ahead?

The UKLA 2010 research found that the Summer Reading Challenge works best when libraries, schools and local authorities work together, and this approach is built into its future plans. For example, The Reading Agency is looking to strengthen the partnership it has with schools and to integrate the Summer Reading Challenge with its UK network of Chatterbooks reading groups for children that are run in libraries and schools (see www.chatterbooks.org.uk for more information). This would offer children year-round reader development activities within their libraries and schools and would mean that the benefits children gain through taking part in the Summer Reading Challenge could be nurtured and developed by being part of a Chatterbooks reading group – all supported by online reading tools and resources that promote children's literacy.

The funding from John Laing Charitable Trust means that The Reading Agency can develop its youth volunteering programme through the Summer Reading Challenge and tens of thousands of young people will have the opportunity to become more involved with their local library. They will feel that the library belongs to them and understand the role of library services in their local community and, as a result, libraries will become more relevant to their lives.

We may even see the Summer Reading Challenge broadened to a challenge that works for the whole family, using the summer break to boost library visits and provide rich, rewarding reading experiences for everyone.

In a pilot activity in 2010, library authorities encouraged parents, especially those with poor literacy skills, lapsed readers, or those who had English as another language, to take part in The Reading Agency's adult reading challenge, the Six Book Challenge (see www.sixbookchallenge.org.uk for more information), alongside their children. The feedback was positive and we expect to see more library authorities running the two schemes together in the future.

> The fact that the two challenges were running in parallel seemed to work well. It was a way for parents to be seen to help their children while also helping themselves. It's been so successful that we'll do it again.
>
> (Dudley Libraries, in ASCEL and The Reading Agency, 2011)

Looking forward to 2012 and the London Olympics, the LOCOG (London Organising Committee for the Olympic Games) Cultural Olympiad team is committed to making the Summer Reading Challenge part of the 2012 Festival. The London 2012 Festival will be the biggest ever arts festival, with more than 1000 events across the UK. It will provide a fantastic opportunity for local library authorities to promote the Summer Reading Challenge and the wide range of cultural activities that they run to support the Challenge. An official link between the Challenge and the Cultural Olympiad 2012 Festival will mean that library authorities have something ready made for the Olympic celebrations, and that association may also unlock local funding.

When the Summer Reading Challenge was first launched in 1999, 80% of library services bought into the Challenge and around 450,000 children took part. In 2010, 95% of library services signed up and 750,000 children took part, which was an increase of 35,000 on 2009 (Figure 5.2). Boys made up 44% of the participants, and 431,250 children completed the Challenge by reading six books over the summer – 57% of participants. By the end of the summer there were 53,000 children signed up as new library members and more than three million books had been read by children taking part in the Challenge. The Space Hop website attracted 68,000 visitors, who visited the site 140,000 times, with 1.6 million page views. The libraries organized 15,000 Space Hop events which 225,000 children attended, and 2000 young volunteers helped out in over a third of library authorities.

The Reading Agency is planning to build on that impact. So far, 97% of UK library authorities have signed up for the Summer Reading Challenge in 2011: Circus Stars. This is the same level of participation as in previous years, despite the fact that the picture for libraries in the UK is very bleak at the

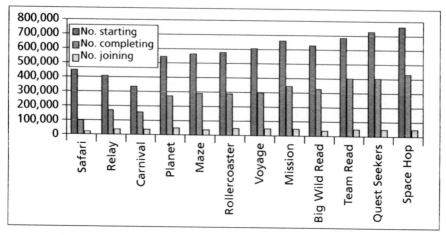

Figure 5.2 *Growth of Summer Reading Challenge, 1999–2010*

moment. Public sector cuts mean that many libraries are losing staff, reducing opening hours or being shut down altogether. This level of take-up is real evidence of the value that libraries place on the Summer Reading Challenge and how far it has become embedded into their work.

Summer Reading Challenge director Anne Sarrag says:

> The Challenge is now enjoying the level of awareness that comes with years of development and tried and tested activity, family recognition, and evidenced benefits. I no longer have to explain what the Summer Reading Challenge is and how it works, I am greeted with enthusiastic responses about displays in local libraries, their child's medal, or the leaflet that came home from school. When the Challenge was mentioned in the *Guardian*'s education blog recently I realized how far we had come!

The Reading Agency's ambition is that one million children will take part in the Summer Reading Challenge in 2013. With a history of such growth and with the support of libraries and other partners – we may just do it.

References

ASCEL and The Reading Agency (2011) *Linking the Six Book Challenge to the Summer Reading Challenge 2010*, www.summerreadingchallenge.org.uk/libraries.

Kennedy, R. and Bearne, E. (2010) *Summer Reading Challenge 2009 Impact Research Report*, UKLA, www.readingagency.org/children/summer-reading-challenge.

Laws, B. (2011) *The Reading Challenge in British Council Centres 2010–11 Evaluation*

Report, The British Council, www.summerreadingchallenge.org.uk/libraries.

The Reading Agency (2009) *Report on the Summer Reading Challenge 2008,* The Reading Agency.

The Reading Agency (2011) *Report on the Summer Reading Challenge 2010,* The Reading Agency.

See www.summerreadingchallenge.org.uk and www.readingagency.org.uk for more information.

6

Stockport does Book Idol! A case study linking libraries and schools to inspire reading for pleasure

Nikki Heath, Eddy Hornby and Jenny Barber

Introduction

As we are told in the School Library Commission Report *School Libraries: a plan for improvement*, 'One of the key agencies which school libraries and school library services could and should be working more closely with is the public library' (Douglas and Wilkinson, 2010). Stockport Public Libraries was pioneering in offering a structured programme of class visits across the borough and has worked closely with schools to deliver these. This chapter describes how working in partnership with secondary school librarians to deliver a new Year 6 class visit, which takes place in the summer term, dovetails naturally into the national Summer Reading Challenge and both informs and assists the transition from primary to secondary school. As Jim Knight MP, Minister of State for Schools and Learners in 2008, said at the launch of the Enjoying Reading[1] project: 'Children's enjoyment of reading is critical to their life chances but schools alone can't crack this. The Department for Children, Schools and Families believes more joined up working between schools and libraries can make a big difference' (The Reading Agency, 2008).

The Stockport Libraries perspective[2]

The Stockport Libraries Class Visits programme was developed in 1995 in response to changes in the school curriculum and the need for a consistent offer to schools across the whole borough. Visits are offered to Years 1, 3, 4 and 6 and cover an introduction to the local library, non-fiction books and their arrangement, fiction books and their arrangement, and culminate with the Year 6 visits, which were originally intended to be a recap of what had been learned on previous visits.

Stockport Libraries, the local school librarians and the School Library Service have been working closely together for four years to promote their Year 6 class visits and to begin to use them as a starting-point to advertise the national Summer Reading Challenge, which is, of course, a wonderful opportunity for students to celebrate reading for pleasure over the summer holidays, as well as to encourage them to continue with their reading whilst away from school. The Challenge takes place from mid-July to the beginning of September and preparation begins in Stockport's public libraries with the eye-catching promotional posters and leaflets going up towards the end of June. Librarians start their school visits at this time, too, and in 2010 Stockport librarians visited 65 schools in the borough, usually having time in a school assembly to talk about the Challenge, explain the theme for the year and show the posters and prizes that were on offer. Invitation bookmarks may be handed out, as well as advocacy leaflets targeted at schools and posters for the school librarians to display and base any of their sessions around.

However, as a result of feedback from teachers over the period since 1995, it was decided that the Year 6 visit needed remodelling, and in 2007 the working group of educational advisors, secondary school librarians, teachers and staff from public libraries came up with the idea of 'Book Idol'. They wanted the new visit to be a lively, pupil-centred experience that concentrated on reading for pleasure and which encouraged children to challenge their established reading choices. Book Idol taps into the popular TV elimination format of *Pop Idol*, *The X Factor*, etc., but centres on the children selling a contemporary fiction title to the rest of the class in teams. Votes are cast over three rounds (cover, 'blurb' and a brief reading), with the winning title crowned the class Book Idol and taken back to school for the remainder of term.

It was acknowledged that the summer term is a busy time for Year 6 classes, with SATs (Standard Assessment Tests), transition visits to secondary schools, recreational trips and school-leavers' assemblies to plan for, so there was a need to work harder to get schools to come along. However, the chance to remind children that the public library is still there for them in secondary school, promote the Summer Reading Challenge and work together with school librarians to share the joys of reading for pleasure far outweighed those difficulties. So a strategy was developed of recruiting the local secondary school librarians to alert their partner schools where possible.

The structure of the public library service in Stockport is such that the learning support function shares line management and office space with the School Library Service. There is a strong culture of working together and the learning support librarian is able to attend the termly meeting of secondary school librarians (chaired by the School Library Service) to promote and report back on the programme of class visits. The concept of the visit was received enthusiastically by the secondary school librarians, who viewed this as another opportunity to ease the transition of their new pupils from primary school. Joint planning, visits and feedback are vital to the success of Book Idol and the visit is a great advertising platform to encourage participation in the Summer Reading Challenge.

It is imperative that students come away having enjoyed their time in the public library. The Year 6 students will be becoming increasingly independent learners over the next five years and the visit is also an ideal opportunity to remind them what the library is for in addition to reading for pleasure. Secondary school students need to have multiple research facilities available to them, with friendly, approachable, non-threatening staff to support them should they need help. Some of the students arriving for Book Idol may not remember being in a public library, and others may not have set foot in a library since their last class visit. Stockport libraries want them to come back over the summer, so a lively, friendly and 'fun' activity is essential!

As the Book Idol invitations are accepted by schools, the learning support librarian co-ordinates visits and lets the secondary school librarians know dates and times so that they can get involved if they wish. The learning support librarian also circulates a Book Idol booklist, which gives the secondary school librarians the chance to purchase the books for their school libraries, if they are not already in stock. From a reader development point of view, it is preferable that the books used in Book Idol are contemporary and lively, but the policy is to try to steer clear of blockbuster authors and titles that the children may have already encountered, whilst contributing to the Stockport Schools Book Award, for example (Table 6.1). The aim is to get

Table 6.1 2010 Book Idol Titles			
Title	Author	Publisher	Date
Hostage	Malorie Blackman	Barrington Stoke	1999
The Beasts of Clawstone Castle	Eva Ibbotson	Macmillan	2006
Mo	Geraldine McCaughrean	Hodder	2006
Meet the Weirds	Kaye Umansky	Barrington Stoke	2003
Help! I'm a classroom gambler	Pete Johnson	Corgi	2006
Kiss of Death	Malcolm Rose	Usbourne	2006
Frozen in Time	Ali Sparkes	Oxford University Press	2009
Broken Glass	Sally Grindley	Bloomsbury	2008

them to try something different and think about what factors influence their reading choices.

The set of books used for the visit is common to all libraries in the borough and is purchased centrally by the Support for Learners team. Each summer a set of the eight titles is issued to each library, which, given that the average class size is currently around 27, gives the session leader some flexibility and allows the game to be tailored to lower/higher-ability classes. After each visit, the session leader informs the learning support librarian of the winning title and a replacement copy is sent out from a central pool. The initial investment in running the visit was 30 copies each of eight titles, plus extra stock copies where required in libraries. Books that have fallen out of vogue or have failed to transmit to the fast-paced format of the game have been changed for different, but always lively and contemporary, titles.

Werneth School[3] experiences Book Idol

Nikki Heath is one of the Stockport librarians who became involved in Book Idol through the secondary school librarians' meetings. She has worked at Werneth School for over six years. She describes the experience of a class visit at the local public library in Bredbury:

'When the class arrives at the local public library, the member of staff who is leading the session welcomes and introduces him/herself and the secondary school librarian. Book Idol is explained to the students, with the sparkly bags on display. The key points to be highlighted are that it will be a *team* challenge, and all students in each team have to work together in order to promote their book. There is usually anticipation, and general curiosity is in the air as this is explained, and questions about the contents of their bag have usually already been whispered about at this stage, which is great! Students are then split into pre-arranged, teacher-allocated groups of five or six and each "team" chooses a name, and then a sparkly bag. Each bag contains a "mystery" book. A student from each group, chosen by the group, is invited to come to the front and choose their sparkly "mystery" bag. As you would expect, this is down to personal choice and has no relevance at all to the book inside! As soon as the students all have their bags, the first round begins.

'Watching the faces of the students as they pull the book out of the bag is fascinating. Some will beam and others will groan. Some students have heard of the authors, and the books cover a range of ability levels, but on the whole, the reception is extremely positive. At Bredbury Library I don't remember anyone asking to change their bag – not that we'd let them anyway!

'There are three Book Idol rounds, based on the book's appearance and content. After each group has had time to assess and explore its book, a spokesperson or persons will promote it to the rest of the class. The first round is always based on the cover – does it promote the book well? What was their reaction when they saw it? If a positive one, why did they like it? If not, why not? How can they change the perceptions of others in the group and make them like it? Subsequent rounds look at the blurb and the book's contents.

'Once each group has had the opportunity to promote "their" book, everyone votes for their favourite, and the votes are totted up. Children are not allowed to vote for their own book. Once all rounds and votes have been compiled, the school takes the winning book back into school for the remainder of the term to read, borrow or just look at.

'At the end of the visit to Bredbury Library, Anna, the librarian in charge, reminds them about being a member of the library. Some of the students will by now be taking a closer look at the shelves and finding books they'd like to borrow, so it is a great time to promote membership. Anna also takes the time to mention the Summer Reading Challenge, and then I talk to them about this, too. At this session, I can begin to make useful contacts with the primary teaching staff, some of whom I will never have met before, remind them once again of the Summer Reading Challenge and its free, downloadable resources and encourage them to advertise this widely within their school.

'The students then prepare to leave, and on their way out are given an origami fortune teller to take away, containing the titles and authors of all the books featured in the visit. Anna encourages them to come back to the library to take out any of the books that we have been discussing – maybe a title has caught their imagination but wasn't the one that won. Stockport Libraries tries to make sure that libraries have enough copies of the books in stock, but where demand outstrips supply, it encourages children to place a free request. Analysis of loan statistics and reservations placed in the subsequent weeks prove that the visits stimulate interest in reading the featured titles.

'Importantly, a lot of this reading takes place during the summer holidays, which helps children to hit the ground running when they start secondary school in September. From a Werneth perspective, it is important that students keep reading regularly over the summer, as the new students will be given an Accelerated Reader reading assessment when they arrive, and it is important that the assessment gives a true picture of where their reading is.' [Accelerated Reader is a reading scheme – see www.renlearn. co.uk for more information]

The school perspective

Sally Apps, Director of Achievement at Werneth, acknowledges: 'It's great to see students engaging with reading on their own terms. Using the talent show format that is so popular with young people has been a real success – and there are only winners in the end. Every child that reads more widely and more prolifically benefits not just academically but in terms of their personal growth. When resources are so stretched, it's great to see school and public libraries working together; it's money in the pockets of our young people in the future.'

Nikki Heath agrees: 'Book Idol is a fabulous opportunity to meet the students who may arrive at Werneth. It is an opportunity for students to meet their school librarian outside of the school environment, and to get to chat informally with them about books and reading before they come in for their "taster day". All Year 6 students in Stockport will be given the opportunity to spend a "taster day" at their secondary school, usually in July. All students are invited to the school and follow a subject timetable for the day. This allows them to familiarize themselves with the school and their journey to and from it, and helps to allay any fears that new students may have about the school. Following a timetable enables the students to experience a typical school day. Students give feedback on their experience at the end of the day, and parents are invited to a meeting that evening to discuss any queries they may have and to learn more about the school.

'As part of Werneth's "taster day", students spend a lesson in the library. The Book Idol books are in stock and displayed prominently, and students are asked which book their class voted for. It gives the librarian an opportunity to talk briefly with the Book Idol student teams about their favourite books and authors, and also to meet their teachers.

'Sometimes, there are students who have not taken part, and if this is the case students from a participating school are invited to explain their class visit, which book was their class favourite and why. This invariably leads to discussions about books and reading. Students are also asked to complete a reading questionnaire about their reading habits, likes and dislikes. This enables the librarian to ensure that the right authors and titles are being stocked in the library, and any new series that have not already been picked up are then purchased ready for September. It also ensures that reading displays and promotions can be accurately targeted at the new students. The questionnaire asks about reading confidence as well as how often the students read for pleasure, which gives an idea of how many of the new students will have enthusiasm about reading for pleasure. Once the results are compiled, they are fed back to staff and students, giving a truthful overview of the reading habits, likes and dislikes of our new cohort, as well as allowing the librarian to identify those who may not have had good reading experiences so far.

'Approximately half of this library session is spent talking about, demonstrating and taking part in an activity based on the Summer Reading Challenge. In past years, the school has been lucky enough to have copies of the Challenge-linked mini booklets. The Challenge booklets are produced to accompany the Summer Reading Challenge, and contain quick puzzles, games and reading challenges, which add depth and breadth to the reading challenge experience. Distributing these again means that the students leave the library with a free gift which they all love, and gives them something concrete to remind them about the Challenge.

'One of the tasks in the Summer Reading Challenge Quest Seekers booklet from 2009 was called "Blue Sky thinking" and asked students to pick a book at random and open it at a certain page to read. This became the Werneth library activity that year. It gave the students the opportunity to browse the library for a good ten minutes or so, and allowed them to pick a book that appealed to them (and some did choose the Book Idol titles), read a small amount and share it briefly with the rest of the group. Students were paired up and asked to talk about their random book, with some then telling the whole group what they had read. Those who enjoyed their choices were encouraged to note down the title in their booklet so that they could either request it from their local library as one of their Quest Seekers books, or find it again once they arrived at Werneth in September.'

Resources for the Summer Reading Challenge were sent into feeder primary schools on memory sticks for the teachers, containing the lesson taught to their students on Taster Day as well as the URL of the Summer Reading Challenge website. A covering letter invited them to share the resources with their colleagues, as the Summer Reading Challenge is for everyone, not just the Year 6 students, and the resources are always easily adaptable for any age or ability group. The letter also reminded them that they could book in for a Book Idol visit at their local library if they had not already done so.

Once the summer holidays arrive, promotion is out of the hands of most school librarians, unless they are a 'coach' or a 'tree person' on the Summer Reading Challenge website. Every year, as well as having authors on the website for the children to send messages to, staff from public and school libraries are invited to be available to answer questions on the website for a fixed period of time. Library staff also have a dedicated space on the Challenge website and children from all over the world may leave questions about their favourite books, ask how they can join in the Summer Reading Challenge or ask advice about what to read next. Apart from this, promotion of the Challenge is in the hands of the public libraries!

In August all Stockport Libraries host an event to keep the enthusiasm for the Challenge high, and these events seem to get more popular each year! In 2010 there were some wonderful craft sessions, with children making spaceships and other out-of-this-world creations, and taking part in treasure hunts for a Space Hop-themed event. The events are an effective way to get students interacting with each other and library staff as part of their reading journey, as well as publicizing other areas of the Challenge such as the activity sheets and website.

At the end of the summer, when students arrive at Werneth, the Summer Reading Challenge is discussed as part of their welcome session. The discussion covers the activities and what they did at primary school with Book Idol, and asks who has completed the Summer Reading Challenge. There are ways of 'bribing' students to admit to this, as many are too shy to, and in 2010 only five students at Werneth would publicly admit to having finished it, although there were probably more. Reward points are offered to 'finishers', although this has not encouraged students to come forward. Those that did take part, as well as all of the Year 7s, were invited to join in the school reading group, which meets on Friday breaks, and whilst initially only one or two of the Year 7s that year joined in, there are now around 10 who come on a regular basis.

Other secondary school librarians have given small 'prizes' or have made up special goody bags. Kathryn Durkan at John Port School in Etwall, Derbyshire has a simple but extremely effective reward in place. All Summer Reading Challenge finishers are invited to a special 'party' in the library. The library is closed to all but them during that time. Last year, this party coincided with a storyteller's visit, and all Summer Reading Challenge finishers were invited along. Kathryn said that as soon as students realized they would be given a reward, more came to see her about the Challenge! It is hoped that the offer of a celebration at Werneth may lead to more students coming forward, as has happened at John Port School.

How Book Idol fits into a wider school reading promotion package

As soon as the students arrive at Werneth, the intention is to try to 'grow' their knowledge of reading and books and to encourage a love of reading. This is done in many ways. From displaying Book Idol books and Summer Reading Challenge material when they arrive, inviting them to choose their Booked Up reading books and allocating a 'Book Champion' for each one, to recruiting new school librarians, setting form challenges for Book Day, holding Drop Everything and Read sessions, using Accelerated Reader – a reward-based reading scheme – as part of their library lesson programme, right through to the whole-school, sports-based challenge at the end of the summer term, there is a constant effort to try to encourage reading for pleasure in all children of all ages and ability. And it doesn't just stop with the students, either.

The school has teamed up all of the Rave Read reading group students with a member of staff, and they are all happily swapping book recommendations, thus increasing the staff's knowledge of children and teen books, whilst introducing the students to authors that the staff may love now, but might equally have enjoyed reading when they were children. The Rave Readers have reviewed books for publishers and authors and given feedback, encouraged others from the school into the library, debated authors and books, made book recommendations to staff and peers, designed displays and run competitions.

The school takes part in the Stockport Schools' Book Awards, and forms vote for their favourite shortlisted book. Over the Christmas and New Year holiday of 2010/11, they will be writing their own stories using Storybird (http://.storybird.com), and the writer of the story judged to be the most imaginative and inventive will win a copy of their own 'book', published through the Storybird website.

The school also uses The Write Path, an international story and poetry-writing venture organized by Bev Humphrey (http://.writepath.ning.com), and a Voicethread poetry collaboration (http://voicethread.com), which encourage both reading and writing for pleasure. Both fit under the school's Global Citizenship theme; indeed, Werneth received an 'Outstanding' judgement for Citizenship in an Ofsted inspection in 2010.

Through Creative Partnerships[4] funding in 2009, which involved the creative agent and three staff members, including the librarian, a group of Year 9 students wrote and performed stories to members of the school as well as to parents and the local community. The 2010 funding will allow Werneth to look at how it can encourage unenthusiastic readers and turn them into enthusiastic ones.

Conclusion

What impact has teaming school and public librarians together had upon the class visits and the Summer Reading Challenge? Reinforcing the message of reading for pleasure at an age where perhaps some children are starting to drift away from reading and libraries has been successful. All teachers and students are sent a Book Idol evaluation form and the learning support librarian received some great feedback from the visits:

> I found out that there's another author I love! (Danielle)

> The children come away very enthusiastic and desperate to start reading *our* book! They also say they are going to join the library. (Mrs Acton)

> If you look into a book it is not just writing on a piece of paper, you can open your mind to a book. (David)

> I enjoyed trying to persuade my friends that our book was fun and adventurous. (Lauren)

> I found out about reading and how fun it is and not just something boring and something that you should do. (Harry)

> It was fun and the books were awesome. (Rebecca)

The Summer Reading Challenge also elicited some excellent comments from both the children taking part in Space Hop in 2010 and their parents/carers:

> Space Hop was really good because it was really good and better than last year.

(Rebecca aged 10)

I enjoyed doing Space Hop and getting stickers. It was good fun and I would like to do it every year. (Nicole, aged 7)

I liked the information books about space. (Adam, aged 7)

I think Space Hop was the best challenge yet! (Siobhan, aged 10)

I really liked it, I have done the Reading Challenge every year since Team Read, I really like reading, and love a good book that I can get stuck into! (Kyle, aged 11)

Lauren didn't really enjoy reading until Space Hop started. She likes reading more now – thank you. (Mother of 6 year-old)

This is a great way to get children into the library during the summer holidays. It's free and fun for them, and they look forward to the free gifts each week. (Mother of 5 and 7 year-olds)

Heather reads a lot but this makes a difference as it gives her a goal to aim for and a chance to talk about her books with different people. (Mother of 11 year-old)

The Summer Reading Challenge nationally and in Stockport has gone from strength to strength. Participation and completion levels remain high, as can be seen from Table 6.2.

Being able to 'connect' with the students arriving at secondary school as a

Table 6.2 *Stockport Summer Reading Challenge statistics*

	Children starting	Children finishing	Percentage completing
2006	3834	1816	47%
2007	3448	1868	54%
2008	3387	2056	60%
2009	3916	2176	55%
2010	3902	2116	54%

result of the visits and the Summer Reading Challenge helps students to feel more comfortable in the school library, and gives us school librarians an immediate discussion point. Instead of being intimidated by coming into the library, it's more like putting on a pair of comfy shoes. They've been before, they know what we will be talking about, and the books on display are familiar to them. Has it been worth the effort? YES!

Notes

1. Enjoying Reading was an initiative funded by the Department for Children, Schools and Families in 2008 to help every child love reading. It encourages schools and libraries to work more closely together. It helps schools to understand how public libraries and schools library services can help them, and how, together, they can get more children reading more.
2. Stockport is a large town in the north-west of England, comprising part of the Greater Manchester conurbation, and located on the River Mersey at the confluence of the rivers Goyt and Tame. Stockport's industrial strength was built on the cotton and hatting industries. The population of the current metropolitan borough is approximately 280, 000. The town has 15 public libraries with 55,381 active members. In 2009/10 there were 1,455,236 visits to public libraries in the borough and 1,625,297 books were borrowed.
3. Werneth School, a College of Performing and Visual Arts is located in Romiley, Stockport and is an 11–16 co-educational school. Its catchment is varied, with 19% of students taking free school meals. GCSE results have increased dramatically in the last five years: from 34% to 84% for 5 A*–C grades and from 41% to 52% in three years for 5 A*–C grades including English and Maths.
4. Creative Partnerships was introduced by the Government in 2002 and supports thousands of innovative, long-term partnerships between schools and creative professionals, including artists, performers, architects and multimedia developers, through a network of local-delivery organizations.

References

Douglas, J. and Wilkinson, S. (2010) *School Libraries – a plan for improvement. the report of the School Library Commission,* National Literacy Trust/ Museums, Libraries and Archives Council.

The Reading Agency (2008) *Enjoying Reading,* primary school advocacy booklet.

Website resources

www.renlearn.com/ar

http://storybird.com

www.summerreadingchallenge.org.uk

http://voicethread.com

www.writepath.ning.com

7

There and back again: restoring reading to the classroom

Bridget Hamlet

Introduction

Reading books for enjoyment in the classroom has been endangered by the emphasis given in the English national curriculum to reading and analysing extracts. As a result, some children may leave school without ever having read a whole book and many teachers become disillusioned. This chapter follows one young teacher's journey from the American Midwest to the English West Midlands; from idyllic teaching to disillusion in the classroom – and, ultimately, to inspiration in the library. It will examine the skills shared between teachers and school librarians, thereby empowering school librarians to be the instigators of a veritable reading revolution. And finally, it will provide practical ideas which school librarians and teachers can deploy to bring reading for pleasure back into the classroom.

First of all, let me enlist your confidence by stating my credentials. I'm not an expert in any field. I haven't won any awards. I haven't invented anything. I am married, with two small children and two small dogs. I live in a house and drive a car. I watch rubbish television and fall asleep on the sofa. I hate doing the dishes and have a minor obsession with tea towels. I'm just normal. The only thing that might separate me from most people is that I love my job. Absolutely, 100%, without doubt. Sometimes I feel guilty about saying that, like it's a confession: *I'm a school librarian and I love my job.*

Of course it wasn't always this way. Nine years ago I loved my job – and I was a teacher. But just one year later, still working as a teacher, I would have said: 'I'm a teacher and my job makes me cry. Every day. I'm a total failure. I want to quit, but if I do I will be deported.' And that lasted for nearly four years. So what had happened from one year to the next?

I had moved to England.

The teaching experience in America ...

Memories are always rose tinted, so I like to believe I was a great teacher in Wisconsin. My final student teaching experience was half in a traditional high school and half in a ground-breaking charter school (these are publically funded but privately governed schools which must demonstrate success or lose their charter). The experience couldn't have been more varied or more enthralling. My mornings were spent up to my armpits in creative endeavours and innovative teaching practices; my afternoons in the familiarity of textbooks, lectures and tests.

I had a leaning towards the ways of the charter school, so when I got my first real teaching job in a small, rural Wisconsin middle school – and discovered I was the only English teacher – I knew I could really teach the way that I loved. I was given anything I could possibly ask for – without asking for it. My classroom was beautiful, with loads of display space and storage, a massive computer room adjoined it, with visibility between rooms, and the library was accessible through the computer room – like a luxury three-room hotel suite geared towards teaching English. I was confident in my abilities and really believed I was making a difference – not only to children's lives but to teaching. In my mind, I was a pioneer.

I was, and still am, a Nancy Atwell convert; her book *In the Middle* was my bible that first year of teaching. Atwell's philosophy is that of a teaching 'evolutionist', and she concentrates on 'learning with students, collaborating with them as a writer and reader who both wonders and knows about writing and reading' (Atwell, 1998). She is the reason I am so passionate about independent learning and the importance of placing learning within a 'real world' context. To this end, I rarely used the pristine, brand-new textbooks ordered by my predecessor and instead read 'real' books to my students. I had a classroom library and comfy reading area, so students could borrow books from me (yes, personally bought – and not one went missing). If I didn't have enough copies of a book that I wanted to read with the whole class, I'd just read it aloud. I introduced them to *Freak the Mighty* by Rod Philbrick, and they forced me to read *Angus, Thongs and Full-frontal Snogging* by Louise Rennison, which I still love.

And when we weren't reading real books, we were writing real pieces: poems to process the confusion of 9/11, after we had all sat in awe on that strange and cloudy day; newsletters to parents all about what was happening in school; scripts for comedies we'd perform to make each other laugh. Of course there were many dull moments trying to understand writing conventions, like how to use an apostrophe and the difference between 'lay' and 'lie' – but that was because I wanted everything the students wrote to be as authentic as possible and to be read by the readership for which it was intended. I didn't want them writing just for a grade.

I know it all sounds very idealized, and I wouldn't blame anyone who found themselves making an involuntary snorting noise just then to indicate what an unrealistic and naïve (perhaps kinder words than you would choose?) young woman I was. But I was a new teacher, and I loved it. Say what you will, but that is important. And not only that, but the students, their parents, my dean of students and principal also enjoyed what was happening in my classroom. I must have been doing something right.

The teaching experience in England

I am convinced I would still be happily teaching at that school had I not fallen head-over-heels in love with an Englishman (as you do). Within two months of meeting my now husband, I moved to England with everything I could cram into four suitcases and began my first year teaching in an English school – a very good, very large comprehensive secondary in a relatively leafy area of Coventry. This was one of the best state schools in the region, but I couldn't see that. All I saw were shabby classrooms, arcane practices of copying from the board and a strict adherence to routines established generations ago.

Then I met the other teachers. Mostly, they were just like me – unhappy with, yet resigned to, the accommodation; frustrated with the government-established curriculum, exam structure and league tables; and desperately afraid of failure. Who could possibly be creative under such conditions? With my work visa hanging in the balance, it wasn't going to be me.

So I slowly learned how my colleagues practised mild forms of subversion to retain their sanity. Like them, I did whatever I had to do and occasionally tried to be different – mostly in summer term, after exams were finished and 'it didn't really matter'. I read some great books with my classes, like *Holes* by Louis Sachar and *Goodnight Mister Tom* by Michelle Magorian. I also read some not-so-great books with my classes, mostly because we had enough copies in the department and it was our turn to do a 'class reader'.

Once, I did something really controversial – I let my students choose their own books to read. Now this wasn't done haphazardly. First of all, they were a 'top set' and so were likely to reach their 'target levels'. Second, they had just completed their SATs (Standard Attainment Tests) at the end of Key Stage 3 (14 year-olds), and in our department we weren't in the habit of starting their GCSE (General Certificate of Secondary Education) studies early, so we had half a term to play with. Third, I had taught all of them for at least two years, so I knew them very well.

Of course they weren't allowed to just read – that would be seen as a waste of time. So I devised a competition to see who could read the most books in the time we had left. To 'prove' they had read a book they had to select one activity to complete from a long list of options (including any of their own ideas), but they couldn't do the same activity more than once. And the books had to have some literary merit and an element of challenge. Naturally, I gave them an exhaustive list of possibilities and allowed them to make suggestions for my approval – basically, I didn't want cheeky Luke to breeze through ten *Captain Underpants* books by Dav Pilkey (which I adore!) while Abdul consumed *His Dark Materials* by Philip Pullman. Under normal circumstances that wouldn't bother me – but with £50 of real money (they each paid £1 to participate and I pitched in the rest) split amongst the winners, I needed to incorporate some boundaries.

I don't remember who won; it doesn't matter. I do remember the excitement of the students, the boisterous trips to the library, all of us sitting outside reading (but hidden behind cars and a large tree so that senior management didn't get involved) and the lovely chats we had about what we were reading. Tara recommended *Purple Hibiscus* by Chimamanda Ngozi Adichie, her favourite book of all time. Becky couldn't get enough John Grisham. We just generally had a delightful, intellectually stimulating few weeks.

We even came up with the idea of organizing a Year 9 talent show for the last day of school. I can't recall how it started, but I guarantee it wouldn't have happened if we were doing a scheme of work analysing 'poems from other cultures and traditions' from the GCSE curriculum, which most teachers were starting early. All I did was get approval to use the assembly hall and allow them time to organize the event in lessons. They did the rest: booking the acts, marketing, rehearsal, audiovisual set-up, judges, prizes, scripting introductions and running the whole show. Maybe it wasn't good teaching, but it was outstanding learning. That half term was delightful, and it just made all of my other lessons even duller by comparison.

The next year I started teaching that brilliant group GCSE English and English Literature, but I didn't complete the course with them because after nearly four years of barely keeping my head above water in the classroom, my husband threw me a lifeline he spotted in the local paper – another very good, very large comprehensive secondary school was looking for a librarian.

Librarian vs teacher ...

It's strange now to think that I didn't always want to be a librarian. I did want to be a teacher for a long time, but my dad said they didn't make enough money and I should be a doctor or a lawyer. Well, I fainted in sixth grade when we pricked our fingers and looked at our blood under the microscope in Mr Lauer's class – so anything in the medical field was swiftly ruled out. I didn't really know what lawyers did, but they always looked good on TV, so for a while when people asked me what I wanted to be when I grew up I said I wanted to be a lawyer.

But when I finally moved to Drake University in Des Moines, Iowa it was to study advertising. I didn't like my Communications lectures, but I loved my English classes (except for the one dedicated solely to Pynchon's *Gravity's Rainbow*). And I didn't like Drake or Des Moines – the combination of too many sororities and corn fields has a way of making one feel utterly alone. But I loved visiting my brother in quaint and bustling La Crosse, Wisconsin, so I transferred there the following year.

The University of Wisconsin-La Crosse was renowned for its teacher training, and so I'd come full circle and finally succumbed to my earliest occupational aspiration: to be a teacher. I earned my degree as a secondary English teacher with an Instructional Media licence. All of my other teacher friends took Spanish as their minor, but I loved books above all things, so adding the librarian feather to my cap just seemed natural. The licence qualified me to be a school librarian from kindergarten to twelfth grade and was valid for five years. If I wanted to be a school librarian after 2006, then I needed to go for my MLIS (Master of Library and Information Science). Since I was planning on teaching middle school English for the rest of my life, it didn't really matter.

Fast-forward to January 2006, when that seemingly miniscule qualification consumed my every waking thought (and some sleeping ones too). I was desperate to land that school librarian job my husband had noticed, and I just had to hope that the people potentially hiring me would accept my Wisconsin qualifications. Fortunately, luck and a fantastic selection panel were on my side; they recognized that my training in America was specifically for school libraries (unlike the other candidates' training) and that it wasn't so strange for a teacher to want to step into librarianship – and, in fact, it could really benefit the school to have someone who had done her time in the trenches.

Little did I know that being a qualified teacher with librarian training placed me in a relatively small pool of school librarians in England. This was strange to me, as it is the norm in American schools, where the vast majority of states require school librarians (sometimes called teacher-librarians) to be state-certified teachers with extra training as librarians. Many require the librarian training to be at master's level. Of the few states that don't require school librarians to be qualified teachers, most require some teacher training beyond the librarian qualifications, for example a set of courses on educational theory, child development and basic pedagogy (Jesseman, Page and Underwood, 2010). In the US, the message is clear: a school librarian is different from other librarians. They need to understand children, their educational needs and development; they need to understand the politics of schools; and they need to be able to teach.

The Australian Library and Information Association (ALIA) and Australian School Library Association (ASLA) adopted their 'Statement on Teacher Librarian Qualifications' in 1994, most recently amended in 2009 (ALIA and ASLA, 2009). In this statement they 'emphasise the unique, integrated nature of the role' of teacher librarian. First and foremost, the teacher librarian is 'a member of the school's teaching team'.

Certainly, in England, with legislation committing local authorities (LAs) to a Single Status policy in an effort to provide equal pay for equal work, so that all employees undertaking the same roles and responsibilities would be paid fairly, this is not always the case. For purposes of employment and pay, school librarians are classed the same as public librarians. The fact that their daily job is different to a public librarian's job goes largely unrecognized by LAs. After a bit more investigating, I was troubled to discover that England is nearly alone in its view of the school librarian's role. Despite Ofsted's emphasizing that 'in the best schools, librarians were given the status and responsibility appropriate to their important middle management roles' and 'the best librarians worked with different subject teachers to teach a coherent and planned programme of IL [information literacy] skills across the curriculum' (Ofsted, 2006), the decision supported by LAs is that school librarians are definitely *not* members of the teaching team.

In its recent report, the School Libraries Commission has, thankfully, addressed this inadequacy by calling for some radical changes in the training of school librarians, teachers in charge of libraries and teachers in general. It recognizes that a school librarian plays a unique role in schools and demonstrates 'vital skills of information management and stock management' as well as 'a deep understanding of learning, pedagogy and child development' (Douglas and Wilkinson, 2010). 'School librarians need to be re-positioning themselves as part of the teaching staff in the school' and, as such, the Commission strongly recommends that all professionals with school library responsibility be given the same opportunity to train in whichever area they are lacking: teachers to learn 'library management and children's reading'; librarians to have training in 'teaching, learning and child development'. What is more, the Commission also recommends that school libraries make an appearance in higher education institutions' librarianship courses and initial teacher training programmes. It also calls for minimum standards of library provision to become part of school inspections; unless this happens I, unfortunately, cannot see many head teachers adopting the other recommendations within the report. The Commission puts forward an excellent case for school libraries and school library services representing good value for money, but, given current financial constraints, I can see how tempting it would be for a school's leadership team or governing body to look to something non-statutory when making cuts, and, sadly, a school could potentially achieve Outstanding status in Ofsted inspection without the presence of a library. We can only hope that students, teachers and parents would protest its absence.

Although other European Union countries have the same battle as the UK to secure funding for school libraries, they at least appear to acknowledge the benefits of having a school library run by a qualified librarian who has also had teacher training. 'Every school in compulsory education in Croatia has a statuory [sic] school library, run by a school librarian who is also a qualified teacher' (Boelens, 2010, 18). It seems that a number of UK school librarians are currently teaching, to some degree, sometimes without appropriate training and frequently without appropriate recognition or pay. There is even a new online network devoted to librarians who teach (Librarians as Teachers Network, http://latnetwork.spruz.com), which is specifically for library professionals who find themselves in need of advice, inspiration and general camaraderie from other librarians in the same predicament of teaching various library-related lessons, possibly without any formal teacher training. This network confirms the need and desire for librarians to learn teaching skills.

Best of both worlds

So what, exactly, are the professional and personal benefits of this dual qualification? I can speak only from my own experiences and observations, but there are some significant advantages to having teacher training and classroom experience when it comes to managing a school library – and I am certain British school librarians would enjoy many elements of teacher training if they haven't had that opportunity already.

First, you have the confidence to truly collaborate with teachers; you feel more like a colleague and less like a subordinate. When you have an idea you'd like a teacher to try in a lesson, you feel assured enough to discuss that idea with a teacher or team of teachers – and the more often you do this, the more often teachers actually rely on you for adding a bit of innovation to their lessons. For example, recently I had an English teacher ask me what could be planned to really challenge a small group of very talented students who she felt were being slightly short-changed in her lessons because of the vast range of abilities amongst the group. Within minutes I came up with a suitable (albeit haphazard) three-lesson plan (see Appendix 7.1). The students would spend those lessons in the library. After a bit of background information, they would read *Night* by Elie Wiesel over the half-term holiday. The two lessons after the holiday would be spent creating a short presentation or display featuring key quotations from the book and images that illustrate the chosen passages – possibly linking the Holocaust with present-day atrocities.

It's not necessarily trail-blazing, but at a moment's notice I was able to help that teacher, and, hopefully, those students, for a very short period of time. Best of all, I was able to incorporate one of my favourite books into a few lessons that would almost certainly have been devoid of any books had I not been asked to help. It's slightly Machiavellian, but I seek and exploit any and all opportunities to crowbar books into teachers' lessons. And with some teaching experience under my belt, I feel confident that my ideas will meet the needs of both students and teachers. I have an understanding of the focus on learning outcomes, and the pressures teachers are under to explicitly deliver these in lessons; this understanding underpins the majority of my decisions in the library.

With teachers of more applied subjects it's slightly trickier, but again, because of my teaching background, I occasionally manage to tactfully and successfully integrate books into, possibly, the most unlikely subject areas. The crucial factor in this type of collaboration is an understanding of the curriculum – especially the aspects which that teacher or department finds most difficult to deliver – and rooting suggestions within clear subject-specific objectives. This is time consuming because it requires research into various syllabi, meeting time with teachers and organizational time to plan and resource the lessons. If I didn't have teaching experience and a basic understanding of lesson planning, then I would find this level of collaboration either very intimidating or nearly impossible.

But the rewards pay dividends. One of the best lessons we had in the library this year involved a group of girls enrolled on a BTEC (Business and Technology Education Council) Childcare course. They were awaiting their first nursery placements and the teacher had a two-hour block of lessons that she had mentioned in passing as being problematic for a variety of reasons. I instantly saw this as my chance to get a group using our rather large (for a secondary school) collection of children's picture books. It made perfect sense – they were about to learn about children's language development and meet loads of small children; we had a great selection of picture books and two hours in which to discuss visual literacy and practise different methods for reading to children (see Appendix 7.2). You'd have had to see it to believe it: over a dozen teenage girls completely absorbed in listening to me read children's picture books and then clambering over one another to get the best books to read to each other – aloud, with silly voices – for two hours solid. Now they borrow the books to take with them to their nurseries – and that teacher and I have just begun a new 'enterprise' project in which her Year 11 CACHE (Council for Awards in Care, Health and Education) students will write their own picture books using www.storybird.com, which provides beautiful artwork and is extremely teacher-friendly, allowing them to apply what they have learned about visual literacy.

One of the main reasons I love being a librarian more than being a teacher is that I have the freedom to try new things without a debilitating fear of failure. Yet, having been a teacher, I can understand that feeling only too well and it makes me more sympathetic to teachers' needs. I keep at the fore of my mind some great advice from head teacher Graham Tyrer during the annual Coventry School Library Service Reading Celebration Conference (Tyrer, 2010): that any idea you wish teachers to implement must meet three criteria.

1 It must be easy.
2 It must be cheap.
3 It must be extremely effective.

He also advised never to *tell* teachers what to do, but instead to *invite* them to try something, and the success stories will eventually filter through most of the school, so that if it is something worth doing, then most teachers will want to try it anyway. Alongside this, I keep in mind my own line manager's advice to 'stop knocking on a locked door' and concentrate on the open ones.

So how does all of this new-found wisdom translate into ways of getting more books into classrooms and more reading into lessons? One way involves proving how easy, cheap and effective books are – especially if you already have them on your library shelves. Every librarian must feel frustration that so many books go unused in their library; so come up with ways to get those books out there into lessons! Find out which general topics each subject area covers throughout the year and approach the friendliest or keenest teacher (also known as your 'open door') with an idea for a library lesson related to one of the topics.

In Art the students spend a term studying illustration, so naturally I've invited them to visit the library and use the picture books as inspiration. Although this has taken a few years of persuasion, we finally got one Art teacher to accept the offer this year, and she is grateful. A couple of English teachers and I created a challenging poetry-writing project for their gifted and talented classes, which saved our library's poetry books from lying dormant on the shelves (see Appendix 7.3). If you've done most of the work – written the lesson plan, linked it to subject-specific objectives, created and supplied the necessary resources – teachers are highly likely to at least give you a chance. And when it turns out to be an amazing lesson, they will tell the rest of their department, who will practically jump at the chance to book their class into the library for the same lesson.

One such formula (for lack of a better term) that has worked for us in a number of guises is the very simple 'fiction book project'. It's nothing ground breaking, but I think we've managed to vary it in so many ways that teachers find it incredibly easy to simply request a book project based on (fill in the blank), and we both know what that means. It means that we, the library, select and provide the books and they, the teacher, provide the project options sheet (any variation of Appendix 7.4) and manage the students and the timeline. Generally, students work in small groups, which requires multiple copies of titles and allows for differentiation. Occasionally, a teacher will send small groups to the library during these lessons, either to separate the groups in an effort to achieve more quiet and concentrated working or to provide groups with extra support from teaching assistants or library staff. These projects usually culminate in a celebration lesson in the library in which students showcase their work – and I am always impressed with what they manage to complete in such a short amount of time and under such independent conditions. Topics in the past have included the aforementioned Holocaust literature, Michael Morpurgo books, multicultural fiction, Roald Dahl books, and a particularly successful group who selected their own titles (the only restriction being that we only have multiple copies of some books, which fortunately tended to be books shortlisted for either the CILIP Carnegie Medal or the Coventry Inspiration Book Awards). The elements of choice, group work, independence, opportunity and creativity make these sorts of projects very effective – but only if teachers are highly enthusiastic and involved. And, contrary to popular belief, it still works even if the teacher hasn't read every book.

At the moment, I am in the process of trying to promote this idea across various subject areas in order to encourage students to read more fiction – and to convince them that reading for pleasure can happen outside of English lessons. The Geography department at my school is my greatest ally and it is entertaining the idea of ordering a set of fiction books set in various parts of the world to use for a homework project in which students read a book and confirm which geographical features are factual and which are fiction; we intend to meet in the summer to develop recommended reading lists for the various topics to be included on the school VLE (virtual learning environment). I'm trying to implement a similar idea for the History department to use with historical fiction, and one teacher is currently trialling the idea with her Second World War and Home Front scheme of work. You see, it would be easy for me to just keep plugging away with the English department, but I figure that those teachers are already promoting reading for enjoyment; I'm trying to find areas of the school in which reading promotion isn't necessarily apparent and where I could possibly make a difference. I use this same theory to explain being the only librarian on the planet who hasn't read Harry Potter: my endorsement wouldn't make much of a difference, so I should channel my energies elsewhere.

In finding new and experimental avenues into other subject areas – perhaps those less obviously linked with the library – I find I'm able to influence teachers to view the library in a different light. We are no longer the consolation prize for a teacher unable to book a computer room; teachers are beginning to actually prefer the combination of print, human and online resources we can provide during a research lesson. Even the students are finally accepting the fact that for certain things we have books and journals that meet their needs more quickly, reliably and effectively than the internet.

Constantly having to prove your worth and actively promote your expertise is exhausting and can be frustrating, but if I didn't do it, then the library might possibly disappear from the teachers' radar, and that would spell disaster in the current climate of extreme budget cuts.

What the UK does well

Although I've been far removed from American schools for nearly a decade, I have no doubt that their schools and school libraries face the same pressures and threats as those in the UK. If I found myself moving back to the American Midwest and fortunate enough to get a job as a school librarian, then under such circumstances there are a number of ideas I would migrate from the UK.

School Library Services (SLS) allows for a central collection of resources that can be shared across schools within a specific geographical or metropolitan area. For schools struggling with funding a library, this is a very cost-effective solution. One aspect of the service is a librarians' forum that meets every two months and is absolutely invaluable to my development as a school librarian; I would be like a small boat lost at sea without the SLS forum's support, guidance and camaraderie. The expertise and passion of the SLS librarians is unrivalled; they inhabit a completely unique role somewhere between public libraries, local authorities and schools and manage to maintain effective programmes and services amongst such varied stakeholders. I never came across anything like it in Wisconsin or Minnesota, including no mention of such a service during my school librarianship courses. Developing an SLS would be my first priority if I were a school librarian in the US.

Second on my 'to do' list would be to initiate a Newbery Award shadowing scheme based on the CILIP Carnegie and Kate Greenway Medal shadowing (see Chapter 8), which is so successful in the UK – in fact, I would probably still shadow these awards as well. Obviously, one of the reasons the shadowing scheme works so well is that it is a nationwide programme endorsed by all major players in libraries and publishing and supported by a brilliant website that improves every year. Also, it is the perfect time of year to promote reading, since everyone else is focused on exams and students are starting to get that 'summer' feeling – winding down, thinking about what to do over the holidays. And that's when I strike with this exciting and somewhat rigorous reading club! Because we have the luxury of also following the Coventry Inspiration Book Awards throughout the winter (in which we maintain a very informal atmosphere), I feel justified in keeping the Carnegie Shadowing Group slightly exclusive and really target gifted and talented readers who can keep up with the pace of reading at least one book a week. If a Newbery Award shadowing scheme was able to deliver the same calibre of programmes and resources, then teachers and librarians would be fools not to join in – and if any teachers or librarians in the UK haven't taken part in the Carnegie and Kate Greenway shadowing, then you are seriously missing out.

The last thing that would begin my British invasion of American school libraries would be to develop a summer reading programme. Children in the UK have the wonderful opportunity to take part in the public libraries' Summer Reading Challenge every year – and primary teachers and librarians should definitely get on board with this to make the most of a free, ready-made resource that is a proven success year after year (see Chapter 5). American public libraries run similar initiatives, but again, it's the partnership between the school libraries and public libraries that is interesting here. And what I'm currently developing in my school is a summer reading programme that does not compete with the public libraries, but hopefully complements it.

The Summer Reading Challenge is aimed at children between 4 and 11 years old, but my students are 11 and older, so I needed to devise something specific for my students to keep them reading over the holidays – and potentially get them borrowing books from public libraries. This year I am also reaching out to our local primary schools in an effort to involve transition students (those who will attend our school as Year 7 pupils in September). As this is the third year of our school's summer reading programme (see Appendix 7.5 for an example), we've learned a few lessons and simplified it even more. We've selected our theme for 2011 to be 'Around the World in 40 Days' – in which the 40 days represents the number of days students are on holiday and they will be travelling around the world through the pages of books either set in different places or written by authors from various countries. One of the greatest challenges in years past was the number of students completing the programme – we had about 200 students sign up in 2010 but only about 50 returned the activity sheet. Anecdotal evidence indicated that students who hadn't read the full six books suggested by the activity sheet simply didn't report back to us at the start of the school year, so we want to ensure that this year we get a better return. To that end, we have removed anything that might indicate a suggested number of books, so that students do not feel they have failed even though they read books over the holidays. We have also planned a celebration event for September which all students who signed up will be invited to attend – and this is where they will hand in the activity sheet, which is simply a postcard to the librarians telling us about the best book they read over the holidays. At this event we will reward their participation with some spot prizes (books of course!) and perhaps have some special guests to congratulate the students, through the magic of video technology. If our budget allowed, and hopefully this will be the case in future, we would invite an author to headline this event.

With American school summer holidays being almost twice as long as British ones, I would find a summer reading programme to be crucial to any school literacy plan. Ideally, students would get an opportunity to come to the school library on a regular basis over the holidays to exchange books, socialize and perhaps partake in some fun activities – but this is also where school librarians and teachers have an opportunity to promote local public libraries that already provide this service for young people. This is a fantastic way of getting youth to participate positively in their community and to build relationships that will, hopefully, reach beyond the school gates.

Conclusion: a community of readers

After all, isn't that the goal? Isn't that why we teach them? Isn't that why we want them to be readers? As professionals we know that reading brings people together; a reading culture in school can build a sense of community. And that's what I really miss about teaching in America – when you are part of an American school, particularly if it is rural or suburban, there is an almost overwhelming sense of belonging and community; the local high school is the centre of activity for the entire town. It's where everyone goes on a Friday night to watch football or basketball, followed by a dance just about every other week. Students are part of sports teams and clubs that run until at least five o'clock every night – and yes, there are cliques just like you see in movies and on television, but everyone belongs to some group and is able to find their own flock even if it isn't the 'popular' group. I never felt that way when I was teaching in the UK; the people in my department are still some of my best friends, but we didn't bond *because* of teaching together in the same school – we bonded *despite* the constant barrage of targets, initiatives, inspections and all other top-down directives that some people call teaching but that really are capable of destroying all that is good and true in a teacher. I can see this happening to brilliant teachers every day and

I just thank my lucky stars that I found a new path as a librarian; in this role I feel empowered to create that sense of community within a school through the library and by promoting a reading culture. I really think I can help those teachers and I really think I can instil a love of learning in the children in my school. I may not be as naïve as I was when I first moved to England, but I'm still an idealist and I still believe books and reading can change lives – and that's why what we do matters. That's why I love my job.

References

ALIA and ASLA (2009) Statement on Teacher Librarian Qualifications, www.asla.org.au/policy/teacher.librarian.qualifications.htm.

Atwell, N. (1998) *In the Middle: new understandings about writing, reading, and learning*, 2nd edn, Boynton/Cook Publishers Inc.

Boelens, H. (2010) Spring Conference for Croatian School Librarians, *Newsletter for IFLA section no. 11 School Libraries and Resource Centers*, **50**, www.ifla.org/files/school-libraries-resource-centers/newsletters/june-2010.pdf.

Douglas, J. and Wilkinson, S. (2010) *School Libraries: a plan for improvement*, Museums, Libraries and Archives Council and National Literacy Trust, www.mla.gov.uk/~/media/Files/pdf/2010/policy/SLC_Report.

Jesseman, D., Page, S. and Underwood, L. (2010) *School Library Media Certification by State*, www.schoollibrarymonthly.com/cert/index.html.

Ofsted (2006) *Good School Libraries: making a difference to learning*, www.ofsted.gov.uk/Ofsted-home/Publications-and-research/Browse-all-by/Education/Leadership/Governance/Good-school-libraries-making-a-difference-to-learning.

Tyrer, G. (2010) Into the Golden Cloud: raising standards through building a literacy community, paper presented at the *Reading Celebration Conference held on 9 June 2010, organised by Coventry Schools Library and Resource Services*, Corporate Training Centre, Coventry.

Appendix 7.1 A series of lessons around *Night* by Elie Wiesel

(Could be adapted to another book)

Lesson 1

- Discuss the background of the novel using the KWL model.
- Read chapter 1 (or as much of it as you can) either silently or aloud.

Know	Want to know	Learned
What do students already know about the Holocaust? Have they ever heard of Elie Wiesel or any other Holocaust victims (such as Anne Frank)?	What questions do students have about the Holocaust, the book or the author? You could give them time to find this information or provide them with a brief introduction from your own research.	Collect ideas from the information gathering.

- Discuss the chapter:
  - — What happens?
  - — Is there anything confusing?
  - — Are there any characters who stand out? Why?
  - — Can they add anything to the Learned column?
- Students are sent away to read the book – or time is spent in lessons reading the book.

Lesson 2

- Discuss overall feelings about the book.
  - — Could go back to the initial KWL chart and see if any further questions have been answered (or if new questions have arisen).
  - — Could add to the Learned column.
- Students peruse the book again and select some key quotations they find most interesting, poignant, startling, etc. Provide slips of paper to mark the pages.
- Discuss key quotations.
  - — Were there any in common?
  - — Any common themes?
- Collect one quotation from each student onto a large sheet of paper (or divide into small groups and ask each group to record their quotations onto paper).

Lesson 3

- Find images in books, newspapers, magazines or the internet that illustrate the key quotations. These can be put together into a slide show or added to the large paper to make a display, depending on resources and time available.
- Extension – find one image from the Holocaust and one from the present day to illustrate each quotation (linking history to today).
- Present finished slide show or display to the whole class.

Appendix 7.2 A lesson on picture books and visual literacy

Objectives

- Understand various aspects of visual literacy by reading and discussing picture books.
- Practise different ways of reading picture books to entertain young children

Materials and preparation

- Various picture books such as:

    — *Banana* by Ed Vere
    — *No David* by David Shannon
    — *The Adventures of the Dish and the Spoon* by Mini Grey
    — *Each Peach Pear Plum* by Janet and Allan Ahlberg
    — *Penguin* by Polly Dunbar
    — *I Want My Potty* by Tony Ross.

- A whiteboard or flipchart and pen for recording ideas from discussion.
- Arrange the room so that students can sit comfortably in a circle (like storytime).

Lesson

Ask students to think about what type of things authors/illustrators need to consider before they create a picture book for children, and what they, the students, need to think about when choosing a book to read to children (write on board).

Now read a short picture book aloud (like *No David*) and see if they can come up with any more factors affecting picture book design.

- Ideas to discuss include: age; if it should teach a lesson or skill; vocabulary, sentence structure, language features like rhyming and alliteration; whether it should be read by an adult or by the child; pictures show what is written or fill the gap between what is written and what happens; how crucial are small features of the illustration, like facial expressions (look at *Banana*, for example); making predictions for what happens next; cultural awareness; colours; numbers; alphabet; manners; relationships, fun.
- Emphasize that these are all factors of visual literacy and that picture books are more complicated than the students may initially have thought – and how important picture books can be in the education of a child.

Read a more 'involved' book now (like *The Adventures of the Dish and the Spoon*) but vary between reading it well (vocal expression, pointing out pictures, asking questions) and just plain reading the words straight through. Ask students to tell you how each type of reading made them feel. How would a small child react to each type of reading? What would they do, if given the chance?

Students now select a book, go to their own 'space' and read it through a few times, thinking about the best way to 'perform' it for a small child.

Students get into pairs and take turns reading to each other, role-playing small children if need be. Can they make even more improvements to the reading?

Brave students read their picture book to the whole group.

Emphasize the sophistication of picture books and the importance of good reading.

Appendix 7.3 English/Library Poetry Scheme – Year 9 Summer 2009

(Created by Bridget Hamlet, Becky Ford and Rachel Lingard.)

Objectives

Students will:

- gain an appreciation of poetry
- be introduced to new poets
- present poetry in creative and meaningful ways.

Lessons plans (overleaf pp 126–7)

Lesson	Date and period	Location	Main focus	Starter	Introduction
1			Attitudes to poetry	Poetry word game	Attitudes to poetry survey – discuss results in 'ratings line'
2			Types/structures of poems	Riddle poem	Brainstorm different types/structures of poems. Teacher adds to list
3			Writing poems	Diamond poem writing – give instructions and leave them to it (give example if struggling)	'Your task today is to write a poem. ...' Give some general guidelines (i.e. doesn't have to rhyme). Explain stimulus stations
4			Presenting poems	Give list of presentation types: • art • music • video • PowerPoint • animation • spoken word • print • more?	On computer, find as many examples as possible and save good ones to teacher's PC
5			Preparing presentations	• Show assessment sheets so aware of how being assessed • Delegate and organize selves; prioritize tasks • Importance of saving work	Prepare presentations
6			Preparing presentations	• Show assessment sheets so aware of how being assessed • Delegate and organize selves; prioritize tasks • Importance of saving work	Prepare presentations
7			Presenting to class	Peer/self/teacher assessment	Present
8			Presenting to class	Peer/self/teacher assessment	Present
9			Presenting to class	Peer/self/teacher assessment	Present

Development	Plenary	Homework	Lesson
Find one poem you enjoy and be prepared to say why – use library poetry books on tables	Share poems you like (if time allows). Would you start to rethink your survey answers even now?	Write one poem for next week (due lesson 4)	1
In small groups, create a collage of the different types of poems (as per list) on big paper – using library poetry books and photocopier as well as PCs	Examine others' collages and try to find a type of poem that is not represented	Write one poem for next week (due lesson 4)	2
Stimulus stations: • photos • music • headlines • blindfolded/sense of feel • bag of objects • taste/smell Write poems when ready	Sharing ideas/phrases. Feedback on stimulus activity	Write one poem for next week (due lesson 4)	3
Look at samples saved on teacher's PC and discuss how presentation is linked to meaning (may have bad examples of this to show?) Set project task: Choose a poem to present (own or other's), in pairs or alone; how will you present it best?	Collect/share homework poems	Think about supplies/equipment needed for presentation and e-mail to teacher before next lesson! (Your own fault if you don't have materials for work next lesson)	4
Prepare presentations	Plan for next lesson	Continue work for presentations	5
Prepare presentations	Create rota for presentations (volunteers first, then draw numbers?)	Continue work for presentations	6
Present	Peer/self/teacher assessment		7
Present	Peer/self/teacher assessment		8
Present	Attitudes to poetry survey – 'ratings line'		9

Appendix 7.4 Examples of book project options

These are the sorts of activities students could do after having read a book – they can be adapted for age and ability. Teachers could make them much more specific in terms of the book being read or the explanation or expectations of the project. Teachers could also expect students to create a number of projects which demonstrate varying skills (e.g. one writing project, one art project, one text analysis, etc.)

- Design a new front cover and write a new back blurb.
- Write the next chapter.
- Write a spin-off chapter by taking one character and creating a new story for him/her to become part of.
- Write a series of diary entries for one character.
- Create a scrapbook of words and images that introduces others to some of the book's characters.
- Create a board game that illustrates the setting of the book and the types of dangers/choices characters had to encounter.
- Draw your favourite character and write a paragraph about him/her.
- Research the historical background of the book and create a fact file.
- Write a biography of the author.
- Dramatize a section of the book – or for more of a challenge, dramatize a conversation or action that doesn't directly happen in the book but is alluded to and has an impact on events later in the book.
- Design a quiz based on the book.
- Record a podcast to include an overview of the book, reviews of the book and some extracts read aloud or dramatized for 'radio'.
- Research and create a list of books that would appeal to a similar audience or pertain to a similar theme. ('If you like this book, you may also like …').
- Film a book trailer promoting the book.
- Create an audio playlist that could be the soundtrack to the book.
- For a science fiction book, research and report on the likelihood of some aspect of the book becoming reality in the future.

Appendix 7.5 Tile Hill Wood's Summer Web of Reading

Tile Hill Wood's
Summer Web of Reading
Read it, Think it, Link it!

Here's how it works

1 Tell the school librarians that you want to take part and they will give you a
  Summer Reading Pack.

2 The pack will explain that you must read seven books over the holidays – all
  from different genres. Choose three books from the school library to get
  you started on your summer reading – use the recommended reading lists
  for help.

3 After you read each book, add it to your reading web and write how it
  'links' to the other books you've read. For example, if you read *Twilight* and
  Coraline you could say that they both have 'hidden worlds' in them.

4 Give each book's genre a rating by colouring in the circles. Five circles for
  your favourite genres, one circle for your least favourite.

5 Continue to 'Read it, Think it, Link it' after you've finished the books from
  the school library by borrowing the last four books from your local public
  library.

6 When you return to school in September, return your three school library
  books along with your completed activity sheet. You will receive a small
  prize for participating and also be entered into a draw for one of our
  amazing, stupendous, down-right fabuloso prizes!

Remember: 3 books + 1 activity sheet ≥ 1 prize.

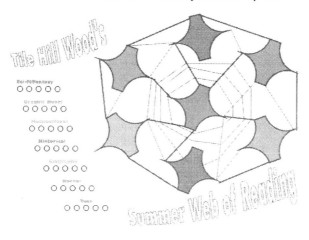

8

Promoting excellence: shadowing the CILIP Carnegie and Kate Greenaway Medals

Kasey Butler, Eileen Simpson and Joy Court

Introduction

CILIP, and formerly The Library Association, have been recognizing and rewarding outstanding literature for children and young people since the Carnegie Medal was established and first awarded to Arthur Ransome for *Pigeon Post* in 1937. A complementary award, the Kate Greenaway Medal for outstanding illustration, followed 20 years later and was first awarded in 1956 to Edward Ardizzone for *Tim All Alone*.

The Carnegie Medal, the UK's first and, arguably, still the most prestigious award for children's literature in Britain, was established with the intention to:

> pinpoint books of excellence in order to provide a basis for selection for anyone attempting to produce a collection of worth to young people ... [as well as to] raise standards in a field where the quality of the books in the Victorian and Edwardian periods had declined considerably. (Barker, 1998, xi)

While recognizing quality children's literature was an aim from the outset, promoting high-quality children's books to both the wider library community and the public was not originally a primary goal. However, the introduction of shortlisting within the judging process enabled a clear direction for promoting and celebrating the best children's fiction published in the UK the previous year and a wider platform to promote the eventual winning titles as well.

In addition the published short list has become a successful platform from which to promote reading. The shadowing scheme born in the early 1990s has developed an infrastructure that schools can use to stimulate reading. Each year CILIP invites reading groups in libraries, schools and other reading environments to sign up for the shadowing scheme. Reading activity takes place from April to June each year, from the moment that the short lists are revealed, to the final winners' announcement. The shadowing process is supported by a dedicated website – www.ckg.org.uk – through which CILIP offers an exciting range of online resources. Once the short list is announced, young readers begin the process of reading books, engaging in discussion in their shadowing groups and tracking their own and other groups' reading-related activity online.

This chapter will look at the emergence and subsequent growth of shadowing and the additional benefits to young people of participating in shadowing, and will demonstrate clearly why shadowing has become an integral part of so many school and public library calendars each year.

Shadowing – how it all began

Whatever one thinks of book prizes and short lists, there's no doubt that the hype surrounding a prestigious award like the Carnegie Medal generates a glamour and excitement that can be used to motivate children to read.

(Inglis, 1993)

Thus Jane Inglis, the librarian from Borehamwood School in Hertfordshire, describes the essential motivation behind school involvement with the Carnegie Medal in an article that is credited with being one of the earliest descriptions of the shadowing process. Jane's school had begun by reading the Hertfordshire Libraries short list for the Carnegie Medal, which was produced by it to facilitate discussion of its authority nomination. From 1993 onwards Jane began using the national short list produced by the judges and 'shadowing' as we know it today was born. That is, voluntary reading groups in schools or public libraries meeting and discussing the shortlist titles selected by CILIP's panel of Youth Libraries Group (YLG) judges and deciding their own winners, which may not, of course, match those chosen by the official judges!

During this time, the awards were benefiting from their first commercial sponsor, and this partnership with Peters Library Service was to prove invaluable both for raising the profile of the medals and for encouraging the development of the 'shadowing scheme'. Lynne Taylor, who later went on to project-manage the shadowing scheme for The Library Association, worked for Peters at this time and by 1996 national publicity materials and a shadowing pack were being produced and sent to schools that registered an interest. In order for schools to be able more easily to study the shortlisted books they needed multiple copies of the books, and it soon became apparent that a system was needed to ensure that schools could get these as soon as the short list was announced. And so the official book supplier was born in 1999 – a role held by Peters until 2010.

In 1997 The Library Association secured funding from Arts Council England to formalize and extend the shadowing scheme. This funding provided the project manager role filled by Lynne Taylor, a printed information pack for schools and the first printed advocacy leaflet 'Can You Spot a Winner?', which quotes Jane Inglis saying: 'We found shadowing the Carnegie invaluable in raising both the status of reading and the profile of the library.'

In that same year an article in the *Public Library Journal* declared:

> The profile of the Carnegie and Kate Greenaway Awards has never been higher; with Peters Library Service's seven year sponsorship coming to an end, we can reflect on the improved status of the awards, with increased awareness in libraries, across the book trade and in schools. Schools have been finding that the librarians' selection of best contemporary children's books – the shortlist for the awards – gives them an ideal vehicle for encouraging reading for pleasure. A growing number are shadowing the awards and finding some surprising benefits resulting. The profile of the school library and the status of school and public librarians is being raised. Students are to view the recommendations of children's librarians with respect and to understand more fully their role in introducing children to books they will enjoy reading.
>
> (Taylor, Clingan and Fraser, 1997, 85)

The shadowing website: creating an online debate

The 1999 report *Becoming a Part of the Story* observed that 'using the Internet to display reviews and responses is an ideal way to cement the idea of a national project and stimulate discussion' and recommended that 'The Library Association should expand their shadowing Web page to provide more information in an attractive format and to encourage the exchange of reviews' (Taylor, 1999, 19), and so, in the early part of the last decade, the shadowing scheme underwent a series of changes and updates – most significantly in relation to the development of the website. Originally, young readers were reading books and their group leaders were e-mailing their reviews in to Library Association staff, but in the years following, a simple, automated system was experimented with whereby group leaders could log in, collate reviews, check and authorize before making them live on the site.

Following a growth in popularity in the scheme, matched with advancements in web technology, in 2003 the team at the newly established CILIP decided to increase the offer for keen shadowers. Tundra*, a small creative team of young web developers and designers, was recruited and managed by Eileen Simpson at CILIP. With the funding of a modest Arts Council grant, it was possible to establish a new shadowing website, building on the core function of readers posting reviews, but now ambitiously expanded.

The new site incorporated specially shot video clips of shortlisted authors and illustrators talking about their books (now known as the 'Watch, Listen and Read' section); it established the Greenaway Gallery enabling groups to send in their drawings, paintings and collages inspired by the illustration books on the list (a feature that was especially popular with participants of primary school age); and poll-style questionnaires for teenage shadowers to answer and contribute to, concerning some of the wider social issues raised in the content of some of the books of the short list, and finding out about reading habits and the effects on readers. There was also an option for readers to submit their questions to authors and for a lucky few to be answered on the site. The idea behind these initial developments was to increase interactivity for the young shadowers, as these quotations from the Writers and Artists Video Survey 2003 show:

> Are their [sic] parts of this story based on real life events which happened to you or someone you know? (Littlehampton Community School shadower Robert's question to writer Kevin Brooks)

> Being a boy yourself, do you understand why people say boys don't like reading? (Norwood School shadower Adeyinka's question to writer Alan Gibbon)

> To all the Illustrators: Are the pictures in your head the same as the pictures in your books? (Owlsmoor Primary School shadower Daniel's question for all the shortlisted Illustrators)

There had been much debate about involving young people in the process of reading the short list and enhancing their reading experience. The inclusion of charts as a web facility was particularly important. This was an automatic chart to plot how many readers had reviewed books and to indicate the most-reviewed book and, more importantly, at the end of the process, for the shadowing group to vote for their favourite book online. This was publicly revealed on the website on the date of the winner's announcement and established a clear public voice for the opinions of the shadowing group. The shadowers' favourite, as we have said, did not always correlate with the judges' final choice!

The 2003 developments also enabled CILIP to gather feedback from its audience that was reported to the CILIP Working Party in 2004. For example, 76% of shadowers said that it's good to talk about books in a group and offered the following comments:

I think that it is a good way to make friends and find out about other people's views! It's a good chance to have fun and learn something! (Amy, 13)

I like reading alone but talking with others helps you see the other sides of the book. (Muinat, 14)

Discussing the book you are reading can help you understand the story more and give you ideas about it and others' opinions! (Himani, 15)

The improvements to the scheme and shadowing website resulted in a clear increase in participation. The number of groups taking part increased by 30% and the number of reviews submitted to the website increased by 38% in 2004. A press release in June 2004 quoted Louisa Myatt, then CILIP Marketing Manager: '[T]here is constant activity on the website ... we've just experienced the highest "hit" rate ever – 10,000 in an hour.'

I think the new design is brilliant! It is much more interactive. (Helen, 12)

The new look is much more snappier than before. ... It's good how we can get more involved now. (Rachel, 14)

These developments were considered a resounding success, delivered by a small team that set up a structure into which the new short list could be fed each year – ensuring that the website had fresh content, including lively graphics and video each year and over the years that followed.

One of the recommendations for future development in the 2004 report was to: 'Produce a support kit, drawn together with input from educational consultants: visual literacy and literacy – working with the criteria and producing a range of ideas to use for successful session.' Thus, the website acquired exciting new sections: downloadable Reader Development Packs and Visual Literacy Packs. In the next section we shall see that the sponsorship and funding opportunities stimulated by forthcoming significant anniversaries really helped to embed this concept of stimulating debate and providing curriculum support.

The Living Archive – a permanent resource

In 2007 the Carnegie Medal celebrated its 70th anniversary and the Kate Greenaway Medal its 50th. The lists of past medal winners celebrated the achievements of the great children's writers and illustrators of 20th and 21st centuries and highlighted the UK's strong tradition of quality writing and illustration for young people.

On 20 April 2007 the general public were invited to vote for their top ten favourite online Carnegie of Carnegie and Greenaway of Greenaway polls. The top ten for each medal were decided by a specially convened panel – including Wayne Winstone from Waterstones bookshops, Jonathan Douglas from the National Literacy Trust, journalist Nicolette Jones and members of the CILIP working party and past chairs of YLG. They selected from a long list created by the public, who had nominated their favourites online. All of the past Carnegie and Greenaway winning books are now housed in the brand new Arts Council-funded Living Archive (www.carnegiegreenaway. org.uk/livingarchive, Figure 8.1). The Living Archive was designed for readers of all ages to swap, share, discover and remember children's books, and readers continue to post a review of a particular title and *tag* the books with a descriptive word.

The top ten contenders were announced at Seven Stories, Children's Centre for books in Newcastle and the winners were announced in June 2007 at a special celebration at the British Library. The winners were: Philip Pullman for *Northern Lights* and Shirley Hughes for *Dogger*. Philip Pullman was unable to attend the ceremony, but offered the following comment in the accompanying press release:

> Every children's writer in Britain feels a particular interest in the Carnegie Medal. If you haven't won it, it's the one you most want to; and if you have it's the one you're most proud of.

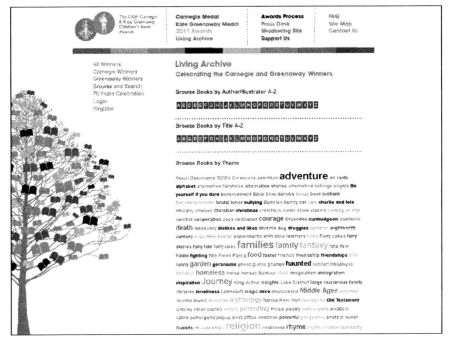

Figure 8.1 *The Living Archive website*

Following the success of the visual literacy and literacy resources developed annually for the shadowing site, Interpreting the Collection was an initiative to take a contemporary look at some of the content of past winners to stimulate debate, encourage critical reflection and be the focus of reading activities. Several anniversary reading resources were commissioned to provide an overview of the Carnegie and Greenaway books, working with a variety of different themes.

The Collection Interpretation Packs were short introductory pieces discussing a number of titles from the past winners' collection in relation to different themes. Aimed at librarians, teachers, the general public and journalists, the packs included a 'suggested reading' list for further information, fact sheets containing key facts and figures relating to the theme and timelines to provide some relevant historical context for each topic. All packs remain downloadable as PDFs (portable document formats) via the Living Archive section of the website.

In the first Collection Interpretation Pack *Home and Abroad*, Susan Tranter, Online Reader in Residence at EnCompassCulture (a worldwide reading group run by the British Council), discussed the theme of how past Carnegie and Greenaway Medal winning books have reflected different ways of looking both at the UK and at the world beyond our shores. She highlights the range of perspectives shown in the selected titles and suggests how librarians/parents/teachers might use the reading lists and other information. She begins:

> All books offer a window on the world – and children's books are no different. … Books which are set in different countries are a great way to introduce young readers to new cultures, histories and peoples. But books set in the UK – whether contemporary or historical – can also reveal some interesting standpoints on our place in the world, and invite some fascinating contrasts. These books can challenge us to think afresh about where we live, how other people view what we call 'home', and what, in turn, shapes our assumptions about others.

Susan chooses a number of titles from the list of past winners – half offer interesting perspectives on the UK, the other half offer contrasting perspectives of other parts of the world, usually as seen through the eyes of British writers and illustrators, including: Beverley Naidoo, *The Other Side of Truth* (CM, Nigeria, 2000); Aidan Chambers, *Postcards From No Man's Land* (CM, Holland, 1999); and Michael Foreman, *War Boy: a country childhood* (KG, UK, 1989).

A closer look at each book offers further relevant reading and points for discussion suitable for using the books in a classroom or reading group. Questions include: 'How do the writers of these books convey a sense of foreignness when describing countries other than their own?'; 'What difference does it make where you read these books?'; and 'What does "home" mean?'

An accompanying timeline includes key dates and events from the last 70 years which relate to the theme:

> 1880–1924 – Over 2 million Eastern Europeans move to America, many of whom are Jews fleeing pogroms in their home countries. (*When Jessie Came Across the Sea*) 1995 – Ken Saro-Wiwa executed along with eight colleagues in Nigeria, following their non-violent campaign against environmental damage in the Ogoni region. (*The Other Side of Truth*)

CILIP also commissioned Michele Gill, part-time PhD student, teacher and children's service manager for Ealing Libraries to write a Collection Interpretation Pack reflecting on the winning titles retrospectively in relation to current understandings/concerns about boyhood, a concern that continues to preoccupy schools today. Michele Gill is writing a PhD looking at the way masculinities are represented in contemporary young adult fiction, and in her Collection Interpretation Pack she takes a look at 'Carnegie Boys', looking at how different representations of boyhood can be traced through a number of the winning books, in relation to changing social expectations around boyhood. In the pack she refers to a number of contemporary titles, but also takes a look at some older titles, including: 1940 Carnegie winner Kitty Barne's *Visitors from London* and 1948 Carnegie Medal winner Richard Armstrong's *Sea Change*.

Visual literacy specialist Liz George has created a Collection Interpretation Pack that provides an in-depth study of the changes in illustration over the past 50 years. This pack provides a fantastic insight into how the past Greenaway winning books sit in a social and political context. From 1950s to the present day she explores developing artistic techniques, themes, attitudes and world events. Of the 1960 Greenaway winner *Old Winkle and the Seagulls*, by Gerald Rose, she writes:

> The new optimism of the 1960s was reflected in a new mood, black and white gave way to a richer palette of colours for artists and designers, coloured sculptures and paintings by pop artists such as Allen Jones, Patrick Caulfield, Peter Blake (who designed the Beatle's Sergeant Pepper album cover), as well as the liberating work of David Hockney with his groundbreaking influence on style and colour. Gerald Rose's illustrations in Old Winkle and the Seagulls, the 1960 winner, are full of life-demanding active engagement, as they unfold the dilemmas of this fishy tale, which spoke of cod shortages even then!

And she continues into the 1970s: 'Perhaps it was Edward Heath's winter of discontent that inspired Raymond Briggs to create such a grumpy and belligerent Father Christmas as he did in 1973, in his book of the same name.' This compelling piece of writing is accompanied by a timeline plotted from the 1950s to the present day. The timeline contrasts historical and political detail with significant moments for popular culture – from felt-tip pens and flared trousers to political tensions and technological advances.

For the final Collection Interpretation Pack, *Outsiderness, Difference and Diversity*, Laura Atkins provides a brief overview of how a selection of the winning books have exemplified some of these themes. Laura notes that children themselves are often outsiders in their own societies (lacking the power and voice of adults). She continues:

Books can also provide both a mirror and a window for readers. The mirror allows those whose experiences are not often reflected in general society to find themselves in a book – allowing space to negotiate their own sense of place and identity, as well as an opportunity to be entertained while more fully identifying with characters. The window allows readers to empathise and relate to stories and experiences outside their own – something which becomes only more important in a time when religious and cultural differences are at the heart of much societal debate.

Her pack reflects critically on the Carnegie and Greenaway children's book awards and she ends the pack with a challenge:

> There is still great potential for the Carnegie and Greenaway awards to do more to reflect the changing and diverse society of the present UK – an area that has been under-represented thus far. ... And as our society changes, there will continue to be more experiences of childhood outsiderness, otherness and diversity that can be told and join the esteemed list of award-winners, giving children from all backgrounds and experiences the chance to find themselves reflected in the best of the books that they read.

CILIP also commissioned anniversary Reader Development Packs and Visual Literacy Packs designed to help readers – young and old – to engage with a range of titles from the past winners' collection in the same way that they are encouraged to engage with the short lists each year.

The Anniversary Reader Development Packs present talking points for a number of past Carnegie winning titles, including: *Flour Babies* (1992), *Millions* (2004), *The Edge of the Cloud* (1969), *The Turbulent Term of Tyke Tyler* (1977), *Tamar* (2005) and *Postcards from No Man's Land* (1999). The packs are designed to provoke interesting and important questions for readers both young and old. The talking points are contrasted with fun activities relating to Carnegie books – including wordsearches, code busting, lateral-thinking puzzles and drawing activities – there's even a book-related recipe for Carnegie Greenaway anniversary parties!

Two Anniversary Visual Literacy Packs take a closer look at some of the past Greenaway winning books, including: *The Jolly Christmas Postman* (1991), *Way Home* (1994), *When Jessie Came Across the Sea* (1997), *Zoo* (1992), *Crafty Chameleon* (1987), *Haunted House* (1979), *Old Winkle and the Seagulls* (1960), *Pumpkin Soup* (1998), *Sir Gawain and the Loathly Lady* (1985), *Snow White in New York* (1986).

The format for the Visual Literacy Packs was based around a double-page spread illustration selected from each book, accompanied by a series of questions designed to encourage readers to thoroughly explore every inch of the page. This technique encourages children to look more closely and critically at illustrations, and the activities and talking points encourage children to offer their personal interpretation of the illustrations and to share and shape their ideas orally in a collaborative setting.

When looking through the responses from website users and participants during the anniversary year we can see that by using 'generic learning outcomes', as specified in the Inspiring Learning for All framework (www. inspiringlearningforall.gov.uk), to measure the impact of improvements to the website in 2007, many 'attitudes and values' were affected – with a generally positive attitude towards the Medals and CILIP and a sharing of responses, memories and feelings towards books. Knowledge and understanding of the books, authors and illustrators that have won Medals was deepened – with an increased activity and progression demonstrated through increased motivation to read more widely. Many developed communication skills by voting online, sharing opinions, comments and knowledge about books by joining the new peer-to-peer network; and finally enjoyment, inspiration and creativity were demonstrated – especially by the younger people that participated in the anniversary celebrations, who had fun, were inspired, and demonstrated innovative thoughts whilst reflecting on the books they had read.

Social networking – the next big thing

The next big innovation to the shadowing website grew from a context of increased social networking and online identity. CILIP wanted to reflect this via the shadowing website and give the shadowers a platform on which to share their opinions and also to establish their reading group online and represent themselves. Sponsorship from ALCS (The Authors Licensing and Collecting Society) enabled this research and development.

Research published by Ofcom (2008, 5) showed that 49% of children in the 8–17 age range who used the internet had set up their own profile on social networking sites. Between 2005 and 2006, the number of visitors to MySpace in the 12–16 age category grew from roughly 3 million to 7.8 million (www.zdnet.co.uk). In 2005 the National Literacy Trust (NLT) carried out a survey of more than 1500 pupils from schools in England. NLT was interested in the reading preferences and habits of children and young people and gathered valuable research on reading incentives. Boys stated that having their own web pages would entice them to read more, and most pupils believed that designing websites and magazines, playing reading games and mentoring younger pupils would interest them and others in reading (Clark, Torsi and Strong, 2005, 38).

CILIP looked at shadowing priorities for the future. These would be to retain their audience and enrich a reading community; to help make reading fun for children and young people; and to promote the library as a democratic, fun place to engage in reading and discussion for pleasure outside the classroom context. As the professional body for librarians in the UK, an important focus for CILIP was also to support school and youth librarians in their roles as shadowing group leaders: to provide the link for librarians to be part of a high-profile, popular national activity run by members of their own profession and provide a website that was free from direct advertising to children and young people. CILIP was determined to continue to innovate and to use the latest technology to communicate effectively with children and young people, librarians and teachers.

In 2008, CILIP invited shadowing group leaders to participate in a survey about the future of shadowing and met with a number of group leaders to find out more about how the shadowing scheme worked for them. Group leaders suggested a number of ways to improve the site, including ways of feeling more connected to other groups such as having more room on the site to tell each other about the work they are doing, connecting groups geographically to enable group leaders to co-ordinate activity in their area and making content more visible on the site – 'shadowers need prompting and reminding all the time about what is available on the site as they forget or miss things'. Further, a need was identified to bridge the gap between the graphics on the website and age of the shadowers. When asked what made the Carnegie and Kate Greenaway shadowing special, one group leader answered: 'The quality of the materials and the variety of books. It makes students read outside of their comfort zone.'

Newly structured Group Home Pages provided a space for each group to develop an identity of their own within basic 'skins' that were created – users could change background patterns, colours and fonts. Shadowers were given their own log-in – with the group leader retaining the overall administrative responsibility for Group Home Pages, including the ability to monitor or delete shadowers' contributions to individual home pages as appropriate. Aside from posting reviews, each group was now offered the opportunity to create its own blog about books, reading and shadowing;

highlight a favourite author or illustrator, with accompanying biography and video footage; design polls and questionnaires; select their favourite three books on their reading barometer; and even upload their own video content charting their shadowing activity. Groups could now see a selection of neighbouring groups in their area, based on a postcode search, and have the option to add other groups as friends. The group leader was also able to mark out a 'star review' or link to an interesting book from the Living Archive and post a photograph of their group with a caption.

Over the year that followed, the groups familiarized themselves with the new elements offered through the website and began to fill and populate their home pages and construct their group identities. In 2010 the shadowing page was further revamped, with active group pages, blogs and videos showcased on the front page. The added improvements made the wealth of shadowing activity across the UK and internationally more visible on the site – showcasing a collection of vibrant Group Home Pages – with room to grow and change for years to come (Figure 8.2).

The web development has been a long-term, evolving process with pockets of funding driving injection of developments to the shadowing scheme and website. The core activity of reading and reviewing books remains central, with new, engaging elements coming on board to enhance the period of reading activity that takes place yearly over an intense three-month period and in order to make reading fun, customized and connected to the world.

Recent feedback on the success of this strategy

The following are a selection of anonymous quotes compiled in 2009 by Kasey Butler, current CILIP Corporate Marketing Manager.

From shadowers

It makes you really proud to visit a website which you partly created yourself. It was great to post your own reviews to be read by others.

I always enjoy doing the 'Carnegie Quiz' about the books which the librarians give us … and I love taking part in the debate over the books at the end.

I liked discussing the books in the book club with the rest of the group. I've read more of a variety of books as a consequence of the Carnegie short list.

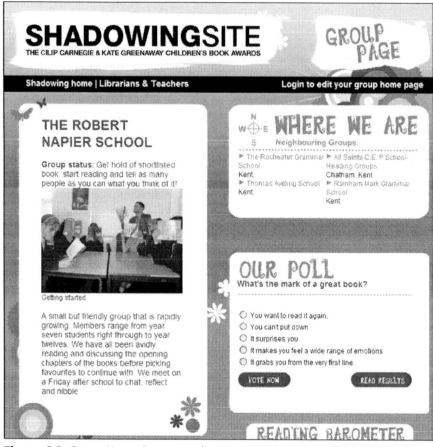

Figure 8.2 *Group Home Page sample*

I really enjoyed doing activities with our group. We did lots of hands on activities. … When our meeting was over shadowing was not because we could go home, read books and post reviews.

I enjoyed talking about my favourite book, and arguing about it, I had to prove it was the best!

From group leaders

I think it was the best year yet of us running the scheme and the improvements in the site have been a big part of this. Thank you.

Our Shadowing Group has been the favourite activity of all the participants. It has inspired them to read, discuss, write; it has encouraged them to make new friends and work together in a close, trusting group. A huge amount of excitement has been generated and they've had great fun while working and thinking hard. Many of them have done wonderful projects inspired by the shortlisted books. I'm going to keep the group running over the autumn/spring as a regular reading group, which will then pick up the 2010 Carnegie Medal trail.

I am a librarian at a girls' school and I lead a shadowing group of girls in years 7–10. It is wonderful to see the young people discussing and debating the strengths and (if any) weaknesses of each book, making friends and growing in confidence. I have a limited budget but make the Carnegie books a priority in my spending, enjoying the interest my girls show in reading. It is an uphill struggle to motivate many of our pupils to read so the shadowing scheme is a valued part of our school year. Well done for giving our young people the opportunity to read quality books which identify with social differences and teenage angst! Long live the Carnegie Medal!

It gave our group a focus with a definite timespan. The talking points were fantastic aids to our discussions and gave the students the confidence to ask questions.

Several boys have said to me that they wouldn't have picked up the shortlisted books if it hadn't been for their commitment to doing so for the reading group. They're so pleased they did read them and say they'll read more widely now, especially taking note of award shortlists and winners.

The positive impact of just getting pupils to read books that they would not normally pick up is justification alone for running the scheme. The impact it has on pupils using the LRC (Learning Resource Centre) and the perception of the LRC being a lively, interesting and vibrant place is a huge benefit. The interaction of all year groups so that year 7 pupils do activities with year 10 pupils in a lively and fun environment cannot be underestimated. The positive and improved links with the English department are great. The involvement of two parents and the positive role models they give out is excellent. The sheer fun and pleasure that I see the pupils get from the Shadowing experience is brilliant. I know they enjoy it and that is why I became a school librarian. It gives some of the quieter pupils the opportunity to blossom in a non-teaching environment and the mixture of year groups participating is great.

The shadowing had a very positive effect on pupils. Shadowing the Greenaway Medal was something I as group leader found very interesting. It was a thrill to see pupils enjoying what would normally be classed as primary books with such enthusiasm. I have now enrolled my students in lessons to observe and then learn storytelling techniques from local public libraries, to tell stories to younger siblings or nursery schools. Shadowing both medals created the opportunity for pupils who may have some difficulty reading, to be part of a wider reading group and indeed encouraged them to see reading as a pleasure not something to be avoided.

The pupils were really engaged in the process and some wrote extremely good reviews. The scheme really encouraged the children to look at books on a number of levels. Several pupils understood the notion of the simple stories being metaphors for other ideas. At the end of the scheme, all said that they had enjoyed it and had read more!

About shadowing now: inspiring and challenging young readers

From its origins in the early 1990s to where the 1999 report told us that 'the shadowing scheme involved approximately 200 schools and reading groups' (Taylor, 1999, 3) shadowing has now grown to a point where the scheme has over 4000 registered reading groups across the UK and internationally engages up to 90,000 children and young people in reading activity.

The shadowing scheme encourages young people to read, enjoy and interact with the very best in children's publishing. Outstanding literary or artistic quality are at the heart of the criteria defined and regularly reviewed by the Carnegie and Kate Greenaway Working Party, comprised of specialists from CILIP's YLG, and this results in a wide-ranging, varied and challenging short list of quality books for young people to read each year.

Why is it so popular? Shadowing is flexible; group leaders can decide how they want to run their own scheme (Figure 8.3). The simplest way is to work with a small group, reading and swapping books, meeting regularly to discuss progress and encouraging readers to review and post online to their Group Home Page. Group leaders can choose to shadow either the Carnegie or the Greenaway Medal or both. Group leaders can follow the whole short list with their group, or choose to make a selection of books from the list to work with, depending on age range, content and suitability.

To help group leaders to promote the scheme, a publicity pack including

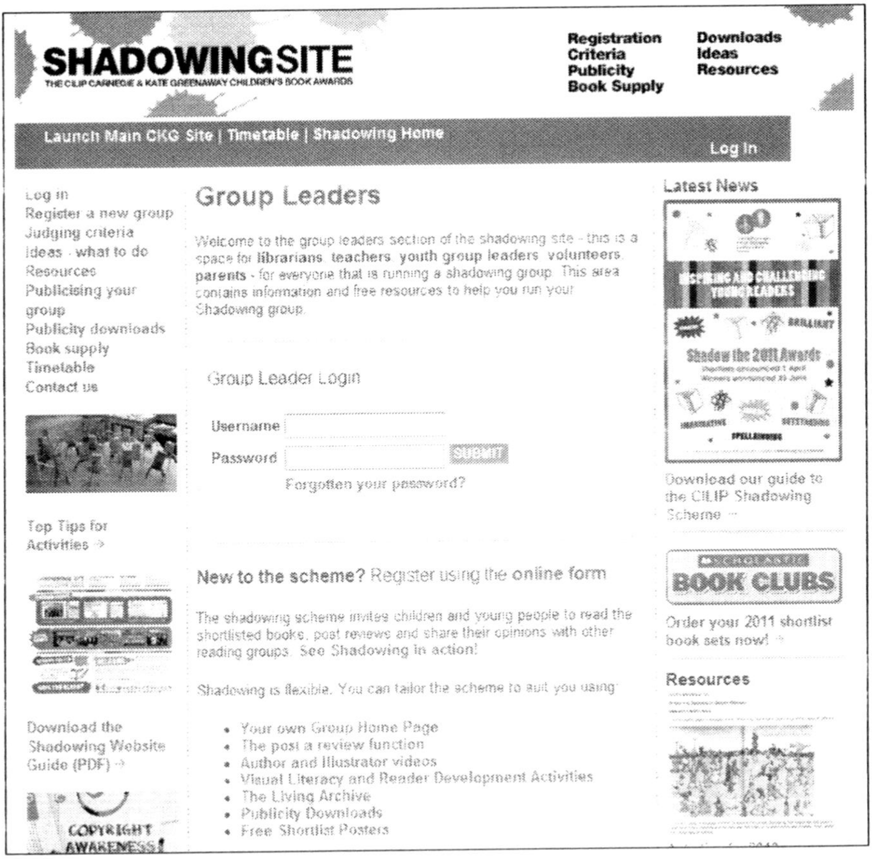

Figure 8.3 *Group leaders' home page*

stickers and posters for shortlisted books is sent to all registered groups on the day of the short list's announcement. In addition, as we have seen, CILIP has developed and continues to offer a wide range of supporting activities for young people to get involved online and resources for group leaders to use with reading groups.

Once registered, group leaders receive regular e-mail announcements of key dates, news and activities; can download publicity material, including certificates, bookmarks and posters; manage a unique Group Home Page for their shadowing group; download Reader Activities and Talking Points for Carnegie Medal shortlisted books and Visual Literacy Activities for Greenaway Medal shortlisted books; and access the judges' blog and Facebook page to interact and exchange ideas with other group leaders.

Shadowing group leaders still arrange their own supply of books. Public libraries and schools library services will provide loan copies of shortlisted books whenever they can. shortlisted titles can still be ordered prior to the announcement at a special discount from the official shadowing book supplier, Scholastic Book Clubs.

Why is it popular with young people? Shadowers can post their own reviews and comments about books and read those of their peers; watch video clips of shortlisted authors and illustrators talking about their work; read about authors and illustrators and post questions; interact with other shadowing groups; explore past winning titles in the Living Archive; create and customize a unique Group Home Page for their shadowing group where they can create their own polls; submit reading group videos; contribute to the Greenaway Gallery, and more.

Feedback via the website shows that shadowing encourages children and young people to read more widely than they might usually, introducing them to new and more demanding literature and illustration. Young people engage in an intense period of reading and vibrant discussion in a supportive environment through which they gain confidence and communication skills. They are encouraged to share their opinions online, to talk about books, to debate and decide on their favourites.

A survey of shadowers for the Carnegie and Kate Greenaway Working Party revealed that, following participation in the shadowing scheme between April and June 2008, 90% of young people read books that they wouldn't have otherwise read, 91% felt they had gained something from taking part, 76% got to know the group leader/librarian better through taking part, 66% found extra time to read, in order to get through the books, 79% thought more deeply about books than they normally did, 82% felt more confident about telling people what they thought about a book and 87% liked talking about books in a group. These statistics are based on 179 group-leader surveys and 286 shadowing-student surveys.

The scheme fosters a sense of community formed around reading – helping to enrich and reinforce a reading culture. Shadowers report that taking part in the scheme enables them to meet new people, both in their own school or library and in other shadowing groups, through organized events. The scheme can be adapted to explore further creative responses to books, including art, drama and writing. ICT skills are also developed through use of the shadowing website, which offers opportunities for young people to use technology to support their enjoyment of reading.

And in the future?

As we move into the 2011 shadowing period we are building on website developments, implemented in the last two years and designed to be populated by groups in the future. Year on year, book reviews, blogs, links to books from the archive, favourite author features, videos and polls are continually added to Group Home Pages by shadowing group members.

With an increasing number of regional book awards across the UK (see Chapter 9) and additional online spaces dedicated to engaging young readers, it is a continuing challenge to keep the CILIP shadowing scheme both relevant and at the forefront of online technologies. As Eileen Simpson says: 'Looking to technological developments in the future, the shadowing scheme will need to address the expectations of shadowers desiring a 21st Century reading experience with creative projects designed to develop better, faster ways to engage with great contemporary literature and illustration.'

Although the core focus of the scheme will likely remain the same – an online delivery portal from which group leaders pick and choose resources and activities relevant to their own group, school, public library or community – the shadowing experience of the future could embrace the digital. This would augment the linear aspects of the reading experience, morphing into more divergent forms, including sensory experiences, such as additional soundtracks, playlists and DJ sets to accompany stories, dynamic links to additional plot information and character profiles, character voices and videos, sound effects and increased imagery.

Gaming with interactive competitive elements could be introduced to encourage participation and to offer readers a more active role in the reading process. 'Gamers and readers are looking for the same thing,' according to best-selling author Rick Riordan; 'they are looking to be dropped into an intriguing story and to become a character in the story' (Rich, 2008). Perhaps shadowers of the future could be offered the opportunity to participate in the shadowing process with the pace and perspective of a video game – advancing forwards with information from the novel and gaining points and rewards for completing shortlisted titles.

Publishers are increasingly using film-style trailers to promote new books and authors and these are already proving extremely popular in schools for use on their school virtual learning environment and on whiteboards or plasma screens in the library. Trailers for shortlisted books would be a valuable additional resource for shadowing leaders to attract new readers to their groups and to promote shadowing to the wider school audience.

Interactivity could be added by inviting shadowers to produce their own trailers, which could be uploaded to their home page. There is also terrific opportunity to work with other material that groups generate and post to their Group Home Page – exploring ways to transform their work into downloadable podcasts, radio broadcasts, video reviews, self-published articles and magazines. All of which have fantastic potential as advocacy tools and could be the basis of shadowing group competitions.

Prizes and competitions of course offer enhanced opportunity for engagement and further reward for the participation of shadowing groups around the country. 'Shadowing group of the year' or 'Shadowing group leader of the year' could be a welcome annual event in the library and information technology world diary – with a shadowing brand established to develop relationships with other successful reading schemes in the UK and internationally, and the opportunity to extend cross-cultural working between shadowing groups in the UK and the increasing number of international shadowing groups – currently over 60.

Informal links between UK and international group leaders currently exist via the awards' presence on social media. A more formal process for contacting overseas groups via the shadowing website could prove a valuable new facility and enhance curriculum opportunities available to school librarians. The new sponsorship from corporate partner Renaissance Learning may also help to bring shadowing to an even wider international audience. The Accelerated Reader quizzes on the shortlisted books, as well as providing additional resources for UK shadowing groups to use, will also be available to all the international customers and could engage more young people with quality books than ever before.

Reading on the move has always been popular with shadowers, with many of them reading to and from school on the bus or in the car. Mobile technology, e-books and e-readers offer the potential for shadowers to download chapters of the shortlisted books to devices that they carry in their pockets. Blurbs, extracts, preview chapters and illustrations could all fuel interest and enthusiasm for reading high-quality literature selected for the Carnegie and Greenaway short lists. Building on the popular review function of the shadowing website, online books could be highlighted, bookmarked and annotated in margins and references linked and shared across peer-to-peer platforms. Reductions in costs, impact on the environment and the speed at which content can be updated or added prompt us to rethink our relationship to reading. Shadowing activity could be developed in tandem with mobile phone technology to insert reading into the flow of entertainment moving between young people via mobile devices.

Shadowers have developed a strong online community and there is potential to build on this to create a series of live events around the country. Theatre, improvised drama and sketches are created in response to the shortlisted book year on year. Events involving shortlisted authors and illustrators, live debates and activities could bring books to life in an exciting series of live events for young shadowers. For example 20,000 pupils from across Scotland tuned in to Scottish Book Trust's latest live streaming Meet Our Authors event with Eoin Colfer on World Book Day in 2011 (www. scottishbooktrust.com/authors-live-with-eoin-colfer). Live, interactive web chats or webinars with shortlisted authors and illustrators is a highly likely future development. On the Scottish Booktrust model this could incorporate a school host for the event with a live audience from around their region.

The current Living Archive is, essentially, a fixed searchable database of past winning titles. Expanding this to include video footage of winners' acceptance speeches and interviews would considerably enhance the user's experience. In addition, with the increasing media profile and recognition of being shortlisted for the Medals each year, there is also potential to extend the archive to include information about past shortlisted authors and illustrators. This would likely form a video archive section of the Watch, Listen and Read resources each year. This would be housed within the overall Living Archive and could include an advice portal for budding young writers and illustrators.

Given that the appeal for group leaders in using the shadowing website is that it provides a safe online environment for young people, it is ideal for any new developments to be retained within the site itself rather than directing to other internet sites, which might be blocked by school firewalls.

Following a small research project tracking shadowing activity in 2011, much thought will be put into ways in which to distribute the findings of this research. In an increasingly difficult landscape of public funding it is essential that librarians have access to clear evidence to advocate their involvement with shadowing on the basis of impact upon student engagement and attainment. The research for the Carnegie and Kate Greenaway Shadowing scheme should be used to capture the attention of both the public and potential funders in an engaging way and to bring 'shadowing stories' to life to reveal the genuine enthusiasm for reading and the great work taking place in libraries and schools up and down the country. Recording these stories in audio-video format would create a series of compelling documentaries and a video archive of shadowing group activity that could be reflected upon ten years in the future.

The long history of the CILIP Carnegie and Kate Greenaway Medals in celebrating excellence in literary and artistic quality has contributed to a lively and vigorous children's publishing industry. For as long as the quality and range of publishing remains, there will always be an interest from schools, librarians and young readers in the very best books available, as represented by the Medal short lists each year and CILIP, together with its activists and corporate partners, will be developing the 'shadowing' experience to enhance reading pleasure and visual experiences for all.

References

Barker, K. (1998) Introduction. In Barker, K. *Outstanding Books for Children and Young People: the LA guide to Carnegie/Greenaway Winners 1937–1997*, Library Association Publishing.

Clark, C., Torsi, S. and Strong, J. (2005) *Young People and Reading: a school study conducted by the National Literacy Trust for the Reading Champions initiative*, National Literacy Trust.

Inglis, J. (1993) *Shadowing Carnegie*, http://booksforkeeps.co.uk/issue/82/childrens-books/articles/otherarticles/shadowing-carnegie.

Ofcom (2008) *Social Networking: a quantitative and qualitative research report into attitudes, behaviours and use*, Ofcom Research Document, www.ofcom.org.uk.

Rich, M. (2008) *Using Video Games as Bait to Hook Readers*, www.nytimes.com/2008/10/06/books/06games.html.

Taylor, L. (1999) *Becoming a Part of the Story: shadowing the Library Association Carnegie and Kate Greenaway Medals in schools and libraries*, Library Association.

Taylor, L., Clingan, S. and Fraser, D. (1997) Carnegie Shadows, *Public Library Journal*, **12** (4), 85–7.

9

Choice and motivation: local book awards

Jean Wolstenholme and Jacob Hope

Introduction

A book awards programme that is devised and run in their immediate locality offers young people a unique opportunity to respond to texts, to encounter the past, to imagine different ways of leading their lives and to come into contact with new ideas and thinking. Rigorous discussion and debate arise as a consequence of appraising the books, and awards present an ideal way to break down some of the stereotypes that perpetuate notions about boys not reading and young people's apathy.

The longest-running local book award in the UK is the Lancashire Book of the Year. It was first awarded in 1987 to a relatively unknown Philip Pullman for the first of his Sally Lockhart novels, *The Ruby in the Smoke*. The award was the first local one where young people were solely responsible for the judging, selecting their own short list in addition to choosing the overall winner. This chapter will focus on the Lancashire Book of the Year, exploring some of the challenges and opportunities that arise from running local book awards. It will include practical methodologies for helping to embed awards by maximizing their impact and ensuring sustainability.

A brief history

The 1980s were a rich era not only for the creation of children's books, but also for celebrating core excellence within the field. A host of awards gave opportunities for authors, illustrators and individual books to gain recognition. The Library Association-administered Carnegie and Greenaway Medals were flourishing, respectively recognizing excellence in fiction for children and in illustrated books for children. The Guardian Award for Children's Fiction was similarly an established part of the landscape of children's literature. Newcomers during the decade included the Kurt Maschler Award, presented in recognition of a synergy between text and illustration, and the Mother Goose Award, which gave the chance to reward new talent in the field of children's book illustration. The winners of all of these awards, however, were determined by adult commentators on the world of children's books.

A change occurred in 1981 when a new award was launched – the Children's Book Award. Administered by the Federation of Children's Book Groups (FCBG) and spearheaded by their former chair Pat Thomson, the award was unique in that it offered children the opportunity to judge the books targeted at them, and in so doing to identify the titles they regarded the most highly. A model was set whereby publishers submitted titles and children drew up their own short list and chose the overall winner.

The importance of children's own views on the books created for them was given another national stage in 1985 with the establishment of the Smarties Book Prize. This award presented children with a short list of titles compiled by adults; the children themselves would then choose the winners of the award from these pre-selected lists.

With two models emerging on the national stage, it was a natural development for local awards to be established, with the aim of empowering and motivating young readers. The Lancashire Children's Book of the Year award was established with precisely that aim in mind. It followed the model of the Children's Book Award in its endeavours to minimize adult intervention by allowing publishers to directly nominate those titles they wished to see considered for the award. A panel of children was then responsible for reviewing and critically appraising these before deciding upon its choice of short list and going on to select its overall choice of winner. Unlike the Children's Book Award, the intention was to bring together children from a defined locality to use books as a vehicle for social interaction and critical discussion in a purposeful way, with the clear rationale that they would be selecting the book they felt most suitable for their peers in the 11 to 14 age range.

The award blossomed as the children took to their task with a real sense of dedication and seriousness of intent. In its early years, the tastes and discernment of the award's young judges identified luminaries of the children's book world at early points in their careers. Philip Pullman was the award's inaugural winner, and Brian Jacques followed shortly after, as too did Anthony Horowitz, and, as such, firm foundations were laid.

During the 25 years that the award has now been running its core purpose

– allowing young people the opportunity to decide their choice of winning book without adult intervention – has remained constant. Against that backdrop, numerous subtle changes have occurred to strengthen and maintain the longevity of the award by allowing it to respond to cultural shifts.

The heralding of a new decade, a new century and a new millennium in the 2000s saw several small, although significant, changes occur that have helped to ensure that the Lancashire awards remain fit for purpose. With the emergence of more definite teenage and young adult markets, the decision was made that the award's focus would narrow to cover 12–14 year-olds. This change was prompted by changes in the way readers responded to texts written for the younger range, as can be illustrated by a letter of criticism (3 July 1993) received by Anthony Masters concerning his novel *Crab*, where the critic stated: 'It was an unsuitable book for this award and should never have been nominated. The High School students should have been spared the waste of their time in reading it and I could have been spared the distress of reading their criticisms of work aimed at a quite different age level.'

After extensive consultation with publishers, schools and young people the decision was reached to locate the award firmly in the secondary age range. 'It would be a great shame if the more challenging books that a fourteen-year-old might enjoy were left off the list because they were felt to be unsuitable for eleven-year-olds. There are, after all, other awards which cover the younger age ranges' (Emma O'Bryen, *Piccadilly Press*, 10 July 2000).

In the early 2000s schools' child protection policies meant that, in addition to the pupil from each individual school that sat on the final judging panel, increasingly an additional pupil was brought to county meetings to meet with schools' safeguarding needs. In response to this, in 2004 the decision was made that each school would be allowed two judges to represent it, a choice that instantly doubled the size of the judging panel but that had a knock-on benefit of meaning that the judges now had peers in their own school with whom they could discuss and debate the shortlisted books. One of the most significant changes occurred in the mid-2000s, when the title of the award was subtly altered from the Lancashire Children's Book of the Year Award to the Lancashire Book of the Year, a fact determined by local research at the time, which identified that young people of this age identified more closely with adults than they did with children. This ability to alter organically in order to best place itself to meet the needs of young people and the educational, political and cultural contexts within which they lead their lives has enabled the award to develop, grow and have its longevity assured into its 25th year. We hope that, with such solid foundations, the award will continue for a further 25 years and for many years to come even beyond that.

Impact of local awards

Considering the impact of administering and hosting a local book award can help to determine whether this fits with existing plans that you have for promoting reading. Awards have many benefits and can be a lively way to create focus and inject excitement into an annual reading-development calendar. They can bring together schools from different communities and with very varied intakes, and create a commonality of purpose and shared interest. They can empower young people, in so doing creating a flagship event within local authorities that highlights the imaginative and creative aptitude that young citizens are able to contribute to society. Crucially, they can also provide young people with an early taste of democracy in action, with all of its associated joys and, at times, frustrations!

Local book awards offer libraries the opportunity to engage young people, to stimulate young minds in creative reading opportunities, and so provide positive interaction with books. In addition, they provide a chance to promote the library service and the type of provision on offer there, showcasing it as relevant, modern and engaging. They also help to break down the stereotype so often – and tiresomely – perpetuated by the media in the UK that young people are all 'promiscuous, unhealthy and violent' (Verkaik and Akbar, 2006).

For librarians themselves, involvement in local book awards gives an insight into the tastes and views of young people, and so can help inform and determine the selection of stock. Book awards provide a tangible rationale for establishing and maintaining links with local schools, working collaboratively to develop a culture of reading and to create a buzz around the exchange of thoughts, ideas and feelings. Awards give the opportunity to promote the books that young people themselves view most highly, as a part of a truly reader-centred approach to reading development.

For schools, local book awards present a key opportunity to promote reading for pleasure and wider reading. They can help to contribute to young people's educational outcomes through developing their skills in critical appraisal. They provide a profile for the school, an opportunity to gain professional knowledge and expertise through links with librarians and the chance to meet authors. Through feedback received from teachers for the

Lancashire Book of the Year award, we know that having a collection of brand new books, often by debut authors, provides a bedrock of knowledge and understanding of the most recent titles for young people, as can be shown by a letter received from David Foster, Head of English at Longridge County High School, commenting on the Lancashire Book of the Year booklet:

> I must applaud the scheme as a whole and congratulate the reviewers on the quality of their work. I certainly use it when I am considering purchasing books for the library or the English department, and it is well read from the magazine shelves in the school library. (19 July 1999)

Titles selected as winners of the Lancashire Book of the Year, or that have been chosen to be on the short list, have often been used very successfully by teachers as a class read – testament to the discernment brought to the task by the young judges.

Local book awards also provide benefits for publishers and authors. They offer an excellent access route for introducing new authors to their target audience. Being shortlisted and winning the award can be a real boost and a statement of support in praise of an author's work. The effects of this were made clear in 2006, when, after winning the award for the second time, Anthony Horowitz described in his acceptance speech how his first win, for *Groosham Grange*, had helped to inspire him to continue writing for young people. Feedback from teenagers on the books nominated for the award gives a unique and invaluable snapshot of views and opinions from the intended audience for the books. Through breaking down stereotypes of reading, local awards can provide a robust means for developing and growing the market for books and for reading and give opportunities to create audience loyalty, developing a fan base for authors.

Most impressive of all, however, are the outcomes for young people themselves. After 25 years, the Lancashire Book of the Year award has alumni of past judges whose achievements have been remarkably inspiring. Reading provides opportunities to reflect, to contemplate, to understand and to harbour a capacity for compassion. Discussing books boosts confidence and self-esteem and raises articulacy. It is no surprise, therefore, to learn that many of the judges of the Lancashire Book of the Year award have gone on to become sports captains, head boys and head girls in their respective schools, and, in some instances, even to win national debating competitions. We know from feedback from teachers, from the parents of judges and from the young people themselves that they view having taken part in the book award as a component of their achievements, as indeed the following comment in 2001 from the Learning Resources Coordinator from Our Lady Queen of Peace Catholic High School shows.

> We know how invaluable this initiative is, especially to pupils as they get such a wide range of experience, not only in reading, but in presenting and sharing their views with others. Some of our pupils who took part later went on to do public speaking and won an award.

Although it may sound grand, through investing in the growth and development of young people it is no exaggeration to say that we secure the future of our communities and of our society.

Whilst discussing the impacts for different organizations and individuals in isolation, as above, presents clarity in identifying these, it is also artificial, in that it negates one of the major impacts of administering an award, which is in the area of developing partnerships. Working in partnership creates a shared purpose and builds a stronghold for reading. When teachers, librarians, publishers, authors and young people come together to promote the vibrant and personalized experience that reading is able to give, a palpable sense of enthusiasm and excitement builds and balloons.

The award programme

As shown above, the outcomes of choosing to host a local book award for young people are manifold. The practicalities of running an award, however, can be intensive, laborious and at times exasperating. This section will explore the way the Lancashire Book of the Year award is administered and will emphasize particular points for consideration when running an award elsewhere.

Running the Lancashire Book of the Year award can feel rather like painting the Forth Bridge. It's an endless task in that, literally, no sooner has one award ended than the next is immediately set into motion. The award follows the academic year and, in readiness for this, schools are invited from late June to register their interest in taking part.

Lancashire County Council has over 80 secondary schools within its geographical area and these are spread across 12 districts. To ensure equality of access to the award, each district has one school representing it annually. The school selected from those that register an interest is the one that last took part longest ago, thereby guaranteeing fairness of participation.

During the summer vacation for schools, publishers are contacted and invited to put forward the titles of books they wish to be considered for the award. Publishers are provided with criteria against which to match potential nominations, and a list of key titles identified by our children's specialists are highlighted to publishers as potential contenders. Our criteria are deliberately loose, to try to ensure that young people's views are given the centre stage in the selection process. We request that all titles that are nominated for entry in the award are suitable for 12–14 year-olds. This avoids embarrassment to authors of work that is evidently either too young or too old in its content. We also ask that all titles should have been first published between 1 September and 31 August of the award's focus year. Titles should be a first work of original fiction or a collection of short stories by a single author. The author must be resident in the UK or Eire. The criteria are intended to ensure that all titles under consideration have an equal possibility of being shortlisted and, indeed, of winning the award. We request that the author is resident in the UK or Eire in order that we can secure the greatest possible opportunity for young people to meet with the author of the book they choose as the winner. With the exception of Robert Westall in 1993, who had, sadly, died earlier that year and Tim Lott in 2008, who had a prior commitment judging a book award in Malaysia, every winner has been able to attend the ceremony.

The award begins in earnest each September, when children's librarians from across the county visit Year 9 groups – pupils aged 13 to 14 – in each of the successful secondary schools. Each school is partnered with another from a neighbouring district, and between them they share a complete set of the long-listed titles. The long list is split in half by author surnames, one school receiving one half and the other receiving the remaining titles. Teachers are provided with a teachers' pack that outlines the various stages of the award and also gives guidance on administering the award within the school. Best practice from former years has shown that the award tends to be most successful in schools when delivered jointly by the English department, which is often able to provide time for reading and reviewing the books, and by the school librarian, who is invariably skilled at loaning books, keeping track of these and chasing up returns where needed! Key dates are decided in advance and are provided for the teacher, with an outline of action that is required by them so as to give schools maximum notice. Each school is provided with photographic consent forms to be completed for the pupils taking part at this stage, in order that these are ready and available further into the award when publicity begins properly.

A review proforma (see Appendix 9.2) and guidance on writing reviews are also given, as one of the outcomes of the Lancashire Book of the Year award is the production of a glossy, full-colour booklet that provides an overview of each book and gives insight into the young judges' views on them. Schools are given until November for their pupils to read their first set of books.

A meeting is arranged between each set of two partnered schools in November. Each school is invited to select four young people to attend, and these are often the judges who have read the most books, reviewed the most or given the most discerning, well-constructed views and arguments. The judges who attend the meeting discuss the books that they have been reading, outlining any that have stood out through being particularly well received in their schools and providing an insight into why that may be. Discussion also focuses on those that have been less appreciated, and the reasons behind this are discussed. Doing this gives schools an early flavour of the type of reception that titles have been receiving. At the close of the meeting, the schools swap their halves of the long list and are given until early February to read the remaining books, in order that each school has read all of the long-listed books.

By February, the process is beginning to hot up as each of the sets of partnered schools meet up once more. At this meeting the four judges from each school debate the books they have read and come prepared to vote for the books they want to see reach the short list of ten. Each school's votes are noted down and are sent in to library headquarters, where they are collated. Each school is also asked to put forward its choice of two judges who will go on to the final panel. It is a baseline requirement that the judges commit to being able to attend both county meetings and that they agree to read all of the ten shortlisted books. Panellists' names are collected centrally, along with the voting. A book that is voted in at first place receives ten points in our system, whilst one voted in at number ten will only receive 1 point. The points are added together and the ten top-scoring books go on to form the short list for the award.

A race then begins to have all the pieces in place for the first county meeting, when the panel, comprised of two young judges from each of the participating secondary schools, meets for the first time. All of the shortlisted books are ordered in quantities of 16, meaning that each school gets one set, the chair of the judging panel gets one set and there are contingency copies so that if, for any reason, the chair is unable to attend, there is a band of people ready to step into the breach who have read the books. Publicity materials are designed and printed, featuring each of the shortlisted books, and reviews for every long-listed book are collated, with the best reviews for each title being selected and typed up to form copy for the review booklet.

In early March the first county meeting is held and the chair of judges, currently acclaimed author and critic Adele Geras, expertly guides the young people through a half day of activities and discussions aimed at teasing out the concepts and features that characterize an exceptional, award-worthy book. The chair's role is to provide impartial moderation throughout the discussion, and an author fills this role so as to be able to feed in information on the mechanics of the books. Each pair of judges from the schools is given a complete set of the long list and schools are provided with publicity materials – posters and bookmarks – to enable the promotion of the award locally. Following the meeting, publicity material is sent out to every high school in Lancashire, to every library in Lancashire, to every member of the Association of Senior Children's and Education Librarians (ASCEL), which ensures that every local authority in the UK is informed, and to each of the publishers with a title featured on the long list for the award.

Judging

Judges have until late May to read each of the 10 shortlisted books. At this stage they come together for the final county meeting. This is, again, chaired by Adele Geras, and is a whole-day meeting. Each book is discussed in turn, with all judges having the opportunity to comment upon the title. Adele asks a series of probing questions based on each of the books in turn. This is to aid consideration of key elements of the book's make-up: characterization, plot, setting and atmosphere. The morning is taken up with discussing each of the books in turn, and immediately prior to lunch the pressure is turned up a notch as each of the judges has the chance to vote for their top three books. Votes are collated during the lunch break and the afternoon session is dedicated to discussing the relative merits, as well as any weaker elements, of each of the three books that successfully make it through to this stage. This is done in small breakout sessions, thereby ensuring that every panel member has an opportunity to contribute fully to discussions and to the final decisions. The panel convenes after the breakout session and spends time in a final group discussion prior to voting for its choice of overall winner. After collation of the votes, the winner is announced by Adele Geras and, if the telephone number of the author concerned is available, the judges themselves ring the winning author to notify them of the exciting news!

Awards

Following the announcement of the winner, the publisher of the winning book is contacted to arrange attendance at the award ceremony. The publisher of each of the shortlisted books is also notified and the authors of these books are invited to attend and also to take part in a panel discussion on their books. Authors are provided with accommodation and subsistence, on the agreement that their fee is waived. This mechanism allows the judges to meet with the authors whose work has resonated with them so fully and for authors to develop and grow their audiences. Copies of the winning book are ordered for each of the panellists, to acknowledge their sizeable contributions throughout the year, and the winning book is given a special feature in the review booklet which, at this stage, is now ready to go to print.

In late June the weekend of celebrations that forms the climax of the award takes place. This kicks off with a shortlist panel event where the shortlisted authors are each invited to introduce their work during a five-minute talk. Following their introductions, discussion is then opened up through questions from the floor and authors also have an opportunity to ask follow-up questions of the young people themselves. Schools from across the county are invited to this special event, which is hosted by our sponsors, the University of Central Lancashire.

Following the author panel event, there is a celebratory dinner held in the University's restaurant. The winning author and each of the shortlisted authors are invited to attend this and we have a number of past judges from the previous year attend to offer a more in-depth overview of what is involved in being a judge and how being involved in the award has affected them. Their speeches are always delivered with care, eloquence and often with great humour. This event helps to recognize and acknowledge the ten shortlisted authors' achievement in being selected by young people from the initial 100 books.

The next morning sees the award ceremony. Judges from the current year talk about their experiences and give their views on the books and the winning author is presented with the award. The ceremony concludes with an acceptance speech by the winning author, after which there is an opportunity for young people to purchase books and have them signed. The celebrations conclude with a buffet luncheon served in the prestigious

County Hall, headquarters of the County Council, and the meal is hosted by the Chair of the County Council. Immediately after the award ceremony, review booklets are sent out to every high school and publisher of young adult books, along with an invitation to register an interest in taking part in the award either as a participating school or by nominating eligible titles for the next year. The process begins again!

Sustainability

Running a book award for a single year involves a great deal of work; however, devising methods to ensure sustainability and longevity is crucial to securing the long-term future for the initiative. One of the first areas for consideration with regard to sustainability is deciding who is responsible for the administration of the awards. In the case of some local awards, notably the Manchester Book Awards, this is carried out by a dedicated award co-ordinator. For many local authorities, however, this lies out of reach, and duties fall to children's librarians in the public library service or the school library service. Having an award co-ordinator provides a single point of contact for the award, thereby creating a culture that is conducive to developing and building upon the successes of the award. Having an existing member of staff responsible for running the award can help to integrate it more successfully with existing provision. As demonstrated, there are benefits associated with either model.

Funding is always a key issue for local book awards. Libraries are often able to provide stock (from resource budgets) and staffing as in-kind support. Many authorities running awards have elected to pre-select a short list of books, which can be an excellent way of keeping costs down. Financial consideration will need to be given to publicizing the award, as well as to the overall prize. In an era where funding is increasingly tight, affiliations can be established to provide added value at a low cost for services. Exploring the use of county buildings – town or county halls – for the final events can lower overall costs significantly. Having a non-monetary prize, but rather something that reflects the aims and ethos of the award, can similarly be a way of lowering expenditure. In the first year of the Salford Children's Book Award, local artist Harold Riley was commissioned to draw a pen-and-ink portrait of famous local artist L. S. Lowry for presentation to the winning author. Similarly cost-effective alternatives can be explored.

Off-setting some of the costs through sponsorship can be another valuable way of lowering overheads for the library service, whilst similarly integrating the award within the locality. In Lancashire we had sponsorship from the NatWest Bank. When the bank's policy on community support altered, new sponsorship was sought, and at the start of the new millennium a new sponsorship deal was secured with the University of Central Lancashire. This felt like a holistic and mutually beneficial relationship because the award raises literacy levels – the key access point for all education – and was also able to bring local pupils into a tertiary education setting with first-class facilities, thereby raising aspirations and stimulating thought on the availability and provision of higher education within the locale.

Political context has played a significant role in assuring the longevity of the award. Each year, key dignitaries from the County Council attend the ceremony: the Chair of the Council; the councillor who is the portfolio holder for libraries; and the children and young people's champion, whose role is to advocate children and young people's involvement in the community. This has helped to integrate the award as a part of the County Council's annual calendar and has raised its profile within the Council to a flagship event for young people. That in turn has meant that support from the corporate communications team for media coverage has been forthcoming, as has support for room bookings and from other departments within the County Council.

The Lancashire Book of the Year award has received relatively few complaints; there have been two cases where individual secondary schools requested that their pupils not read one of the books on the long list. One of these was *Angus, Thongs and Full-Frontal Snogging* (Louise Rennison), doubtless caused in this case by the title – which is somewhat more provocative than the book's actual theme!

In dealing with these sorts of issues we are always keen to promote the level of maturity that the young judges bring to their tasks and the open discussions they hold with regard to suitability, controversy and the appropriateness of language and particular subjects to the story as a whole. Where these issues have arisen, we are careful not to ostracize schools by enforcing reading, but equally emphasize that young people's views are imperative. Clarity of purpose combined with this soft-handed approach has helped to keep schools on board with the award programme.

Devising child protection policies to safeguard young people's welfare and interests has also been a way of maintaining longevity, as it has ensured that the award has kept up to date with the strategies schools are now developing and adhering to. Similarly, we have undertaken to ensure that risk assessments are available for the County Council venues used for the panel meetings, and these can be provided upon request.

Embedding the award

Awards generate local interest and create a focal point for the types of engaging and creative reading development activity that make a real impact on young people. This section will explore ways of maximizing outcomes and making the energy and enthusiasm injected by young people all the more purposeful, through embedding the initiative in the locality.

Creating and maintaining partnership links with relevant groups and businesses can be an excellent way to raise the profile of the award and to ensure that the choices made by young judges are widely recognized. In Lancashire we have made links with the teacher advisory team in the local authority, who have helped to promote the award and disseminated information and publicity with the schools that they liaise with. We have forged connections with our virtual schools team, a group that works to ensure the best outcomes for children looked after in residential care, and have worked in collaboration with it to make copies of the Lancashire Book of the Year titles available to children in residential care, as well as ensuring that places have been reserved for any of those interested in attending the celebratory events. We have loaned collections to the county youth and community team in order for their groups to have access to the books. Additionally, we have formed links with local book retailers and ensured that they are aware of the short list in order that titles can be stocked. We provide them with copies of the publicity for the award in order to create display and promotion opportunities in store.

Award shadowing

In 2006 nearly three times as many schools registered interest in the award as we had places to offer. As a consequence, we were keen to capitalize on the interest that had been generated and to capture that enthusiasm. We thus established an award shadowing scheme as a means to allow more limited involvement both by these schools and also by some of those partnership groups listed above. We were eager to provide a package that enabled meaningful involvement in the award. The shadowing was devised to begin at the shortlist stage of the award. Working in collaboration with one of our local, independent bookshops we were able to offer a complete set of the shortlisted titles at a discounted rate. We provided each participating school with sets of publicity material and with a shadowing pack containing guidance on how to appraise the books (see Appendix 9.3), which was developed by the original chair of the award, Hazel Townson, and ideas for how to create displays and run themed activities in schools. We allowed schools the opportunity to vote for their favourite book via the website and agreed that the combined voting would count as one overall vote at the final judging stage. We wanted young people who had been involved in shadowing to have their voices and views heard, but equally we felt strongly that this needed to be counter-balanced against the fact that, unlike the panellists, there was no guarantee that they had read each of the shortlisted books, nor had they received the personal guidance from Adele Geras that panellists would have done. We were able to provide contact details for other schools shadowing the award so that network opportunities existed, should these be desired. As a final component of the package we were also delighted to be able to offer a limited number of places at the award celebrations. These were offered on a first come, first served basis because of their finite number.

A similar shadowing offer has been made to reading groups within libraries. They have been given publicity for the award and access, through the library system, to each of the shortlisted books. Some groups have written reviews that have been displayed in libraries, helping to further advocate the shortlisted titles. Reading group members have also been offered the opportunity to attend the celebratory events.

We encourage staff to shadow the award and have a 'just for fun' vote to see how closely our views match those of the young judges. Encouraging staff to read the books means that they are better able to promote them face to face. In 2010 we liaised with our University sponsor and the newly established postgraduate course it runs, 'Writing for Young People', to host an adult shadowing with students and library staff alike. This was also hosted by Adele Geras so as to achieve synergy with the young people's judging. Working more closely with the University has integrated the award and its role as sponsor more closely.

For several years now we have been embarking on a programme of library refurbishment in Lancashire, known as 'Regenerate'. The look of the libraries at the end is clean, fresh and modern. Each refurbished library has had plasma screens installed, meaning that we have been able to create rolling PowerPoint presentations using the design concept for the shortlist publicity as a backdrop. This has created an eye-catching and modern way of promoting the books.

Conclusion

Developing the book awards means growing readers, and accordingly we've looked to widen our impact. We now have a book award, 'The Fantastic Book Awards', for primary-school-age children run by our School Library Service, and our Early Years manager is looking towards establishing a book award for pre-school children. As for the Lancashire Book of the Year itself, in its 25th anniversary year we want to produce a celebratory booklet that will underpin a family reading promotion exploiting the present interest in cross-over fiction and also be a legacy document about the award and its history. We also aim to produce a more detailed website, thus giving access to the backlist of young people's views and opinions on 25 years of publishing in the UK. Year on year, the delivery of a successful local book award provides young people with engaging and positive encounters with the public library service. It stimulates a culture of wider reading in schools and encourages debate and critical discussion. Through equipping young people with skills, it turns the page to the future.

Reference

Verkaik, R. and Akbar, A. (2006) Behind the Stereotypes: the shocking truth about teenagers, *Independent*, 23 October.

Appendix 9.1: Previous winners

Year	Author	Title
1987	Philip Pullman	*The Ruby in the Smoke*
1988	Brian Jacques	*Redwall*
1989	Anthony Horowitz	*Groosham Grange*
1990	Jean Ure	*Plague 99*
1991	Brian Jacques	*Mattimeo*
1992	Robin Jarvis	*The Whitby Witches*
1993	Brian Jacques	*Salamandastron* (joint winner)
1993	Robert Westall	*Gulf* (joint winner)
1994	Ian Strachan	*The Boy in the Bubble*
1995	Garry Kilworth	*The Electric Kid*
1996	Frances Mary Hendry	*Chandra*
1997	Elizabeth Hawkins	*Sea of Peril*
1998	Elizabeth Laird	*Jay*
1999	Nigel Hinton	*Out of the Darkness*

2000	Tim Bowler	*Shadows*
2001	Melvin Burgess	*Bloodtide* (joint winner)
2001	Malcolm Rose	*Plague* (joint winner)
2002	Malorie Blackman	*Noughts and Crosses*
2003	Julie Bertagna	*Exodus*
2004	Chris Wooding	*Poison*
2005	Jonathan Stroud	*The Amulet of Samarkand*
2006	Anthony Horowitz	*Raven's Gate*
2007	Robert Muchamore	*Divine Madness*
2008	Tim Lott	*Fearless*
2009	Sophie McKenzie	*Blood Ties*
2010	Narinder Dhami	*Bang, Bang, You're Dead!*

Appendix 9.2 Review pro forma

REVIEW

School:

Pupil:

Book Title:

Author:

BRIEF description of the story in *my own* words:

What I thought about this book (MY likes/dislikes and feelings):

These reviews are your chance to have your say as well as being your chance to go to print! The booklet of reviews we produce goes to authors, publishers and libraries around the country so what you say really does count... We reward the best reviews so let us know your thoughts on the book... If you need more space do feel free to continue overleaf!

Appendix 9.3 Points for consideration when assessing books

1 — The Story
   a. Gripping?
   b. Fast moving?
   c. Good start on the first page?
   d. Enjoyable?
   e. End on a note of hope?
   f. Worthwhile?
   g. Willing suspension of disbelief?
   h. True to life and convincing?
   i. Original?
   j. If the story had a message, was this well conveyed?
   k. Did the story set you thinking about more than the plot?
   l. Did it make you laugh?
   m. Did it provide an experience you might otherwise never have had?
   n. Would you read it again?
   o. Would you recommend it to others?

2 — The characters
   a. Interesting?
   b. Like real people?
   c. Have they stayed in your memory?
   d. Could you picture them as you read?
   e. Did you identify with one of them?
   f. If fantasy, were the characters convincing enough within the setting?
   g. Predictable actions? Or were they more subtle? Should be consistent.
   h. Well-portrayed relationships with other characters?
   i. Did the main characters mature towards the end of the book? Learn anything from their experience?
   j. Were you entirely comfortable with all the characters' actions?
   k. Did the story avoid sexism or racism? Fall into these traps? Or did it try too hard not to?

3 — Were the minor characters well portrayed?

4 — The setting
   a. Could you visualise it without effort?
   b. Was it right for the story?

   c. Did it improve the story, or would the tale have been just as good if set elsewhere?

   d. Did you feel the author had actually been to such a place?

   e. Did the setting help create the tension or drama of the story?

   f. Did you enjoy this escape from reality?

5 — The style

   a. Easy-flowing?

   b. Did the story move swiftly?

   c. Evocative description?

   d. Special richness of language?

   e. Did any phrases stick in your mind because you admired them?

   f. Would the story read aloud well?

   g. If there was dialogue, was this true to life?

   h. Did you have to look up words you didn't understand? Did this help or hinder?

   i. Was the style suitable for the subject matter?

   j. Humour in the language?

   k. Does bad language spoil the story?

   l. Was there word repetition?

  m. Sense of rhythm in the prose?

   n. Did you wish the author had told you more, or less, about some things?

   o. Were you moved by the book, to tears, anger, pity, indignation?

6 — The overall presentation

   a. Does the book look attractive? (Cover, illustrations, paper, text?)

   b. Was it the sort of book you would have been drawn to without knowing anything about it?

   c. Would you like to possess it?

   d. Is it the best book you have read for a long time?

   e. Would you now look for other books by the same author?

   f. Do you feel moved to tell other people about this book?

   g. Does it deserve to win an award?

10

The sport of reading

Celeste Harrington and Wayne Mills

Introduction

With such an emphasis on reading today it seems unimaginable that 20 years ago good readers went largely unrecognized. Prowess in mathematics and sports was more often rewarded than any propensity for reading. With this as the backdrop, the International Kids' Lit Quiz™ was created in 1991 when Wayne Mills, then a lecturer at Waikato University, realized that students were not being recognized for their reading ability and so formulated and designed the Kids' Lit Quiz.™ The intention of the quiz was to formulate a series of general knowledge literary questions similar in format to Trivial Pursuit, except that all the wedges would be different literary genres. Of course in those early years the quiz was much smaller than it is today and was not internationally known. It has grown from 14 teams in 1991 to over 1000 teams on three continents. This chapter will examine just what factors make the Kids' Lit Quiz™ so phenomenally successful in promoting reading and provides insight into the motivational aspects of an international literature quiz that brings readers in the 10–13 age range together from all over the world to participate in an international literary challenge

History and ethos

The Kids' Lit Quiz™ is open to students aged from 10 to 13 years. School grade eligibility, however, is likely to vary from country to country. The National Endowment for the Arts (National Endowment for the Arts, 2004) found that this was the very age group at which reading began to decline (calamitously), and therefore it was vital to maintain students' interest in reading. The age composition defines the scope of the books that are read for the quiz. This means that adult authors like Jodi Picoult, Dan Brown and

Alice Sebold are not included in the quiz (although some students may be reading them). However, young adult novels such as *The Knife of Never Letting Go*, by Patrick Ness or *The Graveyard Book*, by Neil Gaiman may be included. The participants in the quizzes have all read picture books and junior fiction and thus have these literary experiences in common.

Therefore, the scope is anything written for students, from comics and picture books to non-fiction and teenage novels. Typically, readers entering the quiz always want to read upwards. It is not uncommon to be asked by keen readers to introduce the quiz into high schools. This would not be viable because the scope would then automatically broaden into adult literature and thus result in the boundaries of the quiz losing their constraints. A female student from Palmerston North in New Zealand wrote an e-mail to the organizers pleading:

> I know that next year there will be no quiz for me as I will be in Year 9. But hey, that's given me an idea. Why not let Year 9s do the quiz too? The quiz would become bigger and better and we can again be part of all the excitement. So this is a sincere request from me if you could extend the participation to Year 9 students as well.

Initially, the Kids' Lit Quiz™ was begun to encourage and reward students for their reading ability. However, over time and as it developed, the quiz has motivated and fostered students' reading (boys' in particular), affirmed students' self-efficacy and encouraged students to widen their scope of reading both horizontally and vertically. In this sense, students are reading both 'up' into cross-over literature and 'down' into picture books, as well as reading 'across' authors, so that writers like Michael Morpurgo, with 100 plus titles, will provide keen readers access to a distinctive authorial style they may not have encountered. Of course there will always be students who will relate how they've read each Harry Potter 70 times, or the aficionado of J. R. R. Tolkien who will know that Tolkien was born in Bloemfontein, that Peter Jackson and his Weta Workshop brought the trilogy to the screen or that his wife's name was Edith. However, what it ultimately does is encourage students to read. This then has the result of increasing students' annual exposure to print in excess of four million words (Nagy, Anderson and Herman, 1987).

The quiz began in Hamilton in the Waikato region of New Zealand, but it soon spread outwards to embrace neighbouring regions, and, with the support of a national sponsor in 1997, it finally covered the entire country. This allowed for a national final and an opportunity to display and publicize 'the sport of reading' with students who were passionate about the pastime. These days the national final is held in the Parliament of New Zealand. This has resulted in increasing the profile of the quiz, which further values readers. After the 2010 New Zealand final a mother from the Wanganui Intermediate team e-mailed to say:

> Your Kids' Lit Quizzes are amazing and have changed my son's life and made me go 'hallelujah for Wayne Mills'. All through primary school he achieved highly in his loves of reading and creative writing but always in anonymously labelled groups such as bears, lions and tigers so as to not highlight who was in the bottom and who was in the top groups yet somehow it was fine to post on the school noticeboard all the placings in sports events, including those (usually one of my boys) who came last.

In the late 1990s, teams from Australia took part, but the quiz expanded greatly in 2003 when the Kids Lit Quiz™ was piloted in Newcastle in north-east England. With support from school librarian and literary specialist Eileen Armstrong, it was extremely successful and the *Times Educational Supplement* (Williams, 2003) proclaimed that 'Readers Win in Wayne's World'. This encouraged other regions in the UK to participate and the quiz quickly spread across the UK with support from librarians. From there followed South Africa in 2005, China in 2006 and Canada in 2011. In an open letter to the South African quiz co-ordinator, Marj Brown (2006), quiz participant Carys Evans declared:

> I participated in the 2005 South African KLQ. I would just like to say that you truly made my life coming up with this quiz it gives a chance for all the book worms like me to shine, without having to do sports, which is mainly what my school is all about! Thank you soooooooooo much. God Bless!

One team from each regional heat moves forward to the national final. The gathered teams compete head to head and the winning team progresses to the world final. Each stage is progressively more difficult because the questions are longer and the format changes from paper to buzzer for both national and world finals. The teams of four sit at a table that is electronically wired with a buzzer that connects to a motherboard. The students answer by pressing the buzzer on their table, which lights up on the motherboard. The first team to answer correctly scores two points (but an incorrect answer loses a point). The penalty is unavoidable because it's necessary to prevent a team deliberately interjecting in order to block the opposition from answering correctly. The buzzer is accurate to within 1/10000th of a second and the likelihood of two teams answering at the same split second is unlikely.

School engagement and motivation

Schools began to see that their students enjoyed the challenge of a literary quiz that was really and truly demanding because it had no book list (in which sense it is not a 'test'). This meant that every year more schools began to take part in the quiz. Each year schools receive a quiz pack which includes a welcoming cover letter, a registration form and 50 new pre-test questions. These questions are designed to be given to teams rather than individuals, as the quiz is a team event. Additionally, many schools also seek information about potential students from their librarians and teachers. Schools regularly enter the date for the following year's quiz on their literary calendar and work towards it. Librarians feature the quiz as one of the highlights of the school year and even begin to work with students in the year prior to the quiz. The quizzes work around schools' academic programmes and are usually held during the afternoon. However, the evening quizzes are the ones that have proved to attract the larger crowds because spectators are, by and large, freer after work.

Nowadays, schools are inventive in the ways in which they have implemented and developed a reading culture to foster their Kids' Lit Quiz™ teams. Most organize clubs during lunch breaks, but others with more flexible options conduct a breakfast club where students arrive at 7.00 a.m. for cereal and toast and a book chat, or offer an after-school 'chocolate-biscuit' group where students talk informally about their current reading. A booklist is maintained and later e-mailed around for the group to share. These sessions may include brainstorming a category, where a random topic such as 'mice' is nominated and students rattle off titles and characters such as *Geronimo Stilton*, *Maisy* or *The Tale of Despereaux*. Students are sometimes asked to create a category themselves and prepare a mini quiz for the next meeting.

There are a number of literary quizzes on the web, ranging from easy to difficult, and these are easily accessed by entering keywords such as 'literature', 'quiz' and 'book'.

Some schools seek assistance from past quiz members in mentoring their team or, failing that, ask for advice from librarians or call upon (grand-) parents to help with their team's preparation. Several schools conduct interclass book quizzes, which are run as a fun event during a parents' evening, using a knock-out format. Teams with the widest literary knowledge win through and undiscovered talent may be surprisingly exposed.

Many librarians keep an eye on the international book awards and short lists, as these often exalt noteworthy titles. A case in point is *The Graveyard Book*, by Neil Gaiman, the first title to win both the Carnegie Award and the Newbery Award in the same year. Some groups listen to audio books as a means of broadening their students' literary knowledge. The range of titles is enormous and frequently read by actors with well known voices such as Jim Dale and Stephen Fry.

Book clubs are an excellent idea and, once started, often develop a life of their own. As well as encouraging wider reading, they assist students with inferencing, develop their literary awareness and activate their higher-order thinking as they learn to pose their own questions.

Schools have appreciated the team and individual rewards to be gained from participation in the Kids' Lit Quiz™. Teams can receive books, tokens and travel prizes, and individuals can win on-the-spot cash prizes. With support from parents, schools have been spurred on to enter. One South African parent in 2009 wrote:

> My son, from Grove, had an unforgettable experience. He was at last able to shine doing one of the things he does best. This quiz gives reading currency – literally and figuratively.

Questioning and book promoting

The quiz's oral format means that attention remains focused on the questions. Even when the papers are being scored, individual students are absorbed in attempting to be the first to answer a question from an international final for a cash reward. So, with no downtime for minds to wander, the students don't have time to get bored. A boy from England wrote in his evaluation of the quiz: 'The quiz was challenging and fun. I've read a million books but you always ask the questions on the 10 I haven't read!'

Questions attempt to be 'organic' in construction so that students are motivated to read the book from which the question was derived. For instance: 'How did Katniss defy the odds in *The Hunger Games* (Suzanne Collins) by surviving the fight-to-the-death reality games in the newly formed states of Panem?' Many students are going to know the answer to this, but students who do not know the book are piqued to find out more and beat a path to the library door. Harper (2001) noted that the questions were limited only by Mills' own inventiveness. Dull questions like: 'Who wrote Harry Potter?' or 'What colour was *Black Beauty?*' are replaced with interesting questions that make students want to read the book.

The questions are carefully designed to arouse interest in the book and are not written to be pedantic. In fact some questions are as much general knowledge as they are literary. An example is: 'In Dick King-Smith's novel *Dodos are Forever* on which island in the Indian Ocean was the dodo to be found?'

Parents have an opportunity to witness how the Kids' Lit Quiz™ has excited their children to read, because they are also rewarded with their own adult literary questions. For instance, if the school team was asked a question in the ecology category, like 'Why was McCain genetically modifying crops for Kenya in the Alex Rider book *Crocodile Tears?*' then the adults were also asked a question in that category, like 'What famous book by Rachel Carson in 1962 was widely credited with launching the Green Movement?' Of course the rationale for this is to allow the students to see that their parents are also readers.

The questions used at the national and international finals are more complex. They are longer than those used in the heats, and while they may begin obscurely they slowly unpeel like an onion until sufficient clues have been revealed to make the answer obvious. These questions are delivered orally and may therefore be answered at any stage of the delivery. They always begin vaguely, but do move to the obvious as the question unravels.

The questions at both the national and international finals need to be more difficult, in keeping with the literary knowledge displayed by these top teams. The categories at this level will therefore include questions about titles, authors and illustrators, but may also include categories such as books made into movies, crossover titles, fables, folktales, fractured fairy tales, historical fiction, myths and legends, nursery rhymes, poetry, social realism, speculative fiction or even a specific genre such as steampunk.

Steampunk is an increasingly popular genre with both teenagers and adults that blends the historical, often the Victorian era, with science fiction so that the technology employed is anachronistic for the period. An example of a steampunk question is the following:

Name the novel set in the Victorian period in the back of the black. Space conquest had been achieved with the first moon landing in 1703 following Sir Isaac Newton's discoveries. Alchemists operated the space vessels and the Duke of Marlborough had conquered Mars in the War of the Worlds. The time was 1851 and Britain was getting ready for the Royal Albert Exhibition which was to include exhibits from all over Britain's extraterrestrial colonies such as Mars and Jupiter. The Mumby family's ancient space house had been attacked by highly intelligent spiders, bent upon the destruction of the British Empire, under the control of Dr Ptarmigan because it was believed that the family had the key to instantaneous travel. The children, Arthur and Myrtle, with the aid of space pirates were needed to save the Empire and recue their parents. Written by Philip Reeve, the one-word title was [*Larklight*].

For another category – books made into movies, a question might look like this:

In this movie what was once your life is now your legend. Directed by first-time director Stefen Fangmeier and released in 2006 this was the story of a predestined quest in defence of one's homelands and a coming-of-age fantasy. The movie was a mix between *Star Wars* and Middle Earth and told how the discovery of a large blue jelly bean looking object signalled the beginning of magic and adventure. The movie ended with an aerial dogfight between the hero and a giant dragon and with a promise of more to come. The hero played by Edward Speleers beat 180,000 other hopeful contenders for the role of Eragon. Both title of the book and movie were the same. It was [*Eragon*].

With the range and breadth of the questions, any international winning team can feel justifiably proud of its achievement. The winners are often treated as heroes and feted in much the same way as sports stars. Indeed, schools proudly use the win in their marketing and public relations.

Impact and evidence

The reasons for the success of the Kids' Lit Quiz™ are not merely anecdotal but are well supported by research. Several studies have been conducted that indicate that the motivation to read for pleasure in the 11–13 age group does indeed decline (Hamston and Love, 2003; Krashen, 2004; McKool, 2007). However, in conjunction with this decline there are clearly observable groups of children who continue to read avidly. Research has shown several key reasons for this continued reading for pleasure and the Kids' Lit Quiz™ has featured strongly among them. One student summed up her gains in this way:

I have gained so much knowledge about literature. I have become more organised, my language is better, I am more confident, and I have gained SO many new friends! I wish and I wish that I was Peter Pan and would never grow up.

Recent research by Harrington (2009) with a group of students who had taken part in the quiz found several factors that contributed to their being avid readers. Among the reasons cited were the excitement of taking part in a quiz that had international appeal and the fact that the quiz was not prescriptive with set reading lists (i.e. choice). This was an interesting aspect of much of the discussion with these students, as most of them enjoyed the wide range of reading possible with involvement in the Kids' Lit Quiz.™ Indeed this is supported by other research by Krashen (2004) in which students were found to be motivated not by rewards but rather by having a wide choice in their reading. Those perceived to be reluctant readers were actually only so at school, whilst out of school they made other reading choices.

Even in the interviewing of parents by Harrington (2009), one parent said that their child joined the Kids' Lit Quiz™ club because of the interest in a different quiz held at the primary school. (This quiz was one in which a prescribed reading list is given to contestants, who answer questions based upon those particular books.) What their child liked in the Kids' Lit Quiz™ was the lack of a reading list and the choice to read widely. One parent said their child joined as a result of seeing the final of the Kids' Lit Quiz™ at the Storylines Festival (a large festival of children's literature held in New Zealand and, in the past, the site for the national final of the Kids' Lit Quiz™).

Other studies support this important factor of choice of reading matter among this age group of students. In the main, it was found that students gave three generally agreed-upon reasons for reading: 'fun and relaxation, to learn new things, and because they were bored' (Hughes-Hassell and Rodge, 2007, 24). Some of the reading material identified by this group of students was obtained from three sources: the school library, the public library and the school classroom. Hughes-Hassell and Rodge (2007) found that 43% of the students also purchased reading material from local bookstores. These researchers propose that a wider degree of choice in leisure reading matter should be made available to students and that a new definition of leisure reading needs to be established (Hughes-Hassell and Rodge, 2007). Krashen, Lee and McQuillan (2008) also place emphasis on the importance of the school library, in light of how much children chose to read for leisure purposes. The strong links that all schools who participate in the quiz have with their libraries also provide added value to the motivational aspects of the Kids' Lit Quiz.™

In addition to the reasons cited above, students in the study listed the fact that receiving considerable support from their parents contributed to their reading motivation (Harrington, 2009). Indeed, in numerous studies this factor played a significant contributing role in older readers' desire to read for pleasure. Hamston and Love (2003) examined the leisure reading practices of boys aged between 11 and 17 and the role of their parents, and although the focus was on the concept of 'guided participation' (Rogoff, 2003) the findings demonstrated the importance of the relationship between the boys and their parents.

In families where parents had a positive influence on children's reading habits, books were valued by the family and a 'culture' (Hamston and Love, 2003, 55) of reading prevailed in the home. This suggested that the 'Matthew Effect', a term coined by Stanovich (Cunningham and Stanovich, 1991; Hamer and Adams, 2003) was in operation. The Matthew Effect referred to the 'rich getting richer and the poor getting poorer' (*Good News Bible*, 1994, 1064). According to Stanovich, children who had access to books in which they were interested, through the support of their families, would read more and consequently became better readers. Conversely, those who did not have access to books or supportive parents often lost interest in reading, and without the same practice may not have developed the same level of reading skill (Cunningham and Stanovich, 1991). Those children who take part in the quiz certainly have the support of their parents, as evidenced above and in the research by Harrington. A parent is quoted as saying that she always takes her children to the library as well as buying books: 'I want them to enjoy their books, I want them to keep them so as much as I can afford it, I buy them the books' (Harrington, 2009).

Strommen and Mates (2004) came to similar conclusions, with participants in their study being clearly able to identify someone who inspired them to read for pleasure as a key reason for their becoming 'readers'. Likewise, students who were identified as not reading for pleasure had few influences in their lives in terms of reading inspiration, and even though they had been 'readers' up to the age of around nine this interest waned with the reduction of active adult interest in their leisure reading. 'Apparently, these students did not have the support of a family member who enjoyed reading to suggest and share appropriate books' (Strommen and Mates, 2004, 194).

In several letters to Wayne Mills it was evident that the self-efficacy of being identified as a reader was valuable to the children who took part in the quiz:

> in particular, one member of our team, who is dyslexic, has struggled with reading and English lessons for the past two years. Recently, with the trial Kid's Lit™ Quiz questions, and the Kid's Lit™ Quiz event she has found incredible self-worth and belief in her abilities in reading and writing. Suddenly her interest in comic heroes, television adaptations, myth and legends has been validated and determined to be a source of confidence and pride. This is something class teaching alone can rarely achieve. In short, Mr Mills you continue to be a true hero in the world of literature.
> (Letter received from a teacher who entered a team in the 2007 heats in the UK)

How well children were able to read and how much they consequently enjoyed reading showed how important ability and self-belief were to the continued enjoyment of and engagement in reading (Conlon et al., 2006; Cunningham and Stanovich, 1991; Guthrie and Humenick, 2004; Guthrie et al., 2007; McKool, 2007; McNaughton, 2002). Guthrie et al. (2007) examined reading motivation in a study that took into account a significant number of factors, including motivation to read a variety of texts and the growth of reading motivation relative to reading comprehension. They also examined students' internal motivation in terms of interest, self-efficacy and involvement.

Guthrie and Humenick (2004, 329) 'use the word *motivate* in the sense of engagement in an important task'. The authors' discussion was primarily about how students became intrinsically motivated to read and in this way extended their own cognitive and aesthetic ability and enjoyment. This study was valuable in that there was an attempt to establish the possibility of creating contexts in which children would become long-term readers. Self-perception or self-efficacy was indeed an important 'variable' to be 'included when considering the factors associated with reading performance' (Conlon et al., 2006, 29).

Discussion about the wide range of genres that these children accessed and the fact that entry into the quiz and the associated club was voluntary provided further insight into the links between the social nature of reading (Campbell and Green, 2006) and the value these children placed on participating in the quiz.

Evidence gained during the interviews (Harrington, 2009) showed that they had changed what they read and how they read because of their involvement in the club. Some said that their reading choice was widened as they gained knowledge about different authors and different genres from the librarian both at school and at the public library and from their fellow club members. Others felt that they read more frequently because of involvement in the club. They reported being inspired by the other members to read a wider variety of books.

This suggested an intrinsic motivation on the part of those particular children to be involved in something that they enjoyed doing. 'Internal motivation is the seeking of benefits that the reading activity itself confers on the reader. Internally motivated readers have desires, interests, needs, and dispositions that are satisfied through various forms of reading activities' (Guthrie and Humenick, 2004, 330). The participants in Harrington's (2009, 36) study found the idea of a quiz interesting and challenging – 'they joined the Kids' Lit Quiz™ club because they liked reading and thought it would be fun to meet other students who also liked to read'. Research conducted by Guthrie and Humenick (2004) supported Harrington's (2009) view that students had come to know that reading was valued and were thus motivated to accept the challenge of 'reading widely'. A mother who was interviewed said she was amazed at how her daughter had changed in the selection of books she chose to read.

Another mother in Christchurch, New Zealand related how her daughter, who had only read books about horses in her first year of quiz participation, had subsequently broadened her whole sweep of titles after experiencing the scope that the Kids' Lit Quiz™ offered by way of literary challenge. Thus, children entered the quiz for a variety of reasons. Some reasons were social and based upon a self-motivated love of reading, while other children joined in order to have choice in what they could read rather than bowing to parental pressures or school requirements to read particular texts: 'they liked the fact that the Kids' Lit Quiz™ had no required reading list' (Harrington, 2009, 32).

The meeting of like-minded readers from around the world at international finals has resulted in a number of long-lasting friendships and regular exchanges of book recommendations. Through the quiz students have found an avenue for sharing their literary tastes and swapping ideas about what to read next. 'Readers learn, through social interaction with other readers, that reading is entertaining and stimulating' (Strommen and Mates, 2004, 199).

The data also suggested that children across the countries where the quiz took place were intrinsically motivated to read. Children joined the quiz for reasons that were social and based upon a self-motivating love of reading and a desire to have choice in what they could read rather than parental pressure or school requirement to read. Evidence about the wide range of genres that these children accessed and the fact that entry into the quiz and the associated club was voluntary, provided further insight into the links between the social nature of reading (Campbell and Green, 2006) and the value these children placed on participating in the quiz. When people have queried whether there are any socio-cultural differences between readers from different cultures it has always been apparent that avid readers are avid readers, wherever they live. Any differences are more to do with the titles read and the way in which books are accessed.

The sharing of information about titles and authors at the quizzes was seen as a positive feature of the book selling that Mills engaged in with students. It was a student in Shanghai who first informed him of the attraction of *Twilight* before it became a series. Mills constantly provides the students with authors to read or titles to explore before the end of the month or before they turn 14. He has switched students on to relatively new or unknown authors such as John van de Ruit, Brian Falkner and Echo Freer.

Participating in the Kids' Lit Quiz™ plays an important role in these children's reading lives and fulfils some elements of the desire to be in a social group of like-minded others. As stated above, parents are seen to be important in motivating their children to be the avid readers that they are. This is not by compulsion, but by their tacit and implicit support. They, too, play a role in this social nature of reading (Chandler, 1999; Krashen, 2004). Self-efficacy is also significant in light of motivation, and a strong sense of self-belief motivates readers to continue to be readers (Hughes-Hassell and Rodge, 2007; Krashen, 2004; Strommen and Mates, 2004).

In addition to discussing books that they have read, students liked to have people recommend books to them. In a recent study, McKool (2007, 125) examined a wide range of avid and reluctant readers and her findings suggested that very few of the students who were considered to be reluctant readers had people who recommended books to them, whilst those who were avid readers 'reported that their parents or friends recommended good books to read on a regular basis'.

Research has also shown that a range of choice (Hughes-Hassell and Rodge, 2007; Krashen, 2004) was important to students in this age group and there was a general consensus that advice and recommendations about a wider variety of books were welcomed and made it easier to locate books that interested them. Being involved with a group of like-minded readers was motivational to readers, who broadened their text choices through their involvement in the Kids' Lit Quiz.™

> Kids love to talk to me about books because just as kids like to talk to parents or teachers about books, they know in me they've got someone that's probably read the book that they have read and as we all know it is one of the most satisfying things on the planet to find someone that you can relate to and discuss the same book that you've read. … It's a meeting of minds.
>
> (Wayne Mills in Harrington, 2009)

Conclusions

The Kids' Lit Quiz™ has proved innovatively successful in bringing readers together from around the globe to compete in an all-literary competition. This quiz, by its very nature, fulfils the varied and wide-ranging motivational reasons that promote avid reading in this particular age group. The choice made available, the recommendations of books to read, the parental support and the chance to make friends and be social combine to make this a unique chance for readers to remain motivated in their leisure reading activities. As well as this, the opportunity to travel from one side of the world to the other in 'the sport of reading' has opened unheard of opportunities for kids who love reading, and for this Mills was awarded the prestigious Margaret Mahy Medal in 2008 in recognition of his national and international services to children's literature. In addition to this, Mills was also in January 2011 awarded the New Zealand Order of Merit by HM Queen Elizabeth II. The honour provides a way for New Zealand to thank and congratulate individuals who have served their communities and their country well, and to recognize their achievements. It is a tangible mark of the respect in which an individual is held by fellow citizens.

References

Brown, M. (2006) The Kids' Lit Quiz: welcome to the sport of reading, *Innovation*, **33**, December.

Campbell, R. and Green, D. (2006) *Literacies and Learners: current perspectives*, 3rd edn, Pearson.

Chandler, K. (1999) Reading Relationships: parents, adolescents and popular fiction by Stephen King, *Journal of Adolescent and Adult Literacy*, **43** (3), 228–39.

Conlon, E. G., Zimmer-Gembeck, M. J., Creed, P. A. and Tucker, M. (2006) Family History, Self-perceptions, Attitudes and Cognitive Abilities Are Associated with Early Adolescent Reading Skills, *Journal of Research in Reading,* **29** (1), 11–32.

Cunningham, A. E. and Stanovich, K. E. (1991) Tracking the Unique Effects of Print Exposure in Children: associations with vocabulary, general knowledge, and spelling, *Journal of Educational Psychology,* **83**, 264–74.

Good News Bible (1994), 2nd edn, The Bible Society Australia.

Guthrie, J. T. and Humenick, N. M. (2004) Motivating Students to Read: evidence for the classroom practices that increase reading motivation and achievement. In McCardle, P. and Chhabra, V. (eds), *The Voice of Evidence in Reading Research,* Brookes Publishing.

Guthrie, J. T., Laurel, A., Hoa, W., Wigfield, A. and Tonks, S. T. (2007) Reading Motivation and Reading Comprehension Growth in the Later Elementary Years, *Contemporary Educational Psychology,* **32**, 282–313.

Hamer, J. and Adams, P. (2003) *The New Zealand Early Childhood Literacy Handbook, Practical Literacy Ideas for Early Childhood Centres,* Palmerston North: Dunmore Press.

Hamston, J. and Love, K. (2003) 'Reading Relationships': parents, boys and reading as cultural practice, *Australian Journal of Language and Literacy,* **26** (3), 44–57.

Harper, J. (2001) The Kids' Lit Quiz™, *Magpies,* **4**, September.

Harrington, C. (2009) *What Grows an Avid Reader? An investigation into the motivational factors that impact on the reading habits of students in the 11–13 age range,* Charles Sturt.

Hughes-Hassell, S. and Rodge, P. (2007) The Leisure Reading Habits of Urban Adolescents, *International Reading Association,* **51** (1), 22–33.

Krashen, S. (2004) *The Power of Reading, Insights from the Research,* 2nd edn, Heinemann/Libraries Unlimited.

Krashen, S., Lee, S. and McQuillan, J. (2008) Is the Library Important? Multivariate studies at the national and international level, *International Association of School Librarianship,* August.

McKool, S. S. (2007) Factors that Influence the Decision to Read: an investigation of fifth grade students' out-of-school reading habits, *Reading Improvement,* September.

McNaughton, S. (2002) *Meeting of Minds,* Learning Media.

Nagy, W., Anderson, R. and Herman, P. (1987) Learning Word Meanings from Context during Normal Reading, *American Educational Research Journal,* **24**, 237–70.

National Endowment for the Arts (2004) *Reading at Risk,* Library of Congress.

Rogoff, B. (2003) *The Cultural Nature of Human Development,* Oxford University Press.

Strommen, T. L. and Mates, F. B. (2004) Learning to Love Reading: interviews with older children and teens, *International Reading Association*, **48** (3), 188–200.

Williams, E. (2003) Readers Win in Wayne's World, *Times Educational Supplement*, www.tes.co.uk/article.aspx?storycode=378408.

11

Adventures in the book trade: libraries and partnerships

Jacob Hope

Introduction

Libraries have always been about connections: connecting readers to the past, to other cultures and to the vast range of ideas and thinking that document the human race. In the present day, the cultural context within which libraries sit has changed, and there are expectations that libraries should now act as community hubs or offer access to a range of local council services. Whether social, creative or knowledge-based, connections still remain at the heart of the efficient library service. This chapter aims to emphasize and advocate the importance of connections with the book trade as a key component of successful, imaginative and innovative reading development work.

Issues and opportunities

What do we mean when we talk about the book trade? It can refer to agents, who act as intermediaries for authors, negotiating the best deals and selling the rights to manuscripts and ideas – the raw products of the book industry. It can, of course, refer to the publishers, who collaborate with authors to hone those ideas and manuscripts and who package, design and market them to create books that inform, educate and entertain. It can refer to wholesalers, who establish the lines of supply for those books, ensuring that the titles people want and need are available to them. Lastly, it can refer to retailers, who sell the books to the public, organizing displays and promotions to aid that transaction.

Aspects of the work that libraries are engaged in contribute directly to the book trade, particularly in terms of supply and procurement. Other aspects don't always have that same synergy, and there can be tension between the commercial drive and the ethos of reading development, the desire to engender situations where new readers feel that spark of excitement when a book truly resonates with them and, on the occasions when that happens sequentially, developing a new, dedicated and ardent reader. A prime example of this tension occurred in 2008 when the Children's Book Group of the Publishers Association tried to ensure that all books were age banded. This was based on quantitative and qualitative research commissioned by the Publishers Association and carried out by Acacia Avenue which suggested that gift purchasing of books might be significantly increased if more guidance was featured on the books themselves. Information about this can be found on the Publishers Association website (www.publishers.org.uk).

From a purely commercial angle, it made sense: outline the ideal prospective audience and there will be greater clarity as to the market and therefore, presumably, the market will be more empowered to purchase, and to purchase more. However, just as the progression of events in life is rarely neatly sequential, our reading lives also are more complex than that, and, as any reader knows, just as we may choose to read progressively so as to challenge our thoughts, values and abilities, so too we read regressively to cosset and comfort. Reading is special because it has the capacity to simultaneously mirror and enhance our lives. Forget that dialectic by allowing it to become a purely commercially driven venture, and it is locked down in a cold, dark and constrained environment. In just the same way, ignoring some of the developments that arise from commercial strategies will considerably lessen the potential market for reading. Happily, the ideologies of the book trade and libraries are not always in conflict, and when they achieve shared aims and commonality of purpose, innovative reading experiences can be forged.

The bookshop

Access to books and book ownership are the linch-pins of the library service and the bookshop respectively. Tensions have often existed in the relationship between the two, based presumably on the notion that we share the same core audience and that we therefore impinge upon one another's territories. Whilst it is true that the book-reading public is certainly the core audience for us both, the purpose behind usage of the different settings is often distinct. Libraries offer a no-cost, risk-free opportunity for experimentation: to try new authors; to find out more about an emergent interest area; to take a punt on something different that we would not ordinarily have considered. The bookshop, meanwhile, is a place to consolidate existing tastes and interests. We purchase those books with which we know we feel a strong affiliation and that we are likely to wish to return to time and again as the mood takes us, or else those that we desire to give to the people we care about and with whom we share sets of values and ideas. The two do not have to operate in isolation from one another. Working collaboratively with local bookshops offers libraries with an opportunity to engage in activity that might otherwise not have been open to them.

At the time of writing this article, there are 4125 public libraries in the UK, although media coverage at present suggests that numbers of them may be under threat of closure, given local government cuts. Nevertheless, that's a vast network, which makes public libraries the biggest dedicated reading provider in the UK. There is a real opportunity to engage with the book trade and to be key partners in collaborative work by offering extended reach to the reading public. One of the unique selling points of libraries has always been the personalized service they offer to their customers. Rapport and relationship lie at the heart of this, with staff having knowledge of their core users, their tastes and interests. This is something that the commercial sector has tried to replicate, with book chains seeking to counterbalance some of their corporate and centralized ethos through personal staff recommendations, through establishing reading groups and trying to develop greater audience loyalty. Just as the commercial sector has replicated some of the strengths and mainstays of the library system, cross-pollination can occur in the other direction, with ideas coming from bookstores in terms of signage, display and promotion, all of which are key strategies for leveraging greater customer interest and focus upon stock areas within the library.

The post of Reading and Learning Development Manager with Lancashire Libraries has provided the opportunity to work collaboratively with numerous bookstores. At its lowest and most basic level this has been to hold awareness-raising sessions in stores. We held Bookstart (see Chapter 1 for more information on this project) events in a store based in a retail park situated between numerous housing estates. This provided us with the opportunity to extend awareness of the scheme and, by parading in the car park dressed as the Bookstart Bear – a hot and not entirely comfortable activity in midsummer – it was also possible to increase footfall to the bookshop in addition to reaching audiences with whom both organizations might otherwise have struggled to engage.

Bookshops provide another low-level partnership opportunity in regard to point-of-sale material produced by publishers. Libraries do not always have access to this, or are not always necessarily seen as a priority for receiving it. Having links with a bookshop can provide an inroad to gaining these materials if you've had difficulty getting them through your library supplier.

Bookshops also perform an invaluable role when it comes to author events. Having copies of the author's books for sale allows audience members to take away a special, lasting memory, often signed and personalized by the author or illustrator. Having books available for sale in the library can, potentially, meet with staff resistance, but it is a key part of any author event and can be a valuable measure of impact, highlighting a follow-up action by audience members. If reading development is to be a meaningful part of the modern library message, book ownership needs to be recognized as a core element in establishing robust reading cultures.

During her time as Children's Laureate, Anne Fine established the My Home Library website (www.myhomelibrary.org), the premise of which was the understanding that, in addition to the public library, in addition to school libraries, children also needed to be encouraged to develop their own, personal, home libraries and to nurture their own love of books. In Anne Fine's own words: 'Everyone needs a Home Library. Make sure that yours keeps growing. Don't forget that books furnish the mind, and unfurnished minds are EMPTY and TIRESOME.'

It's always worth asking a local bookshop whether it would be willing to sell books at a library event or, if it is unable to attend, to provide copies. It is imperative, if you do this, to ensure that the audience attending the event are aware that books will be available for sale. When contacting bookshops about library events, be clear about what you want, provide an indication of the projected audience size and the proportion of the audience that have bought books at any similar events you have held in the past. If your library service is able to afford copies of books as competition prizes, that offers a guaranteed core sale that will be attractive to the store. Negotiate with the bookshop and ensure that you receive books on a sale-or-return basis. Not all bookshops are willing or able to do this. One strategy, if they are not able to do this, is to ascertain the cost to the store of carriage and ask whether, if the library covered the cost, the store could then participate. This can often be much more cost-effective and risk-free than having to buy the unsold books. Negotiate with the store, too, to establish whether it is willing to provide any form of discount, both for direct sales to libraries, e.g. of competition prizes, and for sales to the audience at large. Having discounted rates to pass on to customers can often be a significant way of driving up sales. The store may wish to have copies signed for sale in-store as an incentive to shoppers, so make this part of your offer. Working collaboratively can have real benefits for both parties and enhance reader experience in both settings.

Strong links with local bookshops can have other benefits, too. It is possible to work collaboratively to make joint pitches to publishers for author visits. Writing a pitch together can enable bidding for bigger-name authors than either party would ordinarily be able to bid for individually. Through sharing resources and facilities bookshops and libraries can strengthen and bolster one another's positions. Libraries are often able to offer access to venues, either using either library buildings themselves or other local authority premises. Through reading groups, publicity in library buildings and, crucially, through direct conversations, libraries can also offer bookshops with reach to a much wider audience. In turn, bookshops are able to provide libraries with access to their customer base and books for sale – a key component of any author event. Pitching for authors will be discussed later in this chapter, when the types of connections that can be forged with publishers are discussed.

As links with bookshops grow, it is possible to explore more innovative ways of working together. This might include planning events in settings thematically appropriate to a visiting author's book. We have held events in Lancaster Maritime Museum, in castles, theme parks and many other venues that provide added audience experience. Robust links with bookshops also allow flexible positioning, so that new opportunities can be seized as they arise. In Lancashire we have been able to work with local bookshops to arrange author gala days and miniature book festivals with programmed author events that include book sales, taster reading-group sessions, reading recommendation sessions, bounce and rhyme sessions and story times (see Appendix 11.1). In doing this, it has been possible to deliver messages jointly about the library service and the bookshop and to give a particularly strong and powerful message about the importance of reading – which, of course, underpins both.

Publishers

Another key area of the book trade is publishers. Publishers provide access to author events as well as to point-of-sale material – posters, show cards and the like. Looking at a publisher's output, it is sometimes easy to be lured into believing that they are much bigger institutions than in reality they are. More often than not, when contacting a publisher your first port of call will be the publicity department. This is often a very small team of people who are attached to numerous authors and are working to a particularly full schedule. It is important to bear this in mind and to think of pitching for any authors you are interested in holding an event with well in advance of your ideal date, particularly if the author you're most interested in is extremely popular and likely to generate a great deal of interest. The types of connection you will have as a library will be of great interest to publishers, so capitalize on your knowledge of local schools and children's book groups and, crucially, your knowledge of and access to some of your most voracious young readers!

At this point it is worth considering the type of information you should aim to provide in your pitch to a publisher for an author event. First, decide what it is that you want. If you are aiming to hold an event with a specific author and are trying to get them as part of a publicity tour, in order to reduce costs, be warned that most authors do not tour more than once or twice in a year at most, and this will usually be for a week or two around a publication date; check dates on Nielsen (www.nielsenbookdata.co.uk) – a bibliographical database available on subscription basis that provides information on book titles for the trade – or on Amazon (www. amazon.co.uk).

Are you able to contribute towards the cost of the visit? If you are pitching for an author as part of a publicity tour it is usual for the author's fees to be waived, but an offer to cover transport costs or accommodation – if needed – can make your bid more attractive to publishers, as well as make the partnership more genuine, thereby showing publishers that you value these opportunities.

If, however, you want to invite an author to attend an event and are able to offer transport, accommodation – if needed – and fees, address your invitation to the author concerned and send it care of the publicity department of the author's publisher. When it comes to authors' fees, it's worth using the Society of Authors' recommended minimum rates as a guide. They are £150 for a single session or £250 for a half-day event and £350 for a full-day event. The Society of Authors' website is at www.societyofauthors.net and it has a valuable set of guidelines for organizing author events.

Your pitch should include the information needed to make a judgement as to the likely success of your event. Detail your venue, giving information on its location, availability and audience capacity. Next consider audience recruitment, for example, that you are anticipating having an invited school audience. School visits are undoubtedly the easiest events to organize, but if you are planning to invite the school into the library you will need to ascertain beforehand that it will accept the invitation and check the length of notice required by the school. It is often the case that schools have to notify parents in advance, so never be tempted to leave things until the last minute. If your event is a public one, think carefully around how achievable audience recruitment will be. Experience has taught that it is usually the case that audience recruitment is slower and harder than anticipated, rather than quicker and easier! One tip, if you are recruiting an audience, is to think of a core group that you can invite so that you know you will have a minimum number of people. These might be Cubs, Brownies or other youth groups. Equally, you might decide to offer the event to local Chatterbooks reading groups. Showing that you've thought about audience and have identified a core group will strengthen your pitch.

Always be sure to include information on how your book sales will be arranged. As discussed above, working collaboratively with local bookshops is often the least complicated way of arranging this and demonstrates to publishers that you are working jointly with the local bookstores towards shared aims and that your planning is robust. It is advisable always to check with your bookshop, prior to pitching, that it is happy to be included and would support you. Publicity departments may follow up on stores named in pitches – if there were an obvious lack of communication it might well jeopardize your pitch, and, furthermore, the library service's relationship with the publisher. Outline in your pitch any media coverage that you intend to secure as part of the event, as this will help to showcase the author and book alike, providing added value for the publisher and making your pitch a well-rounded event package. List your contact details on the pitch, and be prepared for disappointment, as often there are far more venues vying for authors than it is feasible for any one author to visit as part of a tour.

If you are successful in your pitch, consider asking the publicity department whether it would be able to send you a press release for the book, as well as a biography and publicity photograph of the author. These will be invaluable in preparing your audience. As best practice, I tend to request the first three chapters of a book in electronic format so that they can be used to provide a taster for the audience, helping to imbue in them the ideas and style of the book prior to the visit, and generating further interest. If a local bookshop is arranging sales, it is inadvisable to loan copies of the author's latest title to more than 20% of the audience, as this will adversely affect sales and be detrimental to your partnership with the store. Providing a taster is instead an excellent way of giving a flavour of the book without running the risk of compromising potential sales. It may be that the publisher can provide some point-of-sale publicity material to help generate interest in your event. Even if posters have not been produced for the book or author you will be working with, many publishers will be willing to provide high-quality jacket enlargements, which can create a real splash and interest point in displays.

When researching publisher contacts for your favoured author, the Publishers Publicity Circle is an invaluable resource that is worth its weight in gold. Its website features a directory listing publicity contact names and details for almost every publisher in the UK. If you do not have direct contact details for a particular publisher, this website should always be your first port of call. Having a named contact offers a much better overall chance of success. The URL for this helpful website is www.publisherspublicitycircle. co.uk and the directory section is definitely worth bookmarking!

As part of your post-event evaluation process, it is best practice to follow up with publishers, thanking them for their involvement and support and providing them with a photograph or two (remembering that you will need parental consent for any photographs that include children) from the event, details of final audience figures and book sales. This helps to consolidate links with the publisher and develop stronger rapport, meaning, hopefully, that your service can enjoy a continued working relationship with it in future.

Looking for an author

Many authors are now deluged with event requests, and both they and their publishers have difficulty keeping up with them. Accordingly, a number of authors now work with event agencies, which deal with their bookings and help to ensure that every aspect of an event is in place so as to give it the best footing and chance of success. Two of the largest agencies are Speaking of Books (www.speakingofbooks.co.uk), which has an impressive list of some very high-profile names, and Authors Abroad (www.authorsabroad.com). Both organizations take a percentage cut from the author's fee, which can consequently be higher, reflecting the expert advice and guidance that are provided both to the event organizers and to the authors. Working collaboratively with organizations like these can be especially time-efficient when organizing an author gala day or festival. The Contact an Author website is another invaluable resource for identifying authors and illustrators suitable for particular themes or age groups and is run by The Wordpool children's books website (www.contactanauthor.co.uk).

An organization that is less commercial in nature but is equally valuable as a resource is the Scattered Authors Society (www.scatteredauthors.org). This is a group for anyone who is a published writer for children or young adults. The society is unable at present to accept membership from self-published authors. It has a membership base of about 200 authors from across the UK and its website features a very useful database of authors that is helpfully split down into categories for primary and secondary audiences and details authors' locations and interests in events. In addition to providing a point of contact for authors, the society produces its own blog and holds annual meetings that provide a support network for authors who are geographically dispersed. It is thus worth advocating membership of the group to new authors whom you have visiting the library, as it can offer valuable peer support and can also provide other interested parties with an opportunity to host events with the author.

A further helpful development has been Children's Reading Partners (CRP), a national consortium of children's publishers and librarians set up by The Reading Agency in 2008. This is a major cross-industry collaboration involving the entire UK library network and, to date, 13 publishers. Its aim is to improve the way that publishers and libraries work together to widen children's access to books, authors and reading resources. The network of regional CRP library representatives circulates news of promotions and publisher offers, but it is also worth looking regularly at The Noticeboard on The Reading Agency's website (www.readingagency.org.uk/calendar). Publishers will post details of author tours, free books and competitions. Library authorities can also post details of their own events and requests for author visits.

Lancashire Reads: a case study

The final part of this chapter is a case study focusing on a major reading-development promotion held in Lancashire. The purpose is to showcase how links to the book trade can provide added value, making reading-development promotions more effective, widespread and robust.

In the National Year of Reading in 2008, Lancashire took the ethos of the City Reads promotion and scaled it out across the whole of the county, trying to encourage as many as possible of the county's one million population to read the chosen title. It was decided to replicate this activity, focusing on a different book, in the autumn of 2010. The title chosen was the Carnegie-commended *Up on Cloud Nine* by Anne Fine, as it featured health, education, social services professions and parents. This provided a close match to the Every Child Matters agenda and thus offered partnership opportunities. Every Child Matters is a UK Government initiative established in 2003. Its main aims are for every child, whatever their background or circumstances, to have the support they need to:

- be healthy
- stay safe
- enjoy and achieve
- make a positive contribution
- achieve economic well-being.

Each of these themes has a detailed framework, the achievement of whose outcomes requires multi-agency partnerships working together, and Lancashire Reads matched well to this agenda.

Anne Fine's books are published by five different publishers in the UK, so the initiative gave a real opportunity to join up with each of them. As Anne's writing ranges from picture books for very young children right through to adult novels, there was an opportunity to use the initiative as a family-reading development promotion, spring-boarding people into Anne's backlist of writing, and from there into the wider library catalogue. Each of Anne's publishers was contacted and agreed to provide copies of books as competition prizes and point-of-sale materials, and in one instance we were even able to secure funding to enable the purchase of sufficient copies of an out-of-print title to make it viable to bring it back into print. Keeping publishers up to date with the events that were scheduled, with partners, with details of the promotion and the ways in which we would be engaging with schools, book groups and other organizations leveraged greater support from them and secured their involvement.

Working in collaboration with the publishers, we were also able to ensure that local bookshops were able to participate in the promotion by offering discounted Anne Fine stock as an incentive to customers to buy her books and take part in the initiative. This was achieved through the publishers' local sales representatives, who advocated the scheme and ensured that the stores which they served were aware of it.

Random House Children's Books, who published our focus book, *Up on Cloud Nine*, under its Corgi imprint, was particularly supportive and we were able to liaise with its editorial, design and publicity departments to get quotes from the book and photographs of members of staff so that we could produce an A1 display board tracking the production process of a novel. This began with Anne describing some of her inspirations for writing and then moved on to describe the agent's role (provided by Anne's agent, Anthony Gough of David Higham Associates). The display then moved on to the editorial role, the designer's role in typesetting and in designing the cover of the book and an overview of the publicist's role. It then featured an extract from a newspaper review and ended with comments from one of our own young judges from the Lancashire Book of the Year award, thus charting the production process from the initial idea through to the eventual reader. These boards were then provided to each district central library so as to give library visitors an insight into the publication process of a book and were part of a phased publicity plan that was based on the size and footfall of the libraries. Links with the book trade were integral to our ability to do this.

Links with Anne's agent, Anthony Gough, allowed us access to the filed press reviews and coverage for each of Anne's books, and these provided a fascinating social history that was used as part of a rolling PowerPoint display, created for display on plasma screens in libraries. In many instances an author's agent can be identified via an internet search using the author's name along with 'agent' or 'agency', which in many cases will return a result. If this is not successful, it should be possible to track agents down via the author's publisher, although when you approach the publisher you should outline your reasons for wanting to know. Agents can be a route to contacting authors: for larger-scale promotions; backlist reviews; up-to-date details on film options, audio rights sales and, in many instances, the sale of rights and publication of titles internationally. The latter was used in Lancashire Reads because we forged links with schools in some of Lancashire's twinned towns – towns in different countries with co-operative agreements to share cultural and commercial aims. Links were established with further education colleges in twinned towns that offered modern language courses. We were able to pair up schools and ensure that English students read copies of the book in French and German and that partner schools in those countries read Anne's books in English, providing another level of interest. Tracking down foreign rights was also useful as the starting-point for a display of the various editions and jacket images of the book from around the world, thus giving a global perspective to the project. The display was hosted in three of our libraries with the highest footfall so as to demonstrate the ways that literature is presented and marketed in different cultures.

Working with publishers meant that we were able to liaise with Anne directly early on in the planning process, making her aware of the project and its intentions. As a result, and thanks to the support of the University of Central Lancashire, who provided the means to do this, we were able to negotiate to film Anne for a series of three vodcasts in which she spoke about her work for very young children, gave an insight into the writing of *Up on Cloud Nine* and talked about the inspiration and basis for her adult novels. The vodcasts were uploaded to our website as part of an interactive micro site dedicated to the promotion. We were also able to book a photographer to take photographs of Anne in some of the places in her neighbourhood that were of importance to her and were able to make an agreement to take photographs of her study for a 360-degree virtual tour on our website. This was another route for providing readers with an opportunity to gain rare access to the author's world.

Each year an annual book fair is held in Bologna, Italy. This is a dedicated fair for the sale of rights for children's books. The organizers of the fair are keen to develop the field and raise awareness through a series of awards that recognize key publishers, titles and illustrators who are felt to be worthy of international focus. The selection process for these awards involves an international jury. Each year a prestigious illustration competition is held to leverage the focus on an amazing wealth of international talent and styles. Each of the illustrators selected from among the nominees is published in an annual catalogue and is featured on a dedicated website. Using this catalogue, we were able to identify the selected UK entrants, contact them and commission them to produce an original illustration based around *Up on Cloud Nine* that would be used as electronic postcards to help promote the book and provide insight into its content.

At a more local level, we contacted our local voluntary sector organizations and community literary groups to ensure that they were aware of the promotion. This was particularly successful in the case of Lancaster Litfest. Through liaising with it, we were able to work collaboratively and schedule two events with Anne as part of the programme for its festival – an evening event for adults and a Saturday morning event for families. This brought in an additional partner and widened the reach of the promotion locally.

Engaging with different groups to secure partnership opportunities was vital to the success of this project. A time-efficient way of doing this is to produce a project briefing. For a project briefing, outline:

- the aim of your project
- the objectives that you hope to achieve
- when it will happen, so that the timescale is clear
- how you will go about doing it
- what help and support you need from partner organizations.

A short project briefing will provide clarity of purpose and can produce parity of aims, purposes and values between partner organizations.

Conclusion

Connections with the book trade can provide real opportunities to bolster, add value to and to create reading-development practices. The book trade, like libraries, faces many challenges in these changing times. Printing technology means that print-on-demand holds the promise of ensuring that, effectively, no book need ever go out of print. Electronic books are likely to alter the habits and patterns of consumers and borrowers alike in accessing their reading material. Against all of these changes, however, there will always be a place for informed, knowledgeable ambassadors who are able to advocate reading not as a dull, solitary and outmoded activity but as a creative, engaging and relevant pursuit that in subtle ways can alter who we are and how we think. To achieve this, libraries need to avoid tensions with the book trade and achieve a synergy with it, so that power and thrust can fuel the message about the importance of reading and develop and grow its market through devising new routes into books.

References

Authors Abroad, www.authorsabroad.com.

Children's Reading Partners, www.readingagency.org.uk/children/childrens-reading-partners.

Contact an Author, www.contactanauthor.co.uk.

Every Child Matters, www.education.gov.uk/consultations/downloadableDocs/EveryChildMatters.pdf.

My Home Library, www.myhomelibrary.org

Publishers Association

www.publishers.org.uk/index.php?option=com_content&view=category&layout
=blog&id=256&Itemid=413.

Publishers Publicity Circle, www.publisherspublicitycircle.co.uk.

Scattered Authors Society, www.scatteredauthors.org.

Society of Authors, www.societyofauthors.org.

Speaking of Books, www.speakingofbooks.co.uk.

Appendix 11.1: Sample children's programme

12

The hard-to-reach reader in the 21st century

Andrew Blake, Julia Hale and Emma Sherriff

Introduction

Young people aged 11–19 are perceived as a challenging group to engage in using public libraries. This chapter will examine projects delivered by library services in the most deprived areas of the UK's south-west peninsula, endeavouring to connect with some of the most hard-to-reach groups of young people in the region. Our aim is to identify how libraries can go about removing barriers to library use through innovative schemes of outreach work. We conclude with the reasons for successful outcomes.

What are the obstacles to young people's using public libraries?

This is a question we often hear in dialogues with librarians, youth agencies and young people. One stereotype of the younger library user is of the 'bookish' loner, socially outcast by their peers. There is also the view that libraries are fundamentally 'uncool' and have nothing to offer the 21st-century teenager. Many librarians already doing positive work with teenagers may view these as unfounded prejudices and lazy clichés; however, there is plenty of evidence on which to base these views, confirmed by dwindling borrower figures amongst this age group.

In 2006, reports from the Audit Commission and the House of Commons Select Committee on Culture, Media and Sport had noted the small (and still reducing) use of public libraries amongst 14–35 year-olds. In response, the Museums, Libraries and Archives Council, Department for Culture, Media and Sport and Laser Foundation commissioned *A Research Study of 14–35 year olds for the Future Development of Public Libraries* (2006). This report aimed 'to provide evidence for potential future strategies for the public library service that will result in increased usage amongst the 14–35 age group'. Interviews were held with 15 groups of young people from different parts of the country, chosen without reference to whether they were library members. The researchers found a 'deeply entrenched negative perception' of libraries and that the majority of existing and unmodernized libraries were seen as dirty and uncared for, with old and poor stocks and an oppressive atmosphere. 'Users turned out to be a minority. Even they were reported as disappointed by the breadth and depth of stock and its lack of currency.'

The research concluded that perceptions could be changed when young people experienced modernized services but that libraries needed to address negative perceptions arising from the view that libraries 'are not for me' by providing evidence that library users are 'people like me'. To do this, libraries would need to take into account the differing needs of this age bracket by moving away from a one-size-fits-all approach.

Who are the hard-to-reach?

Attracting young people to libraries is difficult. What is even more challenging is that it is the hard-to-reach young people who need libraries most that are the least likely to use them. In the particular context of this book, they are missing out on the educational, emotional and social benefits that reading provides.

To turn this situation around so that the library becomes an inclusive destination, who and where are the young people that we should especially be trying to target? In Plymouth's and Dorset's libraries there were already services for the engaged, dedicated young reader. Existing teen reading groups and young people's involvement in stock selection kept library collections fresh and appealing in both small community and larger town-centre libraries. The focus turned to the more hard-to-reach young people, those unmotivated to visit the library because they struggle to read because of either a lack of interest or motivation, learning difficulty or disadvantage.

'Hard-to-reach' is a broad term used by agencies in UK local government to describe particular parts of the community that are difficult to involve in public participation. It often refers to a hidden population, those who are slipping through the net because of particular circumstances and are failing to access the services that are available to them (Brackertz, 2007).

Those defined as 'hard-to-reach' are not a homogeneous group. They can but do not always include ethnic minorities, lesbian, gay and transgendered people, drug and alcohol dependents, victims of domestic violence, gypsy travellers, isolated rural communities or people living with mental or physical disabilities.

Although hard-to-reach young people may also belong to one or more of the groups mentioned above, some circumstances are unique to under-18s. These include looked after children (children in care), young carers (children who are the primary carers for a disabled or dependent parent) and young offenders (children who have committed a criminal offence). They can also include those engaging in risk-taking behaviour such as sexual activity and drug and alcohol use from an early age. Many hard-to-reach young people have also suffered from neglect, physical, sexual and emotional abuse or have witnessed domestic abuse in their homes.

The reasons why hard-to-reach young people are of concern in the medical and educational fields is that they tend to have poorer health and educational outcomes. Therefore reaching them is of particular concern to those working with young people and in youth services (Earthman et al., 1999; The Reading Agency, 2008). As Jonathan Douglas, Director of the National Literacy Trust, has stated:

> Libraries make the most difference to those who have the fewest books at home, where parental engagement is likely to be weakest and amongst those least likely to buy books or value reading. Libraries have a disproportionate benefit for the most disadvantaged.
>
> (Douglas, 2010)

How we included hard-to-reach young people in Plymouth and Dorset

The outreach projects discussed in this section are with groups of young people who required support to access library services because they did not use them at all. The focus for the four projects was young people with behavioural problems and learning difficulties (HeadSpace); young people who had offended or were at risk of offending (Literacy with a Twist); young parents (Young Mums to Be [YMTB]); and 16–18 year-olds not participating in any post-16 learning (Entry to Employment [E2E]). (For background information on all projects see Appendices 12.2–12.5). Although presenting different and complex challenges, what all these young people have in common is that their circumstances can often prevent them from accessing mainstream services and they can be classified as hard-to-reach.

Library planning for and identification of hard-to-reach groups requires local knowledge about socio-economic factors and the services already operating in the area. Meeting with other service managers (in particular, the youth service) was key to identifying where need existed and how the library services could fill the gaps in Plymouth and Dorset. This partnership enabled us to incorporate the HeadSpace and Out of the Box programmes – national and regional projects developed in conjunction with The Reading Agency and the National Youth Board.

All the young people in the projects were from a low socio-economic background, living in deprived, predominantly White British urban areas with high unemployment, poor health outcomes and few affordable facilities for young people. Most had low levels of school engagement and qualifications. Low parental education, poor housing and chaotic family backgrounds with a high level of conflict were also common features across the groups, as were short attention spans and poor literacy. Low expectations for the future, including careers or other long-term goals in general, were identified across all the young people.

Since its launch in January 2008, HeadSpace Efford, Plymouth, has engaged over 200 young people who would not otherwise have used a library. The local youth service team leader is impressed by the young people who now regularly attend HeadSpace, because of their previous non-reader status and behaviour.

The experience of the outreach support officer working with these young people was to observe the social context of the neighbourhood, and a culture amongst families and peers that has led to a 'survival of the fittest' attitude. The young person who shouts loudest gets the most attention and is dominant in the peer group, presenting ongoing challenges. Several of the young people regularly get into trouble at school and are difficult to work with at times in the library.

With both the YMTB and E2E groups in Dorset the library service recognized that the first step, as in most work with young people, was getting to know the young people, their interests, their reading experiences and whether or not they used the library (or, in the case of YMTB, if they thought they might when their babies were born). The initial work with the YMTB group then took a two-pronged approach – finding out what the barriers to using the library service were for them as young adults and finding out what the barriers for usage would be for them as parents.

Specific barriers for the hard-to-reach and how they were overcome

Behavioural problems

Behavioural problems can be a barrier to working with young people, but all the projects have chosen to adopt a new approach to dealing with them in the library. The key has been to work closely with partners in youth work and youth offending services and to employ strategies that enable these young people to access library activities and, in particular, to understand that if they operate within given boundaries they will be treated fairly. At HeadSpace several stages are worked through in order to engage hard-to-reach young people in positive activities. Key to this has been a group contract, in which time is dedicated to sitting down as a group and discussing what the staff and young people can agree is acceptable behaviour and how the group can be better organized. This process is called 'group forming' and is a technique commonly used by youth offending services with challenging young people.

Over a number of weeks the signed group contract is applied and the young people go through a process of 'group norming'. This refers to the behavioural norm expected of the young people during HeadSpace sessions. During this time, young people may receive warnings. Some will ultimately be given a weekly ban, as agreed in the contract.

Occasionally a new group or a large number of new members will start to attend sessions and the next stage – 'group storming' – begins as young people test the boundaries in order to find out what is acceptable. This triggers a need to start the forming process again and ensure that everyone is familiar with the contract that needs to be upheld. If the contract is not adhered to, bans will be issued and the individuals concerned will not be allowed to return to sessions for a number of weeks. If the behaviour is not corrected after several opportunities, a young person will be permanently banned. Fortunately, this is very rare, because we do not want to start a pattern of social exclusion in the project.

Self-esteem

Existing negative stereotypes about young people are perpetuated by the media, which can further isolate the hard-to-reach. Young, never-married mothers are stigmatized and young males on the street are viewed as threatening. Many hard-to-reach groups are seen as being 'undeserving' and symptomatic of a 'broken' society.

Young people do not live in a bubble and are well aware of the perceived threat of the 'hoodie' and the 'benefit scrounger' and are sensitive to how people interact with them. This adds to the low self-esteem that many of them already feel and that is disguised behind their acts of bravado and loud behaviour.

Low self-esteem can be a barrier to working with young people in any context and is linked closely with peer relationships, poverty and literacy. Arguably, many young people who avoid talking to librarians or workers behave in this way because of a lack of confidence. Even a young person who is confident with their peers can at the same time be very self-critical and sensitive. Challenging behaviour presented during a library activity can mask the fact that a young person is struggling to read and cannot participate.

Relationships with young people are a key priority. The team of librarians, volunteers and youth workers provides positive role models for the young people. The aim is to develop relationships that enable them to see a future in work or study for themselves. It is important that the team is welcoming, friendly and non-judgemental, with a passion for supporting and encouraging young people to reach their potential in a safe and neutral space.

As a result of forming close working partnerships with the youth service and youth offending service, HeadSpace benefits by having a youth support worker and youth inclusion programme worker from each service, respectively. Their role is to support the lead librarian. The librarians learn from their way of working with young people and develop these skills for themselves. The youth worker leads on accreditation, and young people are rewarded for their efforts in helping the library and community both during and outside of HeadSpace time. The youth worker uses a local youth award and AQA (Assessment and Qualifications Alliance) exam board schemes.

The youth offending worker leads on targeted support for young people deemed to be at risk of offending. The worker meets with individuals from HeadSpace outside of group time in order to mentor them, and sets targets for improvement in a range of areas.

All of the projects worked to increase confidence by getting the young people involved in activities that encouraged their talents, in order to increase their self-esteem. Encouraging young people to give each other compliments and praise was also useful. Providing informal reading and writing support during activities was important for engagement in the projects. There were opportunities for youth workers to discuss personal issues with the young people and make referrals to Child and Adolescent Mental Health Services (CAMHS) if required.

Drug and alcohol abuse

Any young person who is reporting that they are regularly drinking alcohol or taking drugs can be at risk of not focusing clearly on their learning. HeadSpace has overcome this barrier by building in regular youth worker-led informal sessions and quizzes on teen issues. This has sometimes been sparked by young people's remarks and conversations about drink and drugs during the sessions. When library staff were concerned for a young person's welfare, referrals for further advice and support were made through the youth service.

Poor nutrition

At HeadSpace many of the young people were observed to be eating sugary snacks rather than proper meals, which was, arguably, reflected in their ability to function and in their behaviour and appearance. We used our wide selection of recipe books to get them reading, cooking and planning balanced, nutritious menus. Our recent smoothie-making and 'Camping-stove Come Dine with Me' activities covered a range of healthy options and provided them with an opportunity to learn about planning a menu, the importance of healthy diets and cooking skills. A couple of small flowerbeds in the library garden were turned over to HeadSpace in the spring of 2010, giving the young people a place to grow strawberries, tomatoes, salad and herbs. They also planted an apple tree.

Lack of interest in reading

In the local area surrounding the Efford HeadSpace, literacy has been identified as a problem for both adults and young people. In any context this is a significant barrier to library use. Many of the young people do not have books at home, which suggests that reading is not encouraged as a leisure activity. Although most of the activities involve reading in some form or another, it is made clear that young people do not necessarily have to sit and read books in order to participate in a session.

They are much more likely to pick up a book in later sessions than they are at the beginning of their attendance; this is a marathon, rather than a sprint. Similarly, the young offenders in Literacy with a Twist can be very dismissive of reading anything at all on starting the programme, and an E2E case study describes Jade, who sat with her arms folded, saying that she didn't like reading and refused to join in with the weekly one-hour session where the youth workers encouraged the group to relax with books, magazines and newspapers.

A combination of factors will usually determine whether a young person feels this way, and these include: a disengagement with education (and the connection with books); the type of books read in the classroom; absence of books at home; parents with literacy problems; peer relationships; and a reputation amongst peers.

The subject matter can be important when it comes to reading and writing. First you have to get to know what the young people are interested in. This will determine what book they might read in the future – for example, a footballer's autobiography or a book about tattoos. Relevance is the key.

For example, after several sessions of getting to know Jade, it was discovered that although she was not into reading she loved cartoon programmes such as *The Simpsons* and *Futurama*. The librarian then provided the centre with one or two Simpsons comic collections, which were just left on a table in the centre. Jade picked up one of the books and flicked through it, reading it and laughing. She then regularly requested more Simpsons comics until she had exhausted the library service's stock. By this point she was comfortable with reading and moved on to other books that sparked her interest, such as Horrible Histories, other comics and some fantasy/adventure novels.

Similarly, at HeadSpace they ensured that there were plenty of magazines and papers available to browse, based on their young people's interests; for example, many boys were arriving at sessions by bike, so BMX magazines were made available as well as the more common celebrity gossip material aimed at this age group. Regular book buys with young people are also arranged at the city-centre Waterstones. As a result of involving challenging young people in stock selection, the library's book-issue figures at Efford have increased, particularly with manga and graphic novels.

Some of the E2E group asked for books about a number of subjects that they obviously felt the library service would not be able to offer, such as sex and drugs. The librarian took along a selection of books about these subjects and the group was surprised that this stock was available. This led to a number of discussions, first with the youth reading and learning librarian, in order to find out what other subjects were covered by the library service's stock. These discussions also provided the youth workers with a chance to talk about a variety of topics that the young people had asked for books about. From this point on, the link between the E2E group and the library service benefited in two ways: first, it acted as an 'ice-breaker' between the young people and the librarian, and second, the youth workers understood the resources that the library service could provide to support the subjects covered by the course.

Another method used to break down the literacy barrier is hosting author events at HeadSpace. So far, the young people have met top teen authors Joanna Nadin, Cathy Cassidy and Marcus Sedgwick. Meeting the author face to face can help young people to understand the birth and journey of writing a book, and they are then keen to read it afterwards.

Many of the sessions with hard-to-reach young people were based around informal discussions led by library and youth staff, using gossip magazines. Celebrity culture appeared highly influential across the groups, especially among the young women, and particularly with regard to the appearance and behaviour of high-profile young women. Through talking, some young mothers admitted that they felt under pressure to conform to the image of immaculate hair and make-up. These discussions showed that, as the projects progressed, the young people were talking more about their reading, were reading more and feeling comfortable about doing so. Reflection on their reading did require prompting from the workers, so staff needed to persevere in order to keep the discussion on track.

Once a relationship was established with the group, some visits took on a more structured format. For example, in one session the youth librarian discussed the importance of books and reading from a very young age and the variety of materials available to encourage a child to engage in books at all stages of their childhood.

Even these more structured sessions were interactive, with the group being encouraged to pick whichever of the baby books appealed to them, and for whatever reason. This meant that by the end of the session the group had had a chance to look at a variety of books and also to hear about a number of other titles.

Literacy skills

Many of the young people choose not to read in their own time because they struggle to read a sentence on their own. A recurrent problem is that disengaged young people have missed crucial parts of schooling, and this leads to great gaps in their reading skills. Some members of the YMTB group were not confident in their ability to read and some felt that the library was irrelevant to them, an attitude that was mirrored by the E2E group.

However, everyone is visually literate and a double page of a striking silent graphic novel enlarged to A3 size is the perfect way to introduce talking about books (see Appendix 12.3). The young person learns to read the image and interpret the story from pictures. In pairs they can write their own story from the page and decide on the characters, plot line and title. Choosing books with interesting content, like graphic novels and manga, with a small amount of text, can take this activity further.

All the team members – librarians, youth workers and volunteers – are encouraged to look at books, newspapers and magazines during HeadSpace time. In doing this, the aim is to generate an informal discussion of reading likes and dislikes. Informal support with reading and writing is something often provided along with help with homework. Young people can bring in work to complete at any time.

It is important to understand that the young people can find it difficult to participate in an activity in a formal way. Some young people will immediately dismiss an activity if it involves sitting around a table with a blank sheet of paper in front of them, as it reminds them too much of school.

The HeadSpace group has been running for three years and the young people who initially joined at the ages of 13 and 14 are now looking for employment and volunteering opportunities. Librarians will spend one-to-one time with young people at the computer to help put together a good CV that demonstrates their skills and experience, including their learning whilst volunteering or taking part in HeadSpace activities.

The library and librarian stereotypes

If library staff persist in presenting a negative attitude to young people and to working with them, this can be a significant barrier for the hard-to-reach. Library professionals need to look at themselves and their services through the eyes of young people who have a preconceived idea of what a library is. How young people respond to that idea can be a barrier to engaging them. The most common notion at the beginning of the projects was that when in the library you must be silent, you are forbidden to eat or drink and you must read a book! In Plymouth, many young people are shocked to discover that the library is quite a different place during

HeadSpace time on Tuesday evenings.

HeadSpace challenges the stereotype by creating a relaxed, safe space for young people where they can spend time talking with friends and staff, with a hot drink. Young people are asked for their ideas about what activities and projects they should be involved in. Young people are actively encouraged to contribute. This has led to the delivery of a programme of positive and creative youth-led activities.

A big barrier to young people's using the library service comes from the image they have of libraries. In Dorset a member of staff from one of the local libraries attended when the YMTB group was having a focus group about reading and she was able to dispel many of the stereotypical views held – for example, that library staff are always strict and you have to be silent in the library.

Some members of the YMTB group described their local community library as 'not for us', saying that it was only there for older people and they did not feel welcome. When the library manager of this library retired, three of the YMTB group who lived in the area were invited to be part of the recruitment process for a new library manager. They were given training on equal opportunities, looked at the person specification and devised questions that they felt would help to find the ideal candidate for the post. They spent a day interviewing and their opinions formed part of the final decision.

By building up a relationship with the library staff, young people will feel more able to ask about what the library has to offer and to relay their views and fears about using the library. This also means that the library staff can reassure young people that libraries are relevant and welcoming to everyone within the community. For example, before the E2E group visited one of the libraries together, the children and young people's mobile library visited the Weymouth youth centre. This offered the group a snapshot of the stock available through the library service, and another opportunity to meet and have a positive experience with a member of staff from their local library.

By having a good knowledge of the stock available across all areas a librarian will be able to find stock that meets an individual's needs. This will highlight to young people the fact that the library service can cater for everyone, regardless of interests and ability. Through regular contact, the youth librarian was able to provide a stock that was tailored towards the needs of the individuals within the group and aimed at their interests, reading habits and abilities. All of this work helped to break down the barriers that the young people felt were preventing them from using the library.

The Dorset projects succeeded for a number of reasons: in both instances both library and youth service staff were keen for the partnership to form and be successful. Also, staff at all levels were signed up to and keen to meet outcomes that achieved mutual targets. A third factor was the approach with the young people, the relationships that were formed over time and the more structured work that took place once the relationships had been formed. This meant that the young people were, hopefully, seeing the links with the library not as something they were forced to do, but as something that they were actually enjoying.

Special educational needs

HeadSpace members sometimes have a learning difficulty such as dyslexia, or an autistic spectrum disorder such as Asperger's syndrome. In order to prevent this being a barrier to their taking part, staff liaise with parents about any special needs so as to support these young people in the best way possible. The most important thing is to understand properly what the condition means for the young person and to ensure that the activities fit, or to give them an alternative that suits. The second most important thing is to ensure that the group understands their difference and what that means for them. Young people are very accepting, helpful and understanding when they have been given the information.

Peers

Peer relationships can be a barrier in engaging young people in libraries. Some are happy to simply attend sessions, but not to volunteer or make any further commitment. This can lead to issues within the peer group. Bullying has been a serious issue that HeadSpace has had to address frequently. Using 'Teen Talk' materials supplied by the Youth Offending Prevention Team to generate a discussion and get young people thinking about discrimination and name calling has been essential in overcoming this barrier. Setting targets for the young people is also a useful way of shaping their personal development. The outcome has been a much more understanding and accepting peer group who are able to ask questions if they are unsure.

Poverty

Poverty is a highly stigmatized social position and the experience of poverty in an affluent society can be particularly isolating and socially damaging for young people. A young person's experiences of poverty are not isolated from other factors in their lives, and complex social, cultural and economic processes and divisions create particular challenges for families. As contemporary childhood becomes more commodified, it is important to understand the impact of poverty and how it affects young people.

Many of the young people come from poor backgrounds where there are no books in the home and they may not have been able to afford to buy books even should they have wanted to. Neither have they been able to pay library fines if they are existing library members. In Plymouth, they worked with library staff to ensure that the young people were helped to understand that there is no charge for being a member of the library if items are returned on time. Otherwise it can be expensive, especially if you hire DVDs and bring them back late.

When given the opportunity to buy a book for themselves, some of the E2E young people in Dorset said that such a purchase was 'a waste of money'; their financial priorities were rent, food, clothes and leisure interests that they put way ahead of reading. The YMTB group took the most time and care in choosing suitable books for their babies during a trip to Waterstones. However, both these groups took pride in the ownership of their own books and were keen to take them home, rather than to use them as a basis for the next session at the youth centre.

Theft culture

This was a particular issue for young offenders. When the Literacy with a Twist programme started in 2006, librarians were unsure if any of the items borrowed would be returned. Happily, this has not been a problem and very few young people have not returned items. Theft is discussed outside of the literacy sessions with workers and Police Community Support Officers. Staff accepted that there was an element of risk in loaning items to these young people, but also felt that it was preferable to write off any unreturned items if they had kept a book that they enjoyed. It is interesting to note that numbers of unreturned items are no higher in this group than for other borrowers.

Banning orders from local library

Many of the young people involved in the Plymouth projects had received banning letters from the library because of earlier incidents of anti-social behaviour. Supervised visits to the library were agreed, and enabled the young people to meet staff on a more positive footing. The Library Outreach Support Officer built a relationship between the young people and staff to enable a fresh start. This challenged the young people's negative impressions of staff and, as a result, some people apologized for their behaviour. One young person now regularly visits the library to use the computers, and the library staff look after his headphones when he is not there because they are not safe at home.

Top tips for creating access

It is important that we show young people that we understand. We understand that they have busy lives and may not remember to bring their books back on time, and will make more noise when they come in with friends, but library staff can make time to talk to them. We want young people to come to their library and use it.

Libraries need to provide a space for young people where they can see what is relevant to them and use it. Provide dedicated opening times that suit young people and recognize that older young people need a different approach to 11 and 12 year-olds. Young people aged 13 and over may want to go to a group that is open later in the evening – otherwise they might be out on the street, cold, bored and at risk. Explain to young people that they are welcome to visit during the week, but that they need to consider other users at those times.

Building relationships with young people helps us to engage them in discussions about reading. Encourage and support participation. Young people want to be involved in projects, trips and helping out at events. Offer the opportunity to all of the young people but be clear about your expectations, roles and start and finish times. Give clear instructions about the activity and make sure that you have permission from their parents or guardians.

Offer volunteering opportunities and accreditation. Young people are more likely to volunteer to help the library if they have a good relationship with you, and will approach you when they are ready. Once a young person has one volunteering award, this tends to lead them to ask where to go next. Be ready, and make sure that any enquiries from their friends are followed up.

Library activities should be youth-led, practical, relevant, informal and creative. Ask the young people for their ideas and present activities in a way that suits their learning style. Group work may be difficult with young people who have behavioural problems; split them into smaller groups or zone the activities around the library.

Ensure that your expectations are realistic and consider both the young person's ability to read and their attitude to libraries. There are some young people who may never return to the library, or may return when they are adults with children of their own. Relax! This is fine, as everyone's journey is different. An authoritarian approach will not win the war.

Working with partners to improve your service will help you to manage your group and enjoy your role. Partner support will enable you to resolve any concerns quickly and free you up to focus on library matters when you need to.

Invest time in learning about the needs of your young people. There are plenty of free local courses available, delivered by local authorities, as well as charitable and voluntary organizations that can give you a one-day overview of a particular issue. This will leave you better equipped to spot the signs of potential problems and to prevent their escalation.

Enjoy your work and be passionate about libraries. Young people can tell if adults are happy working with them, and are just as perceptive about unenthusiastic body language or tone of voice. At 12 or 13, they may mock you for your love of reading, but by 16 they will be asking you how you got to be in your role and enquiring about work experience and job opportunities.

Conclusion

It is essential that we embed a new approach to delivering library services in order to engage the hard-to-reach young person.

First we should look at altering our view of these young people. Although often challenging, it is also extremely rewarding to work with such strong characters with a spark and passion for what they love and hate. We should encourage and enable them to shape library services for the future; start small and foster growth.

Build respect for the work that you do in libraries and the service that you provide to others, be it with the young people or the partners you work with. Library outreach projects work best when they are delivered in partnership with the professional agencies that already know about young people and what their needs are. Our partners have enabled us, as librarians, to develop the skills to form relationships with young people.

Reaching out to young people and making them feel part of the community, rather than the enemy within, is the most welcoming invitation you can make to engage their commitment and co-operation. From here we can accompany them on their personal journeys to becoming library users and lifelong readers.

References

Brackertz, N. (2007) *Who is Hard to Reach and Why?* ISR Working Paper, www.sisr.net/publications/0701brackertz.pdf.

Douglas, J. (2010) *Libraries Raise Literacy Standards and Must Be Funded,* www.literacytrust.org.uk.

Earthman, E., Richmond, L. S., Peterson, D. J., Marczak, M. S. and Betts, S. C. (1999) *Adapting Evaluation Measures for 'Hard to Reach' Audiences,* Children, Youth and Families Education and Research Network, University of Arizona, http://ag.arizona.edu/sfcs/cyfernet/evaluation/adapeval.pdf.

Museums, Libraries Archives Council, Department Culture, Media and Sport, and Laser Foundation (2006) *A Research Study of 14–35 Year Olds for the Future Development of Public Libraries,* DCMS D3/560, Define 1516, www.bl.uk/aboutus/acrossuk/workpub/laser/news/awards2005/publiclibraries.pdf.

The Reading Agency (2008) *The Library Offer to Young People,* www.readingagency.org.uk/young/library-offer-to-young-people/library-offer-and-young-people.

Appendix 12.1 The National Youth Offer

The National Youth Libraries board laid out 'new solutions to help every young person love reading' in the Library Offer to Young People (The Reading Agency, 2008). The core of the offer is that librarians should enable, support and equip young people to participate in and make decisions about their library service. The rest of the offer makes the case for librarians to develop partnership links and professional skills in the delivery of service – already common practice in the teaching and youth work professions.

The national Library Offer to Young People requires that public library services empower young people by:

- allowing them to participate in the shaping, design and delivery of library services
- providing volunteering opportunities in libraries, and being included in staff appointments
- working with younger or older users and being given accreditation for their time
- developing citizenship and community engagement opportunities.
  In addition, libraries should give young people access to free, safe and welcoming spaces, the internet, and technology and learning opportunities delivered in partnership with other agencies.

Libraries should offer a bank of quality stock, including relevant and inspiring books, magazines and other media. Libraries should highlight these by providing positive and creative activities that give young people a chance to share their experience of reading and culture. Up-to-date information on education, training and careers opportunities should be made available on noticeboards and information stands, and careers advice agencies such as Connexions should be approached when referring young people for extra support and guidance. Reliable information on health and social issues and on local services for young people should also be clearly visible.

Appendix 12.2 HeadSpace, Efford, Plymouth

HeadSpace is a national pilot project, launched by The Reading Agency in 2006 and funded by the National Lottery. There are 20 HeadSpace sites in England across four regions. Each HeadSpace site, whether based in a rural, seaside, city or suburban location, is 'a place where young people can read, listen, surf, talk, meet friends, enjoy a drink or a snack and generally chill, to their heart's and head's content' (http://headspaceefford.wordpress.com). In the South West there are projects in Lyme Regis (Dorset), Padstow (Cornwall), Weston (Somerset), Swindon Central Library and Efford (Plymouth).

HeadSpace, Efford in Plymouth is situated in a suburban area and was developed in close consultation with local young people. SWERDA (South West of England Regional Development Agency) had already targeted Efford as an area of regeneration. It is a post-war housing development with large amounts of council housing. It has an estimated population of 7200. A household survey conducted by MORI in 2002 confirmed that there were a number of problems affecting the Efford neighbourhood. In particular, employment and income levels are low. Only 4 in 10 adults in the neighbourhood have any formal qualifications and low levels of literacy and numeracy remain a barrier to social and economic participation.

The ward falls within the worst 20% of wards in England, according to the Indices of Multiple Deprivation, and within the description of a declining neighbourhood centre. However, of the priority neighbourhoods identified in Neighbourhood Renewal Strategy, Efford received amongst the lowest level of regeneration funding in Plymouth, missing out on a number of occasions to other, higher-profile areas in the city.

Fortunately, Efford was unanimously selected to go forward for consideration as a pilot under the SWERDA's Building Community Initiative as a regeneration area to improve homes and local facilities. As a result, Plymouth City Council, housing associations, schools and the local church developed the scheme of a four-storey building that includes the public library on the ground floor and 40 flats for frail and elderly people above. This library would have a 100 square foot area set aside for the HeadSpace project and was scheduled to be one of the first to open nationally.

Young people from Efford Youth Development Forum (EYDF), Routeways participation group and Lipson Community College took part in a range of local and national consultations during the summer of 2006. This included a range of young people's consumer surveys on: branding, design schemes, furniture selection and activities. Each survey provided the opportunity for young people who completed a questionnaire to be entered into a prize draw to win an iPod nano. One of the young entrants from Efford won the iPod. (Online competitions are a far more teen-friendly solution to engagement and participation than the usual paper-based library surveys.)

Plymouth Libraries also hosted a regional workshop for south west library authorities to brand the project; young people from Swindon, Bristol and Dorset took part to meet designers face to face.

EYDF planned our launch event and chose our first batch of stock and furniture, which is extremely fresh, appealing and modern in colour and style. The current HeadSpace members continue to select stock and replacement furniture, as well as lead on decision making on our programme of events every three months. Young people are invited to volunteer at community events and younger group sessions and they receive accreditation for their time through award schemes such as V-Involved, Duke of Edinburgh's Award and Youth Achievement Award.

Statistics

HeadSpace achievements (June 2010):

- 215 young people engaged in HeadSpace activities (target: 205)
- 91 young people involved in designing and planning the HeadSpace site (target: 30)
- 9 young people undertaking work placements or securing employment with the library service or partners: 3 securing employment, 6 work placements – includes long-term volunteers and work experience (target: 2)
- 100 young people have improved knowledge, understanding or skills (target: 35)
- 92 young people have demonstrated an improved awareness of their own feelings (target: 25)
- 86 young people experience personal development and social progress (target: 30)
- 89 young people discover opportunities for enjoyment, inspiration and creativity as a result of their involvement (target: 140).
  (The targets for each outcome were set by The Reading Agency at the beginning of the project.)

Appendix 12.3 Literacy with a Twist, Plymouth

Plymouth Library Services outreach support officer and the Secondary Inclusion Programme (SIP) team have been collaborating since November 2006 with the aim of improving literacy amongst young people temporarily excluded from school. It has been proved that there is a correlation between social inclusion and a risk of offending behaviour. Some of the group are young offenders on the Youth Offending Team's prevention programme. The young people range in age from 11 to 16 years and have a range of learning needs. Several activities were developed and drawn together to form the needs-led three-week programme Literacy with a Twist, which culminates in a group visit to Plymouth Central Library.

The programme

Week 1: Engaging the group
Introductions and library-joining form
Icebreaker: If I were... I would be...

A 'getting to know you' exercise which informs the team of the young person's interests. The group are asked to write down their response to these statements:

- If I were chocolate I would be...
- If I were a celebrity I would be...
- If I were a car I would be...
- If I were an item of clothing I would be...
- If I were a holiday destination I would be...
  (Reading Agency toolkit)

Reading and writing activity: silent graphic novel or manga

A double page from an exciting graphic novel or manga is used to prompt the young people to form their own interpretation of the story using the pictures and to encourage them to use their imagination as an author would. The young people work in twos or threes to develop their story. The stories are then shared and performed when we meet as a group. The SIP has a stock of books on loan from Plymouth Libraries that enable young people to continue this work outside of the weekly sessions.

Fun reading activity: library karaoke

Karaoke is an informal way to engage young people in a reading activity that can be shared with others and change the young person's view of the library. Custom-made CD+G karaoke discs are used, the music tracks being chosen by young people. The activity is accessible to all, no matter what their reading ability.

Week 2: Developing skills

Icebreaker: magnetic poetry

Young people are asked to work individually to come up with a three-line poem about a topic of their choice using fridge magnet letters. Examples include poems about love, the sea, forests and chocolate. The activity enables young people to be creative with words in a hands-on way without having to write anything down. SIP workers and the library outreach support officer provide help to read the letters and construct the poems. Each poem is displayed on the board and the young people share them aloud.

Reading, learning and understanding activity: Rummikub Word

If any library service has not used the Tomy Rummikub Word board game when working with young people, it is strongly advised to order a set immediately. Using this game with young people is revolutionary in changing their attitude to words. The young people form a team with a worker and the aim is to use all the available letters to win. The *Oxford English Dictionary* is used to learn new words with which to enable each team to victory.

Library visit preparation

The young people are briefed before their library visit in order to prepare them for the environment. We discuss why other people use the library and remind them to consider others' needs whilst they are there. The young people have the opportunity to ask questions about library borrowing, using the internet and the activities they will take part in.

Week 3: Library visit

Icebreaker: library challenge

When young people visit the library they take part in a challenge which enables them to get to know the Central Library, 'supermarket sweep' style. The young people are divided into two teams and given a 'shopping list' for various items (all books). When the young people have completed the challenge they each get to choose a prize.

Reading and writing activity: type up and present your stories

The young people have time using the library computers to type up and present their stories. They are encouraged to add images that relate to key moments from the story. The stories are printed and form part of their folder of work.

Fun reading activity: Driving Theory Test Pro

Many young people are interested in cars and are of an age to be thinking about starting to learn to drive. Using the library service's subscription to Driving Theory Test Pro, young people read and answer ten questions from an example test online based on the examination set by the Driving

Standards Agency. The library outreach support officer shows the group how to navigate the Plymouth cyberLibrary (www.cyberlibrary.org.uk) and access the test. Most of the young people need one-to-one support to read the questions. The group has the opportunity to find out their score and the correct answers.

The project to date has engaged 94 young people, who have all become library members.

Appendix 12.4 Young Mums to Be group, Weymouth, Dorset

Since September 2009 Dorset Library Service has been working closely with a Young Mums to Be (YMTB) group in Weymouth. This initiative was driven by the Out of the Box project, but the work is now part of the library offer. Out of the Box was a national project set up by the National Youth Agency and The Reading Agency. It encouraged stronger partnerships between libraries and youth services to create informal reading opportunities for young people aged 14–19 who are not engaged in formal education or learning.

Many young parents, or young people who are expecting a baby, find themselves thrust into a position of responsibility (as a parent) at a young age. This has meant that, in some cases, their education has been disrupted and, as a result, they are not confident with reading – either for themselves or to their children. Dorset Library Service was keen to encourage young people to see for themselves the value of a library service and to provide creative opportunities for these young people to try to regain their confidence and improve their reading ability.

The YMTB course aims to support young people who are expecting children and provides them with an accredited award. The course has a rolling intake (so turnover of group members is regular) and the young people must complete a set of units in order to achieve the award. The units cover: Antenatal care; Health and Safety; Healthy Lifestyle; IT; Literacy; Numeracy; Care of Newborn and Young Children; Training; Education; and Work.

The obvious links with the library service come in the literacy section of the course. However, there are other areas in which working with the library can be of benefit: for example, part of the IT unit requires planning a book with the theme chosen by the learner, and some people choose to write simple stories for their babies. This can be supported by looking at published baby books and the factors that determine their success with readers.

A variety of sessions were provided by the library service, first to promote reading and second to promote use of the library itself. A library card was created for the centre and a stock of books was allocated to it and stored on the centre's bookshelves; there were a variety of titles, from the latest teen/adult fiction bestsellers, biographies and TV/film tie-in novels, to parenting guides, baby picture books and books about getting back to work. The aim was to provide a wide variety of books for a wide range of abilities and interests. The stock is regularly updated, based on requests from the group or recommendations from the librarian/youth workers.

Over half of the initial group that the library service worked with are now members of the library and use their cards regularly. The library keeps in contact with the group so that new members of the group are introduced to the library service and the benefits it offers to families and young people as individuals.

Regarding library staff, because of their interaction with the YMTB group, many members of staff feel that they are more confident when dealing with young people and young families. The library service benefited from gaining young people's perspectives on a range of issues, from their involvement in the recruitment and selection process, through to general negative perceptions that young people have about using the library service and how these can be overcome.

Appendix 12.5 Entry to Employment (E2E) and Pre-Entry to Employment group, Weymouth

The Entry to Employment scheme is open to all young people aged 16 to 18 who are not participating in any form of post-16 learning. It enables progression to an apprenticeship, further learning or employment. The course covers three areas of personal development: Basic and Key Skills; Vocational Development; and Social Development. It is not time-bound and the learning should fit the needs of the individual.

The library service can be beneficial in all three of these areas. It helps with literacy (Basic and Key Skills) by providing a wide range of stock to suit the interests and abilities of the members of the group. It benefits Vocational Development by providing resources (both stock and access to computers) that can help young people to gain skills, find relevant courses/classes to attend and look for jobs. Social Development is aided by the library service's being able to signpost relevant services, activities and organizations.

The centre was provided with a card for the group and a stock of books that was regularly refreshed through requests from the young people and staff and recommendations from the librarian leading the project. The initial stock was wide ranging: there was a selection of popular children's, teenage and adult fiction; non-fiction books around leisure/interest subjects as well as about gaining skills; and a selection of graphic novels. For the most part, the initial supply of stock was used as a discussion point, providing inspiration and generating links to other books that the group wanted for future visits. Through getting to know the young people and by having a good knowledge of the stock available, the librarian was able to supply stock of interest to individuals within the group.

13

Creative reading and insideadog.com.au

Lili Wilkinson

Introduction

We all know that reading is important, especially when it comes to children. But what do we actually *mean* by reading? Do comic books count? Newspapers? *Goosebumps* books? What about the internet?

Australia's Centre for Youth Literature promotes reading for pleasure, through a variety of onsite, offsite and online programs. The primary principle underlying the Centre for Youth Literature programme is access. Within the limitations of current resources, the Centre aims to maximize geographic, social and cultural access to its programme, which of course is greatly expanded through our online programmes, namely the Boys Blokes Books and Bytes blog (boysblokesbooks.edublogs.org), our Read Alert blog for professionals (slv.vic.gov.au/readalert), and, in particular, Inside a Dog (www.insideadog.com.au), our website for young people about books and reading.

The Centre sits within the State Library of Victoria as part of the Library's youth offer. The State Library strives to provide access to Victorian, Australian and international resources that will enrich young people's cultural, educational, social and economic lives. Its work in achieving these values is informed by the five values of innovation, collaboration, engagement, excellence and respect. Inside a Dog is part of the Library's online offer which, in addition to a corporate site, also includes Ergo – a research skills website and an ongoing digitization project featuring images and manuscripts. The Library also works closely with the State Government Department of Education to develop and manage a series of education-based web projects in partnership with a number of other cultural institutions.

Why read?

Reading brings many more benefits than just improved literacy skills. The rewards of a love of reading last a lifetime: well-being, resilience, communication skills, personal development, imagination, creativity, curiosity.

The Search Institute in the US (Search Institute, 2007) lists 40 developmental assets for young people to make them become caring, responsible adults. The more assets a young person has, the more likely they are to succeed in school, help others, value diversity, maintain good health, resist danger, exhibit leadership and overcome adversity. They are also less likely to use drugs or alcohol, vandalize, choose violence, skip school or become depressed and/or suicidal. One of the key assets is Reading for Pleasure, which goes hand in hand with related assets such as Creative Activities, Community Values Youth and School Engagement. Inside a Dog pulls these assets together through various online literary programmes, including a Writer in Residence, Book Clubs, the Inky Awards and the Inkys Creative Reading Prize.

Adolescence is a critical time in the development of a lifelong reader. There is a sharp drop-off in reading for pleasure between the ages of 9 and 17, and once a young person stops reading, it is statistically unlikely they'll ever start again. A recent US National Endowment for the Arts study (www.nea.gov) reported that less than one-third of 13 year-olds are daily readers, and only 52% say they read for pleasure at all. But reading proficiency scores for 9 year-olds are at an all-time high. One thing that can help to explain the decline in readers is that the definition of 'reading' given in the report excludes non-traditional reading material such as magazines, graphic novels and online reading.

The news is not all bad, however. In 2008, six of the top ten Australian bestsellers in all genres were young adult titles. Book sales globally are in decline, with the exception of YA and children's sales, which in Australia are up nearly 13% (Nielsen Bookscan, 2009). Major book retailers all over the world are closing down unprofitable CD and DVD sections and replacing them with sprawling shelves of YA books, which are becoming the focal point of the bookshop, instead of being relegated to a poky back corner.

Reading online

When we browse the internet, we are not really 'surfing' at all. We are reading. Inside a Dog combines the interactivity and flexibility of the internet with the deeper and more profound effects of book reading.

The internet is an amazing reader development tool. From websites like Inside a Dog, to the personal websites and blogs of authors such as Meg Cabot, Neil Gaiman and Scott Westerfeld, to fan-fiction sites that encourage users to engage creatively with stories they love, to fansites like the Leaky Cauldron and the Harry Potter Alliance, to social networking sites like LibraryThing and Shelfari, the internet has a community for every sort of reader.

In the western world, the 'digital divide' has all but vanished. Broadband-equipped computers are in 97% of state-funded schools, and virtually all children and young adults can access the internet either at home, at school or at their local public library. And they do. A 2009 Pew Internet and American Life Project report found that 78% of American teenagers play games online and 73% use e-mail. In a recent series of focus groups run by the Centre for Youth Literature in Australian schools, 100% of students interviewed belonged to one or more social networking sites such as Facebook and MySpace.

Although there has been a reasonable amount of research devoted to gender and reading among young people, it has almost exclusively focused on boys. On the whole, boys tend to be more reluctant readers. Unfortunately, this not only excludes reluctant girl readers, it also excludes the girls who are book neutral or even motivated readers. Given that more girls read than do boys, and that they tend to engage with literature and story more deeply (the majority of participants on online forums and fan-fiction websites being girls), it seems a shame that the majority of advertising campaigns and reader development programmes are geared towards boys.

In 2001, the Australian Centre for Youth Literature commissioned the *Young Australians Reading* report (Centre for Youth Literature, 2001), an investigation into the reading habits of 10–18 year-olds. The report found that, contrary to media scaremongering, young people liked to read. Over 60% of respondents indicated that they wanted to read, that they recognized the value of reading and would like to read more. But many identified a lack of peer-to-peer book recommendation, and it became clear that there was a need for an online resource for young people to find out about books.

The major challenge in developing Inside a Dog.com.au was creating a website that would appeal to young people. Young Australians are true digital natives and are used to seamless online experiences. They can also sense a try-hard from a mile off. We were very certain that the site would fail if it were called teensreading.com or books-r-kewl.com. Cool was never an option when developing Inside a Dog, so quirky was considered to be the next best thing.

Groucho Marx tells us that 'Outside of a dog, a book is a man's best friend. Inside of a dog, it's too dark to read' (Marx, 2000). Inside a Dog seemed just the right blend of quirky and memorable we were looking for, despite protests from some people who claimed that the website wasn't about dogs, and that perhaps it should be called insideabook.

Insideadog.com.au was launched in April 2006. Since then we have received over a million visits, 6000 book reviews, and tens of thousands of comments, competition entries, votes and other user-generated content. In January 2011 we launched an entirely redesigned site, incorporating social networking functionality to allow users to log in and collect books they've read and books that they want to read, as well as being able to follow other users' reviews, join book clubs and comment on books/book reviews.

Other Inside a Dog features include a blog, with news about book awards, video book trailers and plenty of literary fun and gossip. There is a very active forum where our users discuss their favourite literary kisses, which character from a book they would like to be the President of the United States, and what books make them laugh or cry. A book is featured every month, and five or six free copies are given away to our favourite reviewers. The site has booklists, sample chapters, audiobook excerpts and podcasts. There is also a writer in residence, a different author each month who blogs on whatever takes their fancy. There've been about 30 writers so far, including John Marsden, Garth Nix, Melina Marchetta, Scott Westerfeld and Margo Lanagan, and it's been an amazing experience for both the writers and their young fans.

The 2011 redesign introduced a new Teacher Resources section, with worksheets and lesson plans on creating a dynamic reading culture in the classroom. Resources include strategies on how to write book reviews, create video book trailers, engage a school book group, and ideas for class texts. All of the resources link back into the Australian Curriculum, and also include interactive forums where teachers can share their own successes and challenges. There are also teacher-led book clubs, where the barriers between reading for the curriculum and reading for pleasure are broken down. The social networking aspect of the site has proved invaluable to teachers, who can immediately access a student's page and see the books they've read, the reviews they've written and the other ways they've engaged with the site, the other readers and the writer in residence. This tool is particularly effective for parent–teacher interviews, where teachers can show parents specific and concrete examples of a child's progress.

Inside a Dog gives young people a virtual forum in which to discuss, produce, consume and respond to literature. It is a place where authors and the young people who read them can meet and exchange thoughts, ideas and opinions, and find new ways to creatively respond to language and literature.

The readermakers

There is an assumption that everything a child does must have some kind of educational benefit. They can't watch a TV show or read a novel unless they're *learning* something. I'd argue that any kind of interaction with narrative or media is an educational experience, whether it's a biography of Shakespeare, or an episode of *The Biggest Loser*. And why aren't kids allowed to read (or view) purely for pleasure? *Goosebumps* creator R. L. Stine (2011) once said that 'kids as well as adults are entitled to books of no socially redeeming value', and he was right.

David Fickling has published a wealth of highly regarded writers, including Philip Pullman (*The Golden Compass*) and Mark Haddon (*The Curious Incident of the Dog in the Night-Time*), but he started out publishing *Goosebumps*. And although he has moved on to bigger and better things, he hasn't forgotten his roots. Fickling calls these books – *Goosebumps*, *The Baby-sitters Club*, *Star Wars* novelizations – 'readermakers'. They're easy books, accessible books. They're like the white-bread equivalent of books: light, insubstantial and without much dietary fibre.

But if you're a young person and you're a bit scared of this whole reading thing because you don't really get it and everyone keeps telling you how important it is, a 'readermaker' can be a great thing. Because you pick it up. It's easy to get into. The story rips along. Before you know it, you've finished. You read a whole book. A whole, entire book. And it was *fun*. So you read another one. This reading thing is easy! And because you're breezing along, you're a reading *ninja*, you think about picking up something a bit longer. Something a bit harder. And your love of reading has begun.

The internet is also a kind of 'readermaker', but it doesn't even get the dignity of *at least they're reading something*. The internet is an amazing reader-development tool. Because, after all, what we do when we browse the internet isn't surfing at all. It's *reading*. The internet is primarily a text-based medium, from message boards to Wikipedia to Twitter to MySpace and Facebook. When you're online, you're constructing an identity and interacting with the world through words. Young people are the champions of text – it belongs to them. Young people experiment and play with words in a way that adults don't – they take words (and spelling) to places where adults fear to tread.

Inside a Dog attempts to capitalize on this enthusiasm for reading, language and play with various projects, competitions and challenges. This wasn't necessarily something we initially imagined the site would be used for, but it has evolved from the way teenagers are using the site.

It began with LOLYA. For the unaware, there is an internet meme called LOLcats, where funny captions are added to pictures of cats. The captions have *intentionally bad spelling and grammar*, like I CAN HAS CHEEZBURGER. Because cats can't spell, right?

One of our online writers in residence – US author Scott Westerfeld – started a LOLYA competition, inviting users to make similar captions on YA book covers. The competition was a huge success – with hundreds of entries.

On some levels it seems like a fairly simplistic exercise. But there was some interesting intertextual work going on behind all the fun. Take the caption for Susan Patron's *The Higher Power of Lucky*: **In ur kidz books, teachin em uhnatummy** (In your kids' books, teaching them anatomy). This refers to the first iteration of the LOLcats meme, which ran on the formula: **In ur [noun], [verb]in ur [noun]s** (like **In ur fridge, eatin ur foodz**), while simultaneously referring to the controversial use of the word *scrotum* in this award-winning book, and the censorship that resulted. Similarly, the cover of the final Harry Potter book is captioned: **I can haz closure, plz?** (Can I have closure, please?). Another entry pointed out the recent (and rather disturbing) trend in book covers for teenage girls, where a photo is cut off at the chin, leaving the girl faceless and headless. This entry was captioned: **I can haz eyes?**

So while the competition was fun, and the results were often hilarious, it was not necessarily as simple as it first appeared. To participate meant that you needed a familiarity with the original meme, as well as knowledge of the referenced book and the ability to humorously combine those two elements, often while referencing some broader popular culture phenomenon.

Another US writer in residence, Maureen Johnson, also designed a competition. The premise was simple: everything goes better with zombies. Users were invited to take existing works of literature and add a zombie. Again, we had hundreds of entries. Works zombified included Shakespeare, James Joyce, *The Very Hungry Caterpillar* and *If You Give a Moose a Muffin*. Jane

Austen's *Pride and Prejudice* was zombified on Inside a Dog long before Seth Grahame-Smith's *Pride and Prejudice and Zombies* was announced.

Zombie Idol required not only humour and creativity: it also required a sensitivity and understanding of textual conventions, not to mention an ability to recreate an authorial voice and style. In Victoria, one of the assessment tasks in VCE Literature (the equivalent to the UK GCSE) is to write a short story in the voice of an author, such as Edgar Allan Poe or Raymond Carver. This competition, while obviously shorter and a lot more fun, was not dissimilar. The only real differences were that, with Zombie Idol, children as young as 11 were submitting entries and the hundreds of young people who submitted stories did so *voluntarily*. In their own time. Not for school or anything.

The most popular competitions on Inside a Dog have always been ones where young people respond creatively to literature – fan-fiction competitions, book cover redesign competitions and literary mashups.

We have responded to this enthusiasm for creative reading by establishing the Inky Awards. The Inkys are Australia's only national teen-choice book award and have been running since 2007. A long list of twenty books (ten Australian, ten international) is selected by the Centre for Youth Literature and is then whittled down to a short list of ten by a panel of six judges (four teenagers, two adults). Voting then opens on Inside a Dog, and anyone under the age of 20 can vote. The winning international book gets the Silver Inky and the winning Australian book gets the Golden Inky and a cheque for $2000.

There are also the Inkys Creative Reading Prize, awarded to a young person for a creative response to a book, in any format. Past responses have included video book trailers to *The Hunger Games* and *The Hound of the Baskervilles*, crocheted Harry Potter dolls, a musical score to Markus Zusak's *The Book Thief*, the cover of *The Luxe* recreated in cake and a hand-crafted charm bracelet in response to *Twilight*, as well as plenty of poetry, short stories and other text-based responses. The Inky Awards are open internationally to anyone under the age of 20.

The most popular writers in residence on Inside a Dog haven't been the ones who talk about the daily life of being a writer. Our readers want a chance to interact – whether it's expressing their opinions on the Narnia books or voting for their favourite zombie-modified literature. Young people don't want to sit back and absorb information; they want to be involved in shaping the discussion. It is, after all, *their* literature.

Challenges

After nearly five years of Inside a Dog, it's been useful to look back at the various challenges we've faced, and continue to face. One of the biggest things we thought we'd have to grapple with is moderation. In the original incarnation of the site, every book review, comment and competition entry was moderated by a staff member before it appeared on the site. This would often accumulate into a massive backlog of content, meaning that reviews wouldn't appear for several days. However, after five years of content, we've only taken action on one blog comment – a comment not from a teenager, but from an adult who we deemed was making an inappropriate assumption about our writer in residence's religion. Our teenage users are remarkably restrained and well behaved on the site, and because of this we are moving to a more relaxed moderation system where book reviews that don't contain any 'flagged' words will appear immediately and users can become 'trusted commenters' after they have had 25 comments approved.

The biggest challenge we face is reaching our teenage users. The Centre for Youth Literature's position as Australia's leading youth literature organization means that we have excellent contacts with schools and public libraries, but reaching beyond these 'gatekeepers' to students will always be a challenge. The project runs on a bare-bones budget that can't incorporate the kind of marketing campaign required to reach teenagers, so we are reliant on teachers and librarians and social networking to spread the word.

The support from our network of professional educators has been overwhelming, as has the support from Australian publishers, and authors all over the world. We have an extensive Professional Development Program where we suggest methods of using Inside a Dog in the classroom, which is delivered physically all over the country, and virtually via the Department of Education's Knowledge Bank online conferencing tool.

Funding has always been an issue with Inside a Dog, with the original site being built using funding from the Copyright Agency Limited. The recent rebuild was long overdue – the original site was created before Facebook was public, before the smartphone and before Twitter. Teenagers are used to a seamless online experience, and in its later years the original Inside a Dog site was unable to provide that. However, after over two years of planning and research, we were awarded funding from the Australia Council of the Arts and the Victorian Department of Education, and the development of the new site was finally green-lit.

Impact on public libraries

Inside a Dog has had a profound and lasting impact on youth services in Australian public libraries. It's provided a high-profile promotional tool to engage young people with books and reading – a resource that individual library services couldn't possibly develop independently. Despite most library services having a children's librarian, there is a gap in providing specialist services for teenagers. A declining number of teacher-librarians in schools has increased demand on children's librarians, so Inside a Dog has been an invaluable tool and resource.

The Inky Awards, in particular, is a highlight on the public library calendar – with libraries all over Australia creating Inside a Dog displays featuring the long-listed books (we provide a printable set of Inky-branded shelf talkers – display materials designed to stand out from library shelves – for each of the 20 long-listed books). Many libraries hold their own Creative Reading Prize competitions, as well as internal voting and predictions as to the winner. Libraries send in photos of their Inkys displays, and the Centre for Youth Literature awards a complete set of the Inkys books to the library with the best display, as well as the considerable honour of hosting the next year's Inky Awards Ceremony.

In 2008, the Centre ran a pilot programme called Boys, Blokes and Books (BBB), inviting boys and dads to public libraries to eat pizza and hear from authors and prominent sportspeople. This programme produced a toolkit that has inspired many libraries in Victoria to run their own BBB programmes, as well as programmes with girls and mums and more general programmes inviting families to enjoy and discuss books and reading together.

We're looking forward to working more closely with public libraries with the new, improved Inside a Dog. Many libraries that run teenage book clubs – like the Bayside Libraries Teen Read of the Week – are keen to take their physical book clubs online via Inside a Dog, providing more access to teen readers and more cross-pollination between library branches. We're also working with school and public libraries to incorporate Inside a Dog book reviews into individual library catalogues. This is a reasonably challenging task, as each library service and school runs a different catalogue content management system, but public libraries in particular are keen and are working hard towards achieving this.

One of our most frequent requests is for a 'puppy' – a similar website for younger children. We're aware that this is also a much-needed resource, but, as always, resources and funding are always difficult to secure.

The Australian scene

The majority of Australian publishers have a 'children's' section of their websites, which usually includes teen books, but YA rarely has its own section. Teenage users don't respond particularly well to being lumped in with the little kids, so it's no surprise that the average teenager would never consider visiting a publisher's website to find out information on a book or author.

One notable exception to this is Penguin's betweenthelines.com.au, a website for teens. 'An online book club where enthusiastic young readers come to "rant, rave and review"' is how education sales and marketing manager Kristin Gill describes betweenthelines.com.au. 'We'd like to establish a loyal following of readers who will communicate with us on a range of levels about books, publishing ideas, cover concepts and other issues' (Gill, 2008). It's also a great market research tool. With nearly 300 registered members, the site is growing steadily and Gill and her team are excited about its development and potential. The site offers discussion online with Penguin authors, including Melina Marchetta, Sonya Hartnett and Frank Portman, and aims to introduce readers to a range of Penguin titles in a way that is not overtly hyping them.

Another way young people read online is through blogs. Reading an author's blog alongside their books adds a fascinating layer of interpretation to the texts. Knowing how stories are constructed, how research is carried out and how the editing process works, gives the reader a much deeper level of understanding. And it's not just author blogs. The writers of popular TV drama *Grey's Anatomy* have a blog where they dissect each episode and tell you how it was written. Similarly, TV writer Jane Espenson frequently blogs with advice for new writers. Watching television may not be reading, but it is watching *writing*.

There is a strong YA literature blogging community, which has been warmly supportive of Inside a Dog. Some of Inside a Dog's writers in residence have their own blogs, so Inside a Dog users can follow them back and continue their conversations. 'One of the loveliest things about blogging is that it's not just me,' says New York-based writer Justine Larbalestier. 'There's my readers, who chime in with comments, and then all the other bloggers. I'm part of a writing/reading/blogging community' (Larbalestier, 2008). This is obviously a big draw-card for such a solitary profession.

'It makes me feel a part of things,' says Penni Russon, Melbourne author of *Undine*. 'I'm always surprised at industry functions how many people read my blog' (Russon, 2008).

This desire to be part of a 'community' is certainly the driving force behind authors who blog. 'If the blog was just about promoting my books, I wouldn't do it,' says Larbalestier, whose blog (Larbalestier , 2011) has a vocal and diverse following of teens, other authors and adult fans. And it seems that very few authors blog for publicity's sake. 'I like writing in a different way,' says Russon about her blog (Russon, 2011). 'I don't blog so much about being a writer or the writing process, it's more thoughts, reflections, family stuff – it's a very eclectic mix.'

Beyond reading

Online engagement and literature are leading teenagers to new, sometimes life-changing experiences. In November 2008, the adult citizens of the US selected their next President. American citizens under the age of 18 were not able to cast a ballot, but it didn't stop them from getting involved. An extensive online community sprang up called YA for Obama, comprising teenagers and authors of young adult literature. The site quickly gained thousands of members, all discussing politics, ideas and ways in which they could get involved and make a difference. To be fair, there was also a YA for McCain community, but it only had five teenaged members – and no authors.

Joining one of the YA for Obama live blogging sessions during the presidential debates, you would encounter not only American teenagers, but also British teens (up past their bedtime), and Australian teens in the school computer room on their lunch break. The level of knowledge, enthusiasm and political savvy amongst these young people was extraordinary – probably far surpassing that of many voting adults. The young people from all over the world who participated in the YA for Obama project were passionate, enthusiastic and curious about the world. And they came to it via their favourite authors and their love of literature.

The Harry Potter Alliance is a wonderfully bizarre mashup of an online fan club and an activist organization. Members identify the 'real world Dark Arts' such as homophobia, illiteracy, poverty and genocide and then ask 'What would Dumbledore do?' These (mostly teenaged) fans are achieving genuine results – in 2010 they sent five planes full of aid and medical supplies to earthquake victims in Haiti, as well as raising over $250,000 for a global literacy programme.

Social activist Gloria Jean Watkins says that 'life-transforming ideas have always come to me through books'. It seems that combining a love of literature with the social-networking capabilities of the internet is a perfect recipe for 'life-transforming ideas' (Watkins, 2003).

Is reading online the same as reading books? Does it have the same positive effects? Dana Gioia, chairman of the US National Endowment for the Arts, thinks not: 'Whatever the benefits of newer electronic media,' she says, 'they provide no measurable substitute for the intellectual and personal development initiated and sustained by frequent reading' (Gioia, 2008). Well, maybe not. But I don't think anyone's suggesting that one should replace the other. Spending time online isn't a substitute for reading, but neither is watching TV, or getting plenty of exercise, or eating leafy vegetables. It doesn't mean that we shouldn't do any of those things.

A 2009 article in the *New York Times* profiled Nadia, a teenager who struggles to engage with books (Rich, 2009). She read a book about the Holocaust that she enjoyed, but couldn't get into the fantasy novel that her mother bought her. The article then sadly states: 'Nadia never became a big reader.' It then goes on to detail her obsession with Japanese manga comics and online fan fiction, which she both reads and writes.

Nadia sounds like a big reader to me.

She sounds like someone who loves stories so much that consuming them isn't enough. She wants to spend more time with her favourite characters. She wants to push them into new situations, beyond the ones they experience in the canonical world of the original text.

Every time Nadia reads or writes or watches or hears a story, she deepens her understanding of the way narrative works. And this understanding of story, of the mechanics of story, makes her love stories even more.

Young people have an incredible passion for language: they write poetry, keep diaries, fill notebooks with song lyrics. And they communicate through reading and writing online – shaping their identities on Facebook and Twitter with words. It could be said that today's teenagers are the first true generation of writers – they *all* use the written word to communicate and to present themselves to the world. The immediacy and interactivity of the internet provides them with more creative freedom than ever before, and I'm delighted that Inside a Dog can be a part of capturing that enthusiasm.

References

Centre for Youth Literature (2001) *Young Australians Reading,* State Library of Victoria.

Fickling, D. (2005) David Fickling Presents. Paper presented at the *6th Reading*

Matters Conference, Centre for Youth Literature, Melbourne, 26–28 May.

Gill, K. (2008) Personal communication, 12 September.

Gioia, D. (2008) quoted in Wallace, P., *Literacy and Generations of Change*, http://digitaljournal.com/article/257924?tp=1.

Harry Potter Alliance (2010), http://thehpalliance.org/action/campaigns/helping-haiti-heal/.

Larbalestier, J. (2008) Personal communication, 23 September.

Larbalestier, J. (2011) *Justine Larbalestier*, http://justinelarbalestier.com.

Marx, G. (2000) *The Essential Groucho*, Penguin.

National Endowment of the Arts (2007) *To Read or Not to Read: a question of national consequence*, www.nea.gov/research/toread.pdf.

Nielsen Bookscan (2009) *Press release*, 6 January, www.nielsenbookscan.com.au/press.php.

Pew Internet and American Life Project (2009) *Generations Online in 2009*, www.pewinternet.org/Reports/2009/Generations-Online-in-2009.aspx.

Rich, M. (2009) Literacy Debate: online, R U really reading? *New York Times*, www.nytimes.com/2008/07/27/books/27reading.html?_r=1.

Russon, P. (2008) Personal communication, 11 September.

Russon, P., (2011) *Eglantine's Cake*, http://eglantinescake.blogspot.com.

Search Institute (2007), *40 Developmental Assets for Adolescents*, www.search-institute.org/content/40-developmental-assets-adolescents-ages-12-18.

Stine, R. L., (2011) *Highlights of a Life*, www.ohioana-authors.org/stine/highlights.php.

Watkins, G. J. (2003) *O Magazine*, December.

YA for Obama (2008) http://yaforobama.ning.com [network currently inactive].

Index

The Innovative School Librarian
Thinking outside the box
Sharon Markless (editor), Elizabeth Bentley,
Sarah Pavey, Sue Shaper, Sally Todd and Carol Webb

'... more books of this quality about school libraries are needed.'

NEW LIBRARY WORLD

The Innovative School Librarian should be at the right hand of every ambitious librarian, and is a solid entry into any collection dedicated to library science.'

THE MIDWEST BOOK REVIEW

This book takes a strategic look at some of the issues currently of concern to school librarians. It is not a 'how to run a school library' guide. Instead it raises important questions about the functions of the school librarian and sets out to encourage the reader to think outside the box. It takes a strategic approach to the leadership of school libraries, examining notions of professionalism, their effect on identity and models of library practice. This book aims to inspire and enable school librarians to think creatively about their work and the community in which they operate.

Written by leaders in the field, it addresses the practical issues through the use of vignettes, and appendices offer examples of sample documents. The book is divided into three main areas: Who is the Librarian?; Your Community: from perceptions to practice; and Moving Forward.

Key topics covered include:

- the librarian's vision and values
- how others see us
- bridging the gap between different visions for the school library
- identifying and understanding your community
- making a positive response
- keeping inspired and inspiring others
- integrating the library
- innovating.

This is an essential, thought-provoking book for all school librarians, practitioners in schools library services, and students of librarianship. It has plenty to interest school leadership, headteachers, educational thinkers, public library managers and local government officers and also has an international audience.

2009; 224pp; hardback; 978-1-85604-653-4; £49.95

Reader Development in Practice
Bringing literature to readers
Susan Hornby and Bob Glass, editors

'It is an easy book to dip into, with well-laid-out sections on the author as reader, reader development, works of imagination, future directions and the reader as author. The authors of each chapter are enthusiastic advocates in their area of expertise and often bring very personal perspectives to their particular topic...Reader Development in Practice makes a welcome contribution to the understanding of the process of reading and its impact on readers.'

SCONUL FOCUS

Who is the reader? How do we reach them, and why? To what extent are readers determining what libraries offer? How has that changed since the birth of reader development? And what impact has organizational development had on the publishing and promotion of literature?

This edited collection covers all aspects of literature in relation to readership, exploring the chain of events connecting author and reader. It reflects on the challenges facing information professionals in reader development, looks at current promotion and partnership options, and offers new professionals and students fresh ideas, practical guidance and a firm underpinning knowledge upon which to build.

These user-friendly and clearly structured contributions bring together the work of expert practitioners and academics from both theoretical and practical perspectives. Key topics include:

- regional partnerships and reader development strategies
- social inclusion and accessibility
- emergent readers and social regeneration
- the roles of imaginative fiction in people's lives
- imaginative literature for children and young people
- imaginative literature for adults
- reading and information technology
- promoting books to readers
- sharing the knowledge - developing reflective practitioners.

This contemporary guide is essential reading for library and information professionals, students and academics. It will also be of great value to students taking literature and publishing courses.

Contributors
Ann Barlow, Ann Cleeves, Linda Corrigan, Jane Davis, Mike Garry, Andrew Glass, Calum Kerr, Jane Mathieson, Mike Mizrahi, Francine Sagar, Kay Sambell, Anne Sherman, Claire Warwick.

2008; 240pp; hardback; 978-1-85604-624-4; £49.95

How to order Facet Publishing books

Phone: 01235 827702
Fax: 01235 827703
E-mail: facet@bookpoint.co.uk
or order online at: www.facetpublishing.co.uk

Facet Publishing has a selection of titles available as e-books. We will continue to add titles from our active backlist of over 200 titles. See www.facetpublishing.co.uk for an up-to-date list of our e-books or sign up for our monthly e-bulletin to stay informed about the latest additions to our e-book programme.

Libraries can add Facet Publishing e-books to their digital collections by purchasing through these library vendors:

Dawsonera www.dawsonera.com   MyiLibrary www.myilibrary.com